The Toastmaster General's Guide TO Successful Public Speaking

The Toastmaster General's Guide

TO

Successful
Public Speaking

BY

GEORGE JESSEL

A Stuart L. Daniels Book

HAWTHORN BOOKS, INC.

Publishers NEW YORK

ACKNOWLEDGMENTS

MY APPRECIATION to Mark Wachs, Rosalind Wachs, and Jean Vermes for their editorial assistance and to Sam Carlton and Selden Bennett, my long-time associates, for their encouragement.

G. J.

TO

THE MEMORY OF THE LATE

James J. Walker,

MAYOR OF NEW YORK,

THE MOST ELOQUENT SPEAKER

OF HIS TIME

Table of Contents

A Word to the Reader

IT's BEEN my pleasure to have been a professional toastmaster and public speaker for about fifty years. My career in the world of entertainment and communications began in 1906 at the age of eight, when, with Walter Winchell and Jack Wiener as the Imperial Trio, we sang as accompaniment to illustrated slides, a now vanished entertainment form. Since then I have performed in every area of show business—Broadway, moving pictures, radio, television, night clubs, personal appearances.

I think the role in life for which I would best like to be remembered is that of toastmaster and public speaker. My first important public address came in the early 1920's when I campaigned for the late Mayor Jimmy Walker of New York City. Today I have a syndicated television program based on the toastmaster theme. I have always derived a special sense of satisfaction from addressing a gathering, large or small. I hope you will also find that satisfaction when you are called upon to speak.

I don't think this book will make you a great orator, but it will definitely guide you in how to prepare and deliver a speech. Don't turn down any opportunity to talk to a public gathering. As you may know I never do. With this kind of practice you will become more expert.

This book also contains a large collection of jokes which you may select for any appropriate occasion. They are listed in categories, which make them easy to find. A number are tried and true. Don't be afraid of their vintage, because a really good joke, like a melody, lives eternally. No one ever walked out of an opera house saying "Oh, I heard *Madame Butterfly* before!" You can alter the jokes to fit a particular situation. Believe me, I am

telling you the truth. And the truth may be exemplified by this
incident.

The airlines of Israel are not always complimented with the
services of young, beautiful stewardesses. Most young Israeli
girls spend much of their youth in the military. On one occasion,
after leaving Lod airport, which services Tel-Aviv and Jerusalem,
we were served by a middle-aged lady. In at least five languages
she announced: "We are now leaving for John F. Kennedy airport, New York City, U.S.A. Our flight will take approximately
eleven hours and forty minutes and we'll be flying at an altitude
of 35,000 feet, and the weather will be fine all the way. Believe
me, I'm telling you the truth, because the captain is my son,
and would not lie to his mother."

Just what is a speech? It is simply a method of communication,
in many ways like ordinary conversation. I'm sure you have few
difficulties in carrying on a conversation. So there shouldn't be
any reason why you can't deliver an effective speech.

A speech need not be long and scholarly. Something as simple
as a brief announcement to your club members informing them
of an upcoming event is a form of a speech.

Just remember, long or short, a speech must be carefully prepared. You needn't be a silver-tongued orator to communicate
if your speech is well organized.

In the following chapters you will be reading the techniques of
speechmaking—techniques that have served me well. I believe
that they will help you communicate more effectively and have
fun while you do.

And so, "Ladies and gentlemen, may I have your attention
please. This is indeed an auspicious occasion . . ."

GEORGE JESSEL

PART
I
How to Give
A Speech

Planning, Preparation, and General Presentation

THE PLANNING and preparation of any speech you give are probably the most important factors in its success.

We've all seen humorous sketches of audiences falling asleep during interminable, long-winded speeches. The speaker can avoid this fate by planning his talk so that it gets to the point quickly, makes the point concisely, and leads up to a satisfactory conclusion.

Preliminary Outline

In planning a talk, start by putting an outline on paper. An extemporaneous speaker can work directly from this framework. If you plan to read or memorize your talk you can develop a full-length speech from it, secure in the knowledge that you won't be wandering all over the lot.

Listing your points stimulates your thinking about them. Once the outline is made, the construction of the speech will flow along much more easily. First write down everything you think you want to cover in a series of brief words or phrases, on three-by-five cards. Then rearrange the cards in some kind of order. Now put this orderly arrangement into groups of related points that show a progression of thought from beginning to conclusion. These guidelines are key reminders of specific areas which you might otherwise overlook.

Step by Step

After a brief introduction (discussed in Chapter 2), you will want to plunge right into the body of your speech. The best way to organize the heart of your talk is to put it into a time sequence, if at all possible.

If your talk is descriptive, as in a travelogue, then follow the route of your trip as it was made. Don't jump from London to Rome and then back to Paris, or from the country to the city and back.

Another method of organization is to build up to your main point with smaller supporting points, so that you reach a climax with the principal idea that you are anxious to put across.

Many speeches given in these troubled days are concerned with problems. In that type of talk you should present the problem at the outset and explain why it is of importance to your audience. You may then cover the various possible solutions to the problem in the order of their suitability. Finally, explain why you think certain solutions are best and how they can be brought about with everyone's cooperation.

Perhaps you are making an effort to solve a problem and wish to explain your actions. President Franklin Delano Roosevelt, for example, had to explain why he closed the banks for nine days. In order to do this, he described banking operations in simple, easily understood terms. Then he stated the immediate reason why there was a banking problem—a rush of withdrawals caused by panic. He proceeded to tell about how he closed the banks and why, giving the reasons for legislative extension of the bank holiday and regulations permitting the banks to continue conducting certain necessary operations. This was followed by an explanation of the accomplishments resulting from the bank holiday. He offered a chronological description of the banks that were finally being allowed to open, when they were to open, and why. He explained the hoped-for results and asked for the public's cooperation.

Don't Trust Your Memory

There are a number of methods of presenting a speech. The most difficult one is memorizing it word for word. This is not recommended because it results in so much wear and tear on the nervous system. It requires too much time and effort in preparation. And it never sounds quite natural, except when done by an accomplished orator.

Since memorizing is so difficult and ineffective, you may want to consider reading from a manuscript. This method of speaking lacks spontaneity and divides the speaker's attention between the typewritten page and the audience. However, it does assure that you will say exactly what you wish to say, in the way that you want to say it. The inexperienced speaker sometimes feels safer with everything laid out before him. The person who speaks with the hope of having his speech published is also prepared to present exact copies of his text to the press. Today, we also have the electronic prompter—less awkward than the manuscript, but with much the same advantages and disadvantages.

The manuscript should have wide margins, be double or triple spaced, and not carry over a sentence from one page to the next. Special large type faces for typewriters can be used for better readability. The speaker should have rehearsed sufficiently so that he is able to lift his eyes from the page frequently.

The Card Trick

The speaker who does not care to use a manuscript or trust his memory should have a good supply of three-by-five index cards. If he is an extemporaneous talker, he only needs to have enough material on the cards to make sure of the accuracy of his quotations, statistics, or detailed descriptions.

The less experienced speaker must work from copious notes. Noted on each card will be his opening, a series of highlights, and the conclusion, each signified by a key word or two. The cards should be numbered in sequence, with the material on each card covering one particular thought. The cards can then be held inconspicuously in one hand, raised occasionally for reference. There is no point in attempting to conceal the fact that you are using notes; but they should be used deftly and each card discarded as used. You can always put them on the table or lectern.

Something to Look at

A well-chosen visual aid lives up to its name. It gives the speaker aid and support by providing the audience with a sight stimulus. Pictures and charts can make his words more effective by giving them an added dimension and clarity. Some things can be described only vaguely without slides, drawings, diagrams, or even films. Visual aids can improve the impression made by a speaker who is less than skillful.

Visual aids can be put in the hands of each member of the audience; but it is better to have large illustrations at the front of the room, drawing attention to the speaker. A fund-raising speech can be supplemented by graphs showing the amounts needed for various purposes, the sum already raised, and the figure at which you are aiming. An educational talk can be illustrated with diagrams. A talk on any of the arts or on travel can be highlighted with drawings or slides. Points in a technical talk can be demonstrated by the speaker with the use of chalk and a blackboard. A political speech can be enlivened by a background of appropriate posters. Films can enhance any talk, but they tend to put the speaker in the background, making him simply a commentator.

Making a Choice

Before choosing a particular visual aid be sure to remember the advance preparations. Do you have a large blackboard, chalk, and an eraser available? Can you, or someone you know, draw well enough to make your posters or charts clear and effective? Do you have someone to work with you in projecting slides or movies? Do you have an adequate projector and screen? Will the visual aid enhance your presentation or will it involve too much time and effort?

Whatever your choice, it is wise to prepare or obtain your visual aids far enough in advance of the date of your speech so that you can accustom yourself to handling them and working with them. If they prove too awkward or time-consuming, then it is better to work without them. The simplest are large, easy-to-read, single charts that can be pinned to an easel or board behind you. Then your only other accessory is a ruler or pointer to draw attention to the particular illustration you need.

Timing

The time allowed for your presentation will probably have limitations. You should rehearse your speech in any event, and it is a good idea to time yourself. If you are running longer than your time allotment, or longer than your audience's probable attention span, don't hesitate to pare down your speech. A concise talk is always received with much more appreciation than one that spreads itself all over the place.

Check through your cards or manuscript and cross off anything that is not truly relevant. You may lose your audience by going off on a tangent, and you won't put your points over as successfully. When you have pared down the subject matter, pare down your use of words. Keep it simple. Don't use two words when one will do the job. Don't use a big word where a short one will do.

Biblical Psalms are a good example of brevity and the use of short, simple words. In the twenty-third Psalm, for example, there are only one hundred eighteen words. Of those, ninety-two are words of one syllable. Only five of the other twenty-six are more than two syllables.

Be Specific

It is much more effective to be specific than to generalize. Which strikes harder, the vague: "The garbage collection service in this city is impossible"; or the more concrete: " We have only one garbage truck for every ten thousand people in this city"; or the even more specific: "There hasn't been a garbage collection on West Seventy-second Street in two weeks"?

You would get your listeners' attention and contributions much faster if you were to say specifically, "Our organization has so little money its volunteers have to use a broken-down mimeograph machine instead of a Xerox," rather than, "Our organization has to run an office with inadequate equipment."

If you are telling a story to illustrate an idea, people it with actual personalities. Do not talk of "a married couple," but of yourself and your wife, or your brother and his wife, or a couple called Mr. and Mrs. Abercrombie. Speak not of "a boy," but of Tommy Bingham, not of "a salesman," but of Richard Carlton. Also make your backgrounds and locales definite. Have them walk into the Hilton, not "a hotel." Make them stroll down Fifth Avenue, Broadway, Wilshire Boulevard, or the local main stem, not just "down the street." When you use the jokes and anecdotes in this book, try to personalize them with names or places that are meaningful to your audience.

Project Yourself

The content of your speech can be less than perfect, if you are able to put it over with effective delivery. Lean slightly forward as though trying to get close physically to the audience. Make contact with your listeners by looking directly at them. Look from one section of the audience to another. Don't get frozen in one attitude and, above all, don't look over their heads.

Use your body to emphasize points. This doesn't mean employing the stilted positions taught in an old-fashioned elocution class. Do use gestures and facial expressions that come naturally to you. A raised eyebrow, a shrugged shoulder, a pointing index finger, or a pounding fist can emphasize your points and make you more interesting to listen to. You can become your own personal visual aid.

Radio and Television

Gestures are lost in a radio speech, since you and the audience are invisible to each other. On television, movements are limited by the background and camera angles. In both TV and radio, you are speaking not to a group, but to individuals. You should imagine that you are having a chat with an individual or a small family. The talk should be scaled to the interests and intelligence of all types of people, although the time and nature of the broadcast can determine to some extent who will be listening.

Radio is a fine place to use the manuscript speech, since only the studio audience knows that you are reading. TV, of course, makes use of the well-known teleprompter and "idiot cards."

If the presence of radio microphones or TV cameras is only incidental and you are addressing a particular audience, you will naturally address your remarks primarily to them, trying not to be obvious in your awareness of the other people listening or watching. You owe it to your immediate listeners to concentrate on them.

The YOU Concept

Above all, the successful speaker is sincerely interested in telling his audience something they want to know. If they aren't particularly interested at the opening of your speech, they should be by the time it is done. You must impress them with the idea, "I am making this speech to help YOU, to inform YOU, to entertain YOU, to inspire YOU, to move YOU." You should plan, outline, illustrate, phrase, and deliver your talk with this prospective YOU foremost in your mind, whether the YOU in question is a member of a listening, viewing, or in-the-flesh audience.

Nothing to Fear

Everyone is familiar with Franklin Delano Roosevelt's famous "There is nothing to fear, but fear itself." Paraphrase his statement to read: There is nothing to fear, *not even* fear itself—with regard to public speaking.

No one would deny the tension that accompanies the public-speaking situation. What the inexperienced speaker does not realize is that he can challenge his fears and make them work *for* him.

Everybody Is Nervous

If you are nervous before speaking, realize that it is a normal reaction. Even the most experienced speaker is nervous before he addresses an audience.

The circumstances and pressures that accompany public speaking are a challenge to the ego. I have made over four thousand speeches and have felt some apprehension before every one of them.

I am not alone. In a talk before a group of journalists some years ago in London, the famous British cartoonist David Low said that every time he had to make a speech he felt as if he had a block of ice, nine inches by nine inches, in the pit of his stomach.

When he concluded, he was approached by a member of the audience, Winston Churchill. "Mr. Low," asked Churchill, "how large did you say that block of ice is?"

"Nine inches by nine inches," replied Low.

"What an amazing coincidence," said Churchill. "Exactly the same size as mine."

Countless other speakers have been nervous when they went before an audience, yet their speeches were successful. These are some of the reasons:

> They have their fears under control.
> They have gained confidence from past performances.
> They have prepared themselves well.
> They believe in what they say.
> They have learned to turn tension into vitality.
> They know the audience is with them.

Thousands of ordinary men and women in business and social situations have learned to be equally successful. It can be done.

The best antidote for fear is preparation. You know what to expect. You have a carefully prepared speech in hand along with the know-how and practice in delivering it. You are ready. There is no better way to build confidence and, for that matter, to insure success.

Speak at Every Opportunity

There is stress in anticipation of every new experience, and public speaking is no exception. The human body does have the ability to adapt to circumstances, however. As the unfamiliar becomes familiar, we develop a tolerance for that stress.

If you just take the plunge, you will set in motion what I call the "success cycle." You can reduce tension by exposing yourself to the tension-producing situation (in this case, public speaking). As tension lessens, you gain confidence; as you gain confidence, your tension will decrease even more.

Accept every opportunity to speak that comes your way. Don't allow any excuse to hold you back. Face the speech situation often.

Start Slowly

If you have been hesitant about speaking out in front of a group, delivering an entire speech may be more than you want to tackle at first. It is not necessary to begin by speaking for fifteen minutes or more. Any start will do.

Why not volunteer to make an announcement at your next club or sales meeting? Here, too, proper thought and preparation will help put you at ease. Although the announcement may be the simplest form of public speaking, it has a definite beginning, middle, and end.

The Audience Is with You

Some beginning speakers see the audience as the "enemy," a vague body of people waiting for the speaker to make a fool of himself. Nothing could be further from the truth.

If you have ever been at a function where an unprepared speaker floundered, you will recall that you and others in the audience were sincerely distressed. As listeners, you felt uneasy and suffered along with the unfortunate novice. Simply stated, the audience wants you to succeed. They want to relax and enjoy your speech.

Often you will be called upon to speak because you have some special knowledge. You are the expert. Your audience does not know as much as you do about your subject, and they are anxious to hear what you have to say. That is precisely why they are there.

The audience will appreciate the effort you have made on their behalf. They will admire your ability to get up on the platform and share your knowledge with them. And should you make an error while you are speaking, simply correct it and go on. The audience will respect you all the more for dealing with it calmly and maturely.

Importance of Being Earnest

Approach the speech with the genuine feeling that what you say is important to you and important to the listener. If you don't care, why should anyone else? One prevalent reason for failure in public speaking is a lack of enthusiasm for the subject.

A veteran circus performer was teaching a young man to perform on the flying trapeze. "There is only one thing left to learn, and it is most important of all," he said. "Throw your heart over the bars and your body will follow."

"Heart" is an essential part of any successful endeavor. This does not imply that each speech need be a crusade, but if your talk concerns something that you are enthusiastic about, your tension may well be relieved.

Helping You Relax

Contrary to what many people think, trying to hold trembling arms, hands, and legs still will only increase tension and force your muscles to tighten up all the more. But there are specific things you can do to give yourself relief from the excessive tensions that interfere with your speaking. They are all directed at helping you relax.

Before Speaking (off stage or podium)
Yawn several times to reduce tension in throat and jaw.
Rotate shoulders.
Stretch and loosen arms.
Take slow, even, deep breaths.
While Speaking
Make use of movement and gesture.

Bodily action helps vitalize a speech. Used properly, it puts nervous energy to work, gives added meaning to what you say, and helps relieve stiffness and tension. Avoid pacing up and down or fidgeting.

Practice moving about, shifting foot positions and weight distributions. Use hands, arms, and facial expressions naturally. Highly emotional occasions will demand a greater amount of movement and gesture.

Most important, synchronize your movements with changes of thought in the speech. Reading matter has paragraph indentations that serve to indicate a shift in thought, but in a speech this must be done entirely by the speaker. Change of pace, change of pitch, and change of movement are three methods at your disposal to carry the audience from point to point.

Gestures not only clarify thought, but help intensify ideas and make them more emphatic. If you let yourself go, you will find that when you stress an important word verbally, you also stress it physically. There will be an accompanying vigorous movement of your head, hand, and arm. The actual movement should begin with the shoulders and encompass the entire body. Do not use short, choppy gestures.

Learn to move freely about the platform. If you are incorporating visual aids into your speech, use a pointer to indicate some special feature. Walk to the blackboard. Keep your diagrams well-drawn and simple. Write firmly, then put your chalk down. Never jiggle it from hand to hand. The motion is distracting to the viewers and, for that matter, so is the diagram once you have finished with it. When you are through, erase the blackboard immediately with strong, even strokes. This gives you an opportunity to take a deep breath, loosen any tenseness in your arms, and bring the audience's attention back to you, the speaker.

Some Nervousness Is Desirable

Fear and tension can be a positive influence. In any fear reaction, adrenalin and thyroxin are poured into the blood stream, keeping your senses fully alert. A little nervousness is something to be thankful for. It prevents your delivery from becoming dull and uninspiring.

The famous Roman speech teacher Quintilian considered nervousness to be *crucial* to successful speechmaking. He wrote:

. . . I am not unwilling that the man who has got to make a speech should show signs of nervousness when he rises to his feet, should change colour and make it clear that he feels the risk of his position: indeed, if these symptoms do not occur naturally, it would be necessary to simulate them.

Being a little nervous definitely enhances your effectiveness, so don't worry about it.

Perfection Is Not Your Goal

Most conscientious people want to do their best. But there is a world of difference between *their* best and *the* best. Do not confuse the two. Only a few people can expect to win the Kentucky Derby, but many can learn to ride a horse expertly.

I am reminded of the famous orchestra leader who once walked into rehearsal, bowed to the musicians, and then raised his hands for silence.

"Now, gentlemen," he said, "the opening of this symphony must be *piano*—softly, but very, very softly. It opens like a whisper. Now!"

He raised his baton. Tensely, the men placed their instruments in position, but before a single note was played, the conductor lowered his baton. "No, no, gentlemen," he said solemnly. "Already too loud!"

He was reaching for the impossible.

In speeches, too, we must realize that great orations are the exception. When you face an audience, no one expects you to be another William Jennings Bryan. Don't ask it of yourself.

You already have the basic tools of success at your disposal—words. You have been using words your entire life. Most likely, you have used nearly all the words in this book at some time or other in casual conversation.

What makes a speech outstanding is a *unique* thought in simple words or a *unique* combination of simple words.

Remember, you are not trying to produce great oratory, but rather a good, effective speech:

> Effective speeches are simple.
> Effective speeches are clear.
> Effective speeches are organized.
> Effective speeches contain lively detail.
> Effective speeches are not unlike animated conversation.

It is obvious that setting your sights below perfection does not mean a sloppy effort. Speechmaking at business conventions, social organizations, P.T.A. sessions, club meetings, and so forth, requires properly researched material and the skill to put it across to an audience. And that is something everyone can learn.

2 The Opening

WHEN A SPEAKER rises from his chair to make an address, there are two obstacles he must usually overcome immediately—his own inhibitions, which affect his confidence, and the audience's indifference. The ice can be broken at once with the right kind of opening. There are a number of sure ways to produce the sort of reaction that will build up your confidence and help you hold the audience.

Shock Treatment

You can employ the shock method. You can startle your listeners into attention as Bernard Baruch once did at the opening session of the United Nations Atomic Energy Commission. This is the way he began his speech on the control of atomic weapons: "We are here to make a choice between the quick and the dead."

After that, his audience listened and his suggestions were enthusiastically received.

Smiles, Chuckles, and Guffaws

A joke, anecdote, or humorous remark that ties in with the subject matter is a very important aid in inducing a receptive mood. Adlai Stevenson accomplished this and brought smiles when he addressed a graduating class at Smith: "I am not unmindful of the appalling fact that countless middle-aged moralists like me are rising these days on countless platforms all over the world to tell thousands of helpless young captives the score. . . ."

Mark Twain produced chuckles while talking at a dinner of the New England Society: "I reverently believe that the Maker who made us all, makes everything in New England—but the weather."

It is safer to start with a smile or a chuckle than to try for a loud guffaw right away. A little later on in the speech, when speaker and audience have achieved a certain rapport, the chances of a joke or anecdote producing a big laugh are much improved.

The Recognition Factor

Your first words might open up a line of communication with the audience by referring to something familiar. The old-time vaudeville performer would always insert in his opening remarks a reference to some local personage, problem, or geographic locale.

Many speakers who are going to appear before a strange audience make it a point to find out about idiosyncracies or characteristics of prominent members of that audience. This inside information is then thrown into the speech, supposedly to show how knowledgeable the speaker is about the group he is addressing. I have always frowned upon this practice. Thinking people will realize that the outsider couldn't possibly know these things about members of the group unless he was briefed. Thus the references are insincere and merely a gimmick. My own rule of thumb is "Don't use 'in' jokes unless you are really 'in.'"

However, the speaker *should* remember the nature of his audience, its age, sex, marital status, ethnic background, and economic level. Adlai Stevenson bore this in mind at Smith. As an older man addressing a group of much younger people, he made a point of the age differential instead of indifferently ignoring it.

Draw a Word Picture

A pictorial lead-in can illustrate the theme of the talk and introduce a brief statement of that theme, which will be elaborated on as the speaker proceeds. You may want to stimulate your listeners to fresh thinking and a new approach.

You could do this by relating Philip Wylie's tale of a despondent artist who decided to kill himself. He turned on the gas and sat down with pad and pencil to record his final thoughts. Someone smelled the gas and the police rescued him. As soon as he was revived he asked to see the pad. It was brought to him, and on it were the four words: Think in other categories.

Presenting this picture of a man studying the four words he had written that might have solved his problems is much more effective than merely exhorting people to action.

The First-Person Story

The comedian or master of ceremonies who starts off with, "A funny thing happened to me on the way over here," may sound a bit obvious; but he is using a sure-fire approach. He is taking the audience into his confidence by sharing a recent experience with them. Even though they've heard the line before, and they may suspect the incident's authenticity, there is a feeling of immediacy.

You can vary the "funny thing happened" approach by saying

what I said on one of my television shows: "Quite frankly, nothing funny happened on the way over here. I just got into a cab, drove down, paid the driver, and tipped him. He gave me a dirty look, and I got out."

If you are called upon to speak fairly often, you should make notes of amusing occurrences that can be worked into your opening words, as though they had happened, if not on the way over, at least in the very recent past. Will Rogers did this once in a speech to a group of Columbia alumni:

"President Butler paid me a compliment a while ago in mentioning my name in his introductory remarks, and he put me ahead of the Columbia graduates. I am glad he did that, because I got the worst of it last week. The Prince of Wales last week, in speaking of the sights of America, mentioned the Woolworth Building, the subway, the slaughterhouse, Will Rogers, and the Ford factory. He could at least put me ahead of the hogs."

If you, like Rogers, make yourself the butt of the joke, you will create an empathy with the audience. They will think, "He's not trying to be high hat. He is one of us."

The Personal Reference

A personal reference relating a situation to some aspect of your own life can often be effective. This is especially true if the audience is familiar with your career.

Consider this introduction to an address I made at ceremonies honoring the memory of Haym Solomon, the Revolutionary War patriot:

"Having spent a lifetime in the theater, I find myself again engrossed in a moment of drama. For the period of Haym Solomon is one of the great dramatic stories of the United States of America. It has waited a long time to be told. For this man who gave his time, his money, his heart, and ultimately his life is finally being saluted today."

The Suspense Opening

Another method of holding the listeners' interest is to create an atmosphere of suspense. The Reverend Russell Conwell, active as a lecturer for over sixty years, was a master at this in his talk called "Acres of Diamonds." He began the speech with a story, supposedly told to him personally, about a man who hunted for diamonds all over the world. With tantalizing detail, he kept his audiences anxiously awaiting the outcome. Reverend Conwell then went on, with further illustrations, to a speech about the value of worldly ambition and the folly of looking for success far from home. Incidentally, he made his own fortune out of the lecture, which he gave six thousand times, for a return of eight million dollars.

Winston Churchill's famous Iron Curtain speech opened with a suspenseful sentence: "A shadow has fallen upon the scenes so lately lighted by Allied victory." Who could listen to that ominous opening without anticipating the worst, and wanting to know what that was?

Facts That Jolt

No matter what the subject of your speech, there are a few facts connected with it that can jolt the audience out of complacency. For instance:

> Over a million people take up smoking every year.
> There are 6,500,000 alcoholics in the United States.
> Americans spend $100,000,000 on marijuana each year.
> We spend $50,000,000 yearly on maintaining hunting and fishing areas in this country.
> A study shows that working wives spend 74 percent more money on clothes than housewives and take better care of their figures.

Last year, there were 12,364 commercial and industrial failures in the United States, with total liabilities of $1,265,227,000.

At a time when $24,000,000,000 is spent on trips to the moon, the largest city in the United States cannot get an additional $500,000,000 for educational and social programs.

These and similar figures can be obtained from books in your public library, the big insurance companies, the *World Almanac*, the *United States Statistical Abstract*, and various government, health, and business organizations.

Conversational Openings

A good test of the effectiveness of an opening is to imagine that you are using it an an ordinary conversation. Would you turn to someone and say, "Honesty is the best policy"? Of course not. So you'll very likely lose your audience with that kind of preachy start.

However, you can get across the same idea in a conversational way by saying, "The other day something happened to me that shows it certainly pays to be honest." In that way, you'll be arousing curiosity with a first-person story that is told as though you were confiding in a friend. Then you can startle them with a figure on how much a hotel, department store, or business office loses in thefts in a year at the hands of supposedly respectable customers and trusted employees.

Audience Involvement

You may have noticed that television masters of ceremonies often ask their audiences for a show of hands. The questions they ask and the answers they receive are not particularly important, but they get the audience into the act. They force them to use their brains and their arms, so that they become more than a certain number of bodies settled down in chairs.

You can involve the audience by asking them a question such as, "How many of you have ever known a completely honest person?" and asking for a show of hands.

It is necessary, when asking a question, to have several prepared comments to fit the possible responses. If, for instance, you ask, "How many of you are over twenty-five?" and the show of hands is large, you might say, "You may not realize it, but you are members of a minority group." If the show of hands is small, you can remark, "As you can see, you are members of a minority group."

Then you can go on to explain the population trend toward an under-twenty-five majority. Later on, you might produce another show of hands in order to point out the danger of jumping to conclusions. You could ask, "How many of you are under the age of thirteen?" If it is an adult audience, there will be no hands raised, and you can remind them that the under-twenty-five majority will not be an overwhelming group of teenagers and post-teenagers, but will be composed to a great extent of children. If it is a mixed audience, and there are some small hands raised, your point can be made even more effectively.

Give 'Em What They Want

An old Dale Carnegie trick and audience pleaser is a promise to tell people how they can get something they particularly want: "I am going to tell you how to lose weight the easy way"; "I'll explain how you can succeed in business without a college diploma"; or "I'll describe one sure way to make yourself more attractive to the opposite sex."

In the hypothetical speech on honesty mentioned earlier, you could tell your listeners, "I am going to tell you six ways to lower the number of thefts in your business."

Even if you don't state your message that directly, you can manipulate the subject of any talk so that it affects your audience personally. A talk on slum clearance may leave your listeners cold, unless they are reminded of how the evil of the inner city seeps through to the more prosperous neighborhoods through disease, drugs, muggings, burglaries, and added costs for social welfare. Recall for them the time, in the winter of 1968–69, when the Harlem rats showed up in a colony right in the middle of Park Avenue.

If you make a speech on schools, tell the parents how *they* can increase the quality of *their* children's education. If you talk about law and order, tell the members of the community how *they* can protect *themselves, their* homes, and *their* businesses. Think about what your audience's chief interest may be and concentrate on that.

Eye Appeal

Visual gimmicks are attention-getters that work for some speakers. The best results are obtained when objects used to attract attention are ordinary items usually carried on the person, rather than stagey props. In making a speech on honesty, to come to the podium carrying a lamp, like Diogenes looking for an honest man, would be an affectation. To light a match and pretend to be looking around in the dark for the honest person would be simple and effective.

A speech on finance could be highlighted with an easy coin trick. You'll need only ten pennies, a digest-sized magazine, and a glass or cup. You have three pennies concealed in the magazine, which you hold firmly closed. You loudly count out seven pennies, placing them on top of the magazine, then tip them into the glass or cup, allowing the extra three to join them unobtrusively. Then you pretend to pick three more pennies out of the air and drop them into the container, shaking it to make clinking sounds.

Think how well it would illustrate the rewards of sound investment when you withdraw ten coins from the container into which you had only (supposedly) placed seven!

The Preview

A simple, but effective, introduction is the "preview." By using this device, you can inform your audience what to expect in the speech. If your subject is complex, the "preview" introduction may be the best kind.

The following example is a combination of anecdote and preview. It is from an address by William S. Beinecke, President of the Sperry and Hutchinson Company, before the American Marketing Association:

"My uncle, who has been in management for a long time, has a favorite line about a principle of business leadership. He says: 'If you don't know where you're going, any road will get you there.'

"It is a fair principle, too, that an audience has as much right to know where a speaker is going. It might be helpful if I pointed out the road I am going to take here today.

"First, I intend to define what I believe to be the basic responsibility of a corporate president. Second, I intend to single out what appear to me to be two major misconceptions concerning his job. One has to do with the amounts and kinds of information supposedly available to him: the other with the power he supposedly wields. Third, I intend to set the record straight on both of these misconceptions."

One of the best sources for introductory material is your newspaper. Topical allusions can be great ice-breakers. Reference to an event in the news—particularly one that is peculiar to, or has had a great impact upon, the community in which you are speaking—is virtually certain to arouse the interest of your audience. In most cases, these allusions will be humorous. But be careful not to poke too much fun.

Suit Yourself

In choosing the kind of opening that you prefer, you must use the one that you feel at home with—one that suits your subject and your prospective audience. You would not necessarily want to shock a group of middle-aged clubwomen. Humor would be inappropriate at a memorial service. You can always communicate, however, whatever the occasion, by relating to the familiar, and by drawing a picture in words.

The first-person story is suited to the informal talk, the suspense story to a dramatic speech. Facts are great, if the subject matter lends itself to them. The same holds true for audience involvement. No matter what the subject, every audience wants to be told how its interests can be served.

3 The Use of Humor

THERE IS NO better way to relax an audience and put it in a receptive mood than lightening up a speech from time to time with humor. There are a number of ways to turn even an incidental remark into a laugh-producer. You don't need to be as adept a humorist as I am (after all, I do make a living at it). Your audience doesn't expect as much of you as they do of me. In fact, just *because* you are not a professional comedian, they will find your mildest attempts quite funny. People enjoy humor, and they will like you more for making them laugh.

Surprise Twist

This type of humor consists of starting out with a thought apparently leading in one direction, and concluding it unexpectedly in another. A good example of this is a remark Milton Berle is reputed to have made when composer Dick Rodgers asked him to star in a TV show. When Rodgers asked Berle how much money he would want, he replied: "Dick, I'm so flattered that

you want me that money will be the very last thing I think of—
before I get to sleep tonight."

Robert Benchley was known for his use of the twist ending,
as in his advice on how to write: "The biggest obstacle to professional writing today is the necessity for changing a typewriter
ribbon."

Another example of the surprise twist: "The girls are so beautiful. It's sad to think that twenty years from now, they'll all be
five years older."

That is really a double twist. First, there is the transition from
the beauty of the girls today to the sad thought of the changes
that will take place in twenty years, and then the humorous reminder that they will all lie about their ages anyway. This is also
an example of taking an idea that has been joked about for
centuries—women taking years off their age—and presenting it in
a new context.

The Big Letdown

One of the most effective uses of the surprise twist is anti-
climax, or building up to the big letdown. For instance, Alexan-
der Woollcott's famous quip: "All the things I really like to do
are either immoral, illegal, or fattening."

And John Mason Brown's critique of an actress's performance:
"Tallulah Bankhead barged down the Nile last night in *Cleopatra*
—and sank."

Or Mark Twain's remark: "To be good is noble; but to show
others how to be good is nobler and no trouble."

Take Noel Coward's remark about a fellow actor: "Alfred Lunt
has his head in the clouds and his feet in the box office."

Experiment with this technique yourself by starting out with
a thought that seems deep, inspiring, or noble, and then let it
come to a full stop and go into reverse.

The Tall Tale

Exaggeration, they say, is typically American. When it is carried to absurd lengths, it becomes funny, as in the braggings of Texans and midwesterners. A Nebraskan, boasting about the amount of marijuana grown in his state, is reputed to have said, "If Nebraska ever catches fire, half of Kansas will turn on."

Texas has been defined as "miles and miles of miles and miles." It has been said of Texas that it occupies all of the continent of North America except the small part set aside for the United States, Mexico, and Canada.

Natives of other parts of the country have also been known to use exaggeration with effect. Mayor John V. Lindsay of New York City is credited with this remark on the subject of water pollution: "If someone falls into the Hudson River, he won't die by drowning; he'll be poisoned." This is an example of overstating the truth to the point of absurdity, without losing track of the basic fact—the river is polluted.

Looking for the Absurd

Reread your manuscript or your prompt cards and mentally rehearse your delivery. When you reach a point where you find yourself getting bored, stop there and work out a way to get a laugh. Try to think of something ridiculous that has happened to you which is relevant to that portion of your speech. Set down on a piece of paper a number of straight sentences that you had planned to use, and see if you can't find one that can be twisted around for absurd effect. Bring in some sort of contrast, unexpected turn, or mild shock. And of course, check through the categories of humorous remarks in this book for an appropriate story.

Evan Esar, in his *Comic Dictionary*, defines absurdity as "anything so contrary to reason that it is laughable. Remember Victor

Borge's uncle, the doctor, who discovered a cure for which there was no disease."

Art Buchwald concluded a piece on "adult" movies with a supposed conversation between himself and his wife:

"What was the point of that Mountie kissing his horse?" she inquired.

"Oh, come on. Haven't you seen a man kiss a horse before?" he said.

"On the lips?"

Goodman Ace, at the height of the hijacking of planes to Cuba, reduced that problem to the absurd: "The way hijacking is flourishing now, and with the breakdown of the service on suburban trains in New York, any day some distraught commuter will be on a Florida-bound plane shouting, 'Scarsdale! Scarsdale!'"

Notice how, even in this absurdity, he pointed up another serious problem—the deterioration of service on suburban railroads.

I have used the following introduction at a number of dinners and have found it is almost always well received: "I'm sure you'll agree with me that this was a fine dinner we had tonight, although you can never tell about a person's food preferences. I'm reminded of the two cannibals who were having lunch. One of them said, 'You know, I can't stand my mother-in-law.' The second replied, 'So just eat the noodles.'"

Analyzing Humor

We laugh at jokes and humorous remarks without giving much thought to why they are funny. Too close a study of humor takes some of the fun out of it; but it does enable one to see the skeletal structure and how it produces the laugh.

Art Buchwald's story, for example, had a surprise twist, since kissing a horse is assumed to be a harmless gesture, but he turned it into something suggestive. He exaggerated also in insinuating that movies have become so perverse they would show a man making love to an animal. The pairing of a man with a horse, however, is such an extreme exaggeration that it is not shocking, but merely amusing. The punch line is short and snappy, and should get a quick reaction.

Goodman Ace's joke turned a story about hijacking of planes to Cuba into an entirely different train of thought, the difficulty the commuter has in making the short hop to the suburbs. He used exaggeration to get his laugh, along with absurdity. What could be more ridiculous than a man hijacking a Miami-bound plane and forcing it to fly to Scarsdale?

Borrowing Gags

You can gradually build up a file of humor by adding to my collection of funny stories any examples you come across in newspapers, magazines, and on TV shows. You can use them as is or, if you wish, change them a little to fit them into the particular spot you have chosen for them. For example:

> "The biggest obstacle to preparing a speech today is knowing where to put in a pause for hecklers."

> "All the things we enjoy most are either immoral, illegal, or high in chloresterol. If someone falls into the Houstonic [or Mississippi, or Potomac, or Swanee, or whatever your local waterway], he won't have to worry about drowning, because he'll die of poisoning first."

> "You ladies are so attractive. It's sad to think that twenty years from now, you'll all be five years older."

> "The way hijacking is flourishing, and taking into account the breakdown of service on suburban trains, any day some distraught commuter will be on a Florida-bound plane shouting 'Larchmont!' [or Bryn Mawr, or East Orange, or whatever your local suburb is]."

Insult Humor

Insult humor is very popular today, and there are some comedians who specialize in it. They can get away with it because they are known as insult specialists, and the audience expects it from them.

The ordinary speaker should exercise caution in its use. Be sure that your gag is really funny as well as mildly insulting, and —most important—know your audience. If they are members of a group who know you well, like fellow workers, club members, friends, and neighbors, you have little to worry about. If the audience is more mixed, then be careful about insulting *them*. Use the insult against someone else, to whom they can feel superior. Among friends, the following are permissible:

"If I said anything I'm sorry for, I'm glad of it."
"You don't have to be crazy to talk like that, but it helps."
"I never forget a face, but in your case I'll make an exception" (which Groucho Marx said in one of his movies).
"How much would you charge to haunt a house?" Fred Allen asked a radio performer.

If you are in doubt, you can use the following indirect insults:

"They're a very nice couple—he never goes anyplace without his wife, but his wife will go *any*place.
"He's never been known to steal a thing—we watch him too closely."
"She could dish it out—but she couldn't cook it."
"When she wants to punish the kids she sends them to bed with dinner."

Writer Dorothy Parker was known for her insult humor. On hearing that Calvin Coolidge had died, she said, "How can they tell?" And on being told that a society woman was "awfully kind to her inferiors," she inquired, "Where does she find them?"

Marcello Mastroianni is said to have deflated the ego of a pretty girl reporter when he said, "You know, you remind me of Joanne Woodward." When the girl smiled with pleasure, he added, "You also remind me of Paul Newman."

Self-Insult

There is no better way of ingratiating yourself with an audience than by putting yourself down in a humorous way.

You might say of some important personage, "I told Mr. Hughes how to run his business, and you know what happened? We parted good friends. He got into his private jet and I took the bus home."

Joey Adams, upon receiving a doctorate from a Korean university, deprecated his achievement by saying, "I've been made a doctor so many times that I'm starting to resent socialized medicine."

Irreverence

Humor with a religious angle can be extremely funny, and it is especially appreciated by religious people themselves, as long as it does not offend their beliefs. You may recall that Bishop Fulton J. Sheen referred to his clerical dress by comparing himself to Superman.

You might tell about the little boy who explained why he didn't say his prayers every night: "Some nights I don't want anything."

Or you might ask: "If a missionary is supposed to go to heaven and a cannibal is destined for hell, what happens when a cannibal dies after making a meal of a missionary?"

You might quote Mark Twain's, "More men go to church than want to."

Or you could say, "Adam was a lucky man because when he told a joke, he knew nobody had ever heard it before."

You can also poke fun at respected figures, such as heads of state, prominent businessmen, sports figures, or anyone in authority.

At an Inner Circle dinner, Mayor Lindsay of New York referred to Ralph Bunche's complaints about being snowbound in his Queens home: "Well, what did Dr. Bunche expect? He wanted to live in an all-white neighborhood."

Jack Carter commented on the news pictures of Lindsay walking through the city: "He walks around Brooklyn, around Manhattan, and the Bronx. I know how it is—I can't get a cab either."

If you don't want to lampoon a person, you can make fun of institutions that are sometimes pompous and can stand deflation, such as: the government, the Army, the theater, the opera, the ballet, art galleries, professional sports, and big business.

Believe in Yourself

At first the insertion of humor in your talks will be a mechanical thing, deliberately done. After a while, with practice and experience, it should become second nature. Your subconscious will begin automatically turning out the humorous twists that you must work to achieve at first. The main point is to develop faith in your own ability to make others laugh, and build up your faith with repeated public demonstrations of that ability.

4 Varieties of Speeches

THERE ARE as many different types of speeches as there are occasions on which to make them—formal and informal, entertaining and persuasive, introductory and after-dinner, reports and acknowledgments, speeches to raise funds and speeches to sell merchandise or ideas.

Formal Speeches

Because of the formality of the situation, the audience should be warmed up immediately with an opening that strikes a spark of interest. In a speech to be given to parents on the dangers of driving while drinking, you might start out with "There are a number of youngsters who learn the hard way that gasoline and alcohol don't mix." That will do as an opening, but it will get more attention if you follow it up with "Two thousand highway deaths a year are caused by drunken teen-age drivers."

Your audience may be aroused momentarily by this shocking statistic, but it may sink back into apathy unless you provide a strong link between the general statement and some specific connection with the members of this particular audience, such as, " I bring up this subject because seventy-five percent of our local high-school juniors and seniors have drivers' licenses, and a survey shows that twenty-five percent of them are drinkers."

Now that you have softened up any indifference to your subject among local parents, you can go ahead to make your consecutive points, and come to your planned conclusion. The principal difference between this speech and some more informal types is that you will have the floor and can follow through pretty much as planned, and at as great length as you think necessary.

Conference Speeches

The informal speech, such as that made at a conference table, must be shorter and to the point, since some of the others in the group will also want to present their views. Your first sentence should be a brief presentation of some specific reason why you are for or against some proposed move: "Mr. Chairman, I oppose the construction of a ski lift and lodge on Mount Greylock because it will destroy the nests of a number of wild birds which we promised to protect."

Try to follow this up with some phrase that will be remembered even after other speakers have presented their views, in this case, perhaps, "Broken eggs, broken legs, and broken promises." Then back up your thesis with concrete examples, and end quickly with a restatement of your opening proposition.

The Introduction of Another Speaker

There are a few simple rules to follow in making the speech that introduces someone:

Brevity: Don't keep the listeners waiting more than a minute.

Simplicity: Don't waste time on meaningless phrases, such as "it is indeed a pleasure" or "we are gathered here."

Restraint: Keep your praise of the speaker within bounds. Otherwise you will embarrass him or disappoint the audience.

Modesty: Draw attention to the person being introduced, not yourself.

Order: Make your statements about the guest before mentioning his name and causing him to rise.

When you do announce the name, do so loudly and clearly, facing the audience so that everyone can understand you. Then turn to the speaker with an expression of welcome, and remain standing this way until the speaker rises and makes his acknowledgment.

If you have done your job well, by condensing the speaker's background into a brief description, and arousing audience interest in him and his subject, then both speaker and audience should have a good time.

A brief, well-organized introductory speech was made by Richard B. Walbert for Doctor Norman Vincent Peale:

"Our speaker today was born and raised in Ohio, graduating from Ohio Wesleyan University and obtaining his master's degree from Boston University.

"He has achieved world-wide fame as a minister, lecturer, and author. It would be unlikely that anyone here today has not come in contact in one way or another with this remarkable man.

"Since 1932, he has served as minister of the Marble Collegiate Church, located at Fifth Avenue and Twenty-Ninth Street in New York City, where, in two services each Sunday morning, he preaches before four thousand people.

"He has a constant schedule of broadcasts on both TV and radio. He is editor of the magazine *Guideposts*, which has subscribers numbering over one and a quarter million. His syndicated weekly column, "Confident Living," appears in more than two hundred newspapers, including the *Chicago Tribune*, and he has authored the most popular nonfiction book in recent years: *The Power of Positive Thinking*, which has sold more than two million copies.

"It is a pleasure to welcome back to our platform this forceful, dynamic, and highly influential man who will, I am sure, shortly have you thinking more positively—Doctor Norman Vincent Peale."

Responses

The speaker must then acknowledge the introduction before getting into the talk that he has prepared. Doctor Peale did so in this case:

"I appreciate the kind and felicitous remarks made about me by your very generous president. It rather serves to raise my ego. Those who know me best may doubt that my ego needs raising. but I assure you that it was deflated recently, and I am very glad that it's been upgraded here today."

Doctor Peale then went on to describe an amusing incident which took place in Hollywood, where some friends had taken him to the Brown Derby. A loud, staggering drunk, who had evidently learned of his presence, weaved around the tables calling out, "Where's Doctor Peale?" After a while he located the minister, bent over his table, and inquired, "Are you Dr. Peale?" When Dr. Peale said Yes, the drunk stuck his hand out and said, "Well, whad d'ya know—put her there! I've read all your books. You've done me an awful lot of good."

You can see how the minister tied his response with the introduction, and proceeded from there into an amusing story that tended to temper the high praise given him by showing that he is not always successful.

The Welcome

The purpose of a welcoming speech is to promote friendly relations by a formal greeting on public occasions, such as introducing a new member or newly appointed executive, greeting guests at dinner, or welcoming delegates to a convention. The outline of the speech should follow an orderly procedure, such as:

1. Naming the person or persons being welcomed.
2. Naming your colleagues who are present.
3. Presenting the reason for the welcome.
4. Describing the meaning of the occasion and its purpose.
5. Making a tribute to the accomplishments of the person being welcomed.
6. Expressing the rewards of the proposed association.
7. Restating your pleasure at the presence of the members, guests, or delegates.

There is no need for a long response to a welcome. An appreciative "Thank you," followed by the names of those in charge, is sufficient. If a response is made, it should be short and addressed to the appropriate person or persons. It should express gratitude for the tribute, return the compliment, refer to the purpose of the occasion, and close with hopes for the future.

Eulogies

As you know, I am often called upon to give the eulogy at funerals. This happens so frequently that someone once remarked, "When a dog died in Burbank last week, the owners immediately called on George Jessel."

A eulogy is usually a tribute to a deceased person. It includes the essential details of the person's career, background, and accomplishments, his most admirable traits of character, his favorable impact upon his contemporaries, and his contributions to the future.

You may have heard on television or radio in the past few years the eulogies for Doctor Martin Luther King, Senator Robert F. Kennedy, and President Dwight D. Eisenhower. King, Kennedy, and Eisenhower were not ordinary men, of course; but every man or woman has some outstanding traits and worthwhile achievements that can be remembered and enlarged upon at the time of their passing.

President Richard M. Nixon's eulogy for Dwight D. Eisenhower is a fine specimen of this type of address:

"Mrs. Eisenhower, your excellencies, friends of Dwight David Eisenhower in America and throughout the world.

"We gather today in mourning but also in gratitude. We mourn Dwight Eisenhower's death. But we are grateful for his life.

"We gather also conscious of the fact that, in paying tribute to Dwight Eisenhower, we celebrate greatness. When we think of his place in history, we think inevitably of the other giants of those days of World War Two.

"And we think of the qualities of greatness and what his were that made his unique among all.

"Once, perhaps without intending to do so, he himself put his finger on it.

"It was 1945, shortly after V.E. Day at a ceremony in London's historic Guildhall. The triumphant Supreme Commander of the Allied Forces in Europe was officially given the freedom of the city of London.

"In an eloquent address that day, Dwight Eisenhower said, 'I come from the heart of America.'

"Perhaps no one sentence could better sum up what Dwight Eisenhower meant to a whole generation of Americans. He did come from the heart of America, not only from its geographical heart but from its spiritual heart. He exemplified what millions of parents hoped that their sons would be—strong and courageous and compassionate.

"And with his own great qualities of heart, he personified the best in America. It is, I think, a special tribute to Dwight Eisenhower that despite all of his great deeds and his triumphs, we find ourselves today thinking first, not of his deeds, but of his character.

"It was the character of the man—not what he did, but what

he was—that so captured the trust and faith and affection of his own people and of the people of the world.

"Dwight Eisenhower touched something fundamental in America which only a man of immense force of mind and spirit could have brought so vibrantly alive. He was a product of America's soil, and of its ideals, driven by a compulsion to do right and to do well, a man of deep faith who believed in God and trusted in his will, a man who truly loved his country and for whom words like freedom and democracy were not clichés—but they were living truths.

"I know Mrs. Eisenhower would permit me to share with you the last words he spoke to her on the day he died.

"He said, 'I've always loved my wife. I've always loved my children. I've always loved my grandchildren. And I have always loved my country.' That was Dwight Eisenhower."

President Nixon went on to describe how Eisenhower gave of himself, and how much he loved people, and how much they loved him. He told of his tolerance for others and his puzzlement at the existence of hatred. He told of his strength, shrewdness, and decisiveness. He described how Eisenhower's stature grew after World War Two, and how he met this with becoming humility. Nixon described Eisenhower as a peacemaker who was admired and loved all over the world. He dwelt on his character and moral force, and concluded:

"And, so, today we render our final salute. It is a fond salute to a man we loved and cherished. It is a grateful salute to a man whose whole extraordinary life was consecrated to service.

"It is a profoundly respectful salute to a man larger than life who by any standard was one of the giants of our time.

"Each of us here will have a special memory of Dwight Eisenhower.

"I can see him now standing erect, straight, proud, and tall sixteen years ago as he took the oath of office as the thirty-fourth President of the United States of America.

"We salute Dwight David Eisenhower standing there in our

memories—first in war, first in peace and, wherever freedom is cherished, first in the hearts of his fellow men."

Nomination and Inauguration Speeches

A nomination speech follows a certain formula. It is brief and pointed:

1. The qualifications for the office are described.
2. The candidates are compared favorably.
3. The candidate's ability, morality, and intelligence are praised.
4. The advantages to the audience of naming this candidate are explained.
5. The candidate's name is presented with convincing whole-heartedness.

An inauguration speech can be as brief or as long as the occasion, the time limit, and the speaker's judgment dictate:

1. Thank those responsible for your election.
2. Make known your intention to devote yourself to the good of all concerned.
3. If the choice has been less than unanimous, appeal to all sides to work together in the common interest.
4. Confidently outline your plans for the future and how you intend to carry them out.

After-Dinner Speeches

One of the commonest speeches a person is called upon to make is the after-dinner speech. While most such talks are designed as entertainment, they sometimes, because of the nature of the gathering, have a serious side, too.

The speech should be introduced with an amusing story, in order to fit it into the relaxed, dinner-table mood. This is a sort of appetizer. The main course of the speech should be presented simply, and lightly, with many colorful illustrations and anecdotes to season the meaty content. Try to keep your style conversational and intimate, with as little reference to notes as possible. The speech is usually from twenty to thirty minutes in length, so that the audience is left wishing you'd continue, rather than hoping you'll quit.

The Toastmaster

I was honored by President Harry Truman in 1948 when he bestowed the unofficial title of "The Toastmaster General of the United States" upon me. Hardly a week has passed in my life when I have not served as toastmaster at one function or another. A toastmaster is often responsible for the entire program, and since there is a great deal of information to give, I am providing a whole chapter to guide you (see Chapter 5).

The Chairman

The chairman of a meeting acts as a toastmaster and more. He must control and guide the course of the meeting. He must plan the order of business. This is usually a call to order, followed by announcements, introductions of any guests present, and the reading of minutes of the last meeting. Then come the reports of officers and committees, the main program, and finally the adjournment.

The chairman stands when speaking or spoken to, but remains seated while others are speaking. The chairman does not enter into a discussion. If he wishes to do so, he must turn the chair over to someone else temporarily, ask for recognition, and resume the chair after speaking.

If there is a motion or amendment to be voted on, the chairman must state it exactly before taking a vote. He must indicate how the vote is to be taken—by voice, by a show of hands, or by ballot.

The chairman serves as guide for the meeting, as referee in

discussions, as pinch hitter for a canceled speaker, and as toast-master.

The Speech that Informs

An informative speech can include directions, explanations, demonstrations, or descriptions. It is the simplest and most straightforward type of speech, but it has one stumbling block—the subject matter is so clear to you that you may fail to make it clear to your audience. It is easy to overlook essential details that are second nature to you, like the cook whose recipe never comes out right because he leaves out directions that are obvious to him when he passes it along. Such a speech could be reviewed first before a trial audience of family or friends who might point out the gaps.

Another thing to watch out for in the informative speech is giving information that is not entirely relevant. Stick to the facts. Don't be repetitive. If a thing has been presented clearly once, that's enough.

Although this type of speech is often accompanied by visual aids to help clarify it, it should not be completely dependent on visual assistance. The visual aids should point up the talk, not prop it up.

The Report

A report can be the result of an investigation into a situation by government, business, or some other interested group. It is an impartial story of what *has* happened and *is* happening in, say, education, race relations, transportation, communication, or any other subject of public or private concern. It may include the proposals that have been considered by investigators and a statement of a suggested course of action. The speaker usually divides his report into five parts:

1. Purpose of the survey.
2. Methods of obtaining facts.
3. Summary of results.
4. Detailed results.
5. Conclusions reached.

The Lecture

The lecture is an informative speech that can be purely factual, or it can also present the lecturer's own opinions. He interprets his material, as well as merely presenting it.

The lecturer first presents his facts in orderly fashion, then he relates them to the circumstances of their occurrence. For instance, if he were talking on the subject of law and order, he might refer to student protests. He would report a particular outbreak of violence, and then attempt to place the blame either on the administration, the students, or the police, according to his interpretation of the actions of each group.

The lecturer can then generalize from one incident, or a group of incidents, as to the present significance of such occurrences and their possible future results.

The Sales Talk

A successful salesman, like any successful speaker, should genuinely like people and understand them. He should be one of those "people who need people."

He also should be, like a boy scout, "trustworthy, loyal, helpful, friendly, courteous, kind, obedient, cheerful, thrifty, brave, clean, and reverent," because what he is selling principally is confidence in himself. If his listeners believe in him, they will believe in his product or service and respond to his pitch, whatever it may be.

The salesman must also believe in his product or service in order to present it well. And he must analyze the needs of the prospective buyer or buyers, so that he can stress the qualities of what he has to offer that will most benefit them.

If there are any shortcomings in the product or service, it is smart to admit them. They can even become a sales point, as in Avis car rental's admission that they are second in sales.

The successful sales talk is enthusiastic without being high-pressure. Make sure that your prospect wants what you have to sell, and you can add one more satisfied customer to your list.

In a sense, all speeches are sales talks, since we are trying to sell someone on something, whether it be a service or product, a person, an idea, or a course of action.

5 | Tips for the Toastmaster

YOU ARE probably a member of a social, business, civic, sports, community, school, or charitable organization. You may be a member of several or all of such groups. One day you may be called upon to act as toastmaster for a banquet or luncheon or other function.

The toastmaster's lot can be a happy one, provided that there is proper planning. That old remark about having "an infinite capacity for taking pains" should be a guiding motto to insure your success as a toastmaster.

It is necessary to have more than oratorical gifts. Indeed, it may be that speaking ability is not even as important as the skill of being able to organize things.

In many cases, the toastmaster is responsible for the "whole ball of wax"—he must plan the entire program from benediction to invocation. It is often his responsibility to set the over-all theme for the event and to obtain appropriate speakers.

47

Building the Program

Once the theme has been selected and the speakers engaged, the toastmaster begins to build the program. Here is where the tyro toastmaster often goes astray. Having a good theme and capable speakers is not enough. The program must be properly packaged. The toastmaster must act as stage manager in setting up an agenda. The toastmaster must also assume the role of time-keeper. I'm sure that at one time or another you have fidgeted, squirmed, and yawned through a seemingly interminable banquet. It has been my experience that such occasions can be traced directly to laziness, carelessness, or just plain ineptitude on the part of the toastmaster. Here's another motto: Keep things moving.

The toastmaster will generally be familiar with the nature of the audience. He is therefore in a good position to gauge the attention span of the group. Some audiences remain rapt during long, complex addresses. Others lose interest after only a few minutes, no matter how gifted the speaker. Do not think you will be insulting the speaker if you suggest a time limit for his address. The truly good speakers will welcome and heed your advice.

Though the toastmaster is expected to add zest to the evening's activities, you should always be mindful of the fact that you are not a solo performer. Make your presence felt, but do not hog the spotlight.

There is no sure-fire formula for a toastmaster to follow as he goes about arranging an interesting program. It is most important to know your audience. Be sure that the program and speakers will be of interest to the majority of those present, and remember that there is no such thing as a guaranteed interesting program. Even the finest orator can "bomb" if there is no affinity between him and his audience. Generally, the most successful programs are those that are timely and topical.

A banquet may also be a regularly scheduled meeting of an

organization. In this case, the business portion of the meeting should be held before the actual program gets under way with as much dispatch as decorum permits.

Opening the Program

Try to open the program on a light note. A good anecdote or two will usually put the audience in a receptive frame of mind. After your opening remarks, go into the introduction of the first speaker as quickly as possible. Don't wear out your welcome with the audience. Think of your introduction as a miniature speech. Work on it as carefully as you would an address. Give the audience as much pertinent information as possible about the speaker and his subject, but don't get too flamboyant and flowery. If you are overly extravagant with your praise you may evoke some hostility on the part of the audience and make it more difficult for the speaker. If the speaker is well known to you, you might indulge in a few sallies at his expense, but make sure the audience is aware that the digs are only in jest.

What do you do when there is more than one speaker? If they are of equal repute, I have found it is best to contact them, explain your dilemma, and get their agreement to be slotted alphabetically or by lot. An oversight in billing can result in an unhappy speaker and an unsuccessful program.

If you have more than one speaker, don't put them on back-to-back. Keep the program moving from the speeches to the toastmaster's remarks and back again. A speech—particularly a fairly lengthy one—takes its toll upon the audience. They will need time to recover before their attention is attuned again.

To make sure that the program runs smoothly, you should set up a time schedule. A certain amount of time should be alloted to the opening remarks, to the introduction, and to the speech. Always be prepared to expand or reduce your contributions to the evening's activities. Come to the meeting with some additional anecdotes in case you have to fill in an awkward pause.

Plan carefully with regard to the seating arrangements on the dais. Make certain that those who are going to be called upon to speak have ready access to the microphone.

The toastmaster must carefully consider his own contributions. Putting first things first, the opening remarks should be written down. Often, it may seem as if the toastmaster is ad libbing his initial statements, but take it from one who knows, those seemingly off the cuff remarks are often on paper.

Some of My Openings

An effective method of opening a program is to pay tribute to the organization under whose auspices you are appearing. The following is an opening statement I used when appearing before a group of Elks:

"Brother Elks, here we are again as we meet with malice toward none to celebrate this great occasion. Despite the fact that most of us have been members for a long time, I believe it is necessary, every once in a while, to review the birth of our great organization, to refresh our own memories, and to inform the many guests whom we have with us tonight how we began and how little we were. In that way, we may realize how much we have grown and how well and strong we are today."

I then proceeded to touch briefly on some of the highpoints in the history of this great fraternal organization.

Another method I have employed with great success is the use of a famous quotation. Consider the following. It was delivered to a Friars Club Dinner in Los Angeles.

"The poet Robert Burns, in a melancholy mood, once wrote: 'The best laid plans of mice and men gang aft aglee.' For the non-Scotch it means: the plans of all living things, no matter how great or small, do not end the way they are planned. . . . And as it is with humans, so is it with an organization of a fraternal club, such as ours, the Friars."

I then described a humorous mishap that had befallen the organization.

Many toastmasters prefer to open the evening's activities with a joke or two. I have done so on innumerable occasions. A few cautionary notes about jokes. While it is true that any joke is new if you haven't heard it, select yours with care and an eye to appropriateness. Even if your audience is completely male, do not indulge in ribald humor. You may want to tell a blue joke, but always remember that members of the clergy and others who may find such remarks offensive may be in the audience. As I mentioned before, unless you are really an "in" member of the organization, don't indulge in "in" humor. Unless you are pre-siding at a "roast" dinner, be cautious in your attempts to have fun at anyone's expense.

The introduction of speakers or members of the audience in-volves a certain technique, which I have already described. The following examples of introductions of celebrities were delivered by me at various occasions during the past two decades. Note how the career of each is capsuled in the introduction even though, in keeping with my vocation, it was humorous in nature.

Joe E. Lewis

"If ever there was a man who had his foibles or personal life expounded, it is the next speaker and, significantly, almost every-thing you hear about him is completely untrue. Mis-rumor num-ber one is that he is always drunk when he appears before the public—which is far from the truth. He long ago discovered that if you come out with a glass in your hand and you forget the lyrics or tell the jokes wrong, people will say, 'Isn't that cute, he is drunk.' His other reputation—also false—is that he throws away all his money and that his pockets are always full of losing tickets from the race track. He made his appearance the other night in Miami Beach and, as he came out, he threw hundreds of losing mutual tickets out of his pocket and said: 'This is what

I lost today.' Anyone looking at those tickets would have seen them dated: 'Sheepshead Bay Race Track 1909.' He is not broke. He owns several apartment houses in Chicago, has large bank accounts, and his real name is Abe Marovitz. Ladies and gentlemen, Joe E. Lewis."

Harry Hershfield

"Your next speaker is one of the noblest Friars of them all. He has been speaking publicly since the days of the sainted George M. Cohan. The opportunity to speak on such festive occasions as the Friars was brought about not by his talent as a speaker, but because of his great success as a cartoonist with tremendous imagination—Desperate Desmond, followed by Abe Kabibble, made cartoon history, and his reputation made him welcome as a speaker. Perhaps he was rushed into this avocation too quickly, because for many years, regardless of the subject matter or the guest of honor, as he rose, the occasion always reminded him of two Jews in a delicatessen in Brooklyn. At the passing of a dear friend at which I functioned as the eulogist, our next speaker was also to pay his last respects, and as he looked at the remains, I quickly kicked him, for I was sure he was about to say: 'As I gaze here upon my old friend, it reminds me of the two Jews in a delicatessen store.' However, like many vices which age mellows and time conquers—as I can definitely testify to— he is deservedly known as one of the greatest humorists and one of the sweetest men that this great metropolis has ever known —Harry Hershfield."

In addition to preparing introductions for those scheduled to speak from the dais, the toastmaster should jot down some very brief remarks to be used when introducing dignitaries in the audience. Two or three descriptive sentences will do the job.

There are two other tasks to be performed by the toastmaster. He must make a closing statement. These remarks should summarize the evening's activities and should touch on a few of the high points. Closing remarks should be upbeat—anecdotes and poetry are highly recommended. But above all, they should be brief. Bear in mind that your audience has been bombarded with words for hours. If you hold them when they want to go, you may leave them with an unfavorable impression of the occasion.

Because so many little details are involved in "toastmastering" —opening remarks, introduction of speakers, closing remarks, and so forth—nothing should be committed to memory. I strongly recommend that the entire evening's activities be blocked out on index cards. These should be propped up near the microphone (out of sight of the audience) and referred to frequently. You may also find it useful to employ a stopwatch as a means of keeping the program moving.

Follow the guidelines I have given you here, and you'll have a successful evening. You may even enjoy it yourself.

6 Speech Construction

THE SPEECH that conveys your message best is one that is well constructed, avoids long sentences and unfamiliar words, and keeps the use of slang to a minimum. However, don't strain so hard to express yourself correctly that the result is stiff and dull.

Communicate

Once, at a conference of teenagers at the Waldorf, so much of the audience got up and left during one speech that the man in charge expressed his gratitude "to the faithful few of you who remain." Adults are usually more polite, or perhaps they have learned endurance over the years. But you will hold them in their seats more easily if you keep your talk informal and casual, striving to be grammatically correct, but not being so proper that you fail to communicate.

The best way to establish a connection is through clarity, and that can be done by keeping your written speech or notes as simple as possible. Long words are not always understood. Even when they are, too many of them are boring. At any point where you have written down a long word, experiment with the use of a shorter one without loss of meaning.

Keep It Short

Which of the following words is more effective and more easily understood?

Remonstrate	or	Protest
Accumulate	or	Increase
Apportion	or	Divide
Alleviate	or	Relieve
Unwavering	or	Constant
Communication	or	Letter
Irascible	or	Angry
Culpable	or	Guilty
Meticulous	or	Precise
Similar	or	Alike

The shorter ones, of course!

Sentences can also be shortened to advantage. A five- to ten-word sentence is easily understood. A fifteen-word sentence is still not beyond the grasp of the average listener. Anything over fifteen words is apt to have your audience straining to stay with you.

Compare the effectiveness of: "I burst into tears and cried all the way, as I carried my money to the bank where I keep it in a savings account" to Liberace's actual reply to his critics: "I cried all the way to the bank."

Weed out excess adjectives and adverbs when you can. What if Patrick Henry had said, "Give me complete liberty or give me a quick death"? It would never have been remembered. Suppose Mae West had remarked, "Beulah, carefully peel me a large, purple grape." Nothing!

Make It Active and Direct

In English usage, the passive voice is an indirect way of saying something that can be put directly. It is much more direct to state: "The board recommends" than to say: "It is recommended by the board."

How much more direct is a simple "They told me" than the roundabout "I have been told."

Clarity and directness are much more important in a public speech than they are in the written word. A person who is reading has time to think it over, reread, and look up an unfamiliar expression. He must feel as though you are talking to him.

Avoid indirect openings such as, "As a matter of fact, I discovered. . . . " "Actually, I discovered" would be stronger. Strongest of all is a direct "I discovered," without any introduction. Don't be afraid to use the word *I*, as long as your speech isn't overloaded with *I*'s and *me*'s. Some people use the word *we* instead of *I*, imagining it to be more modest. *We* is an affectation. It should be avoided unless it actually refers to more than one person.

Slang

A touch of slang now and then to emphasize a point, or to get a laugh, or to indicate you are "one of the boys" (or girls) can add color to a speech. It is a mistake to use it too generously, though. Slang often takes the place of other words that could express your idea more exactly. "Let's get down to the nitty-gritty" may be a good way of saying, "Let's get to the heart of the matter," or "Let's face the facts," under certain circumstances.

If you want to color your speech with slang expressions, don't date yourself by using last year's jargon. While some slang words like *graft, mob, humbug,* and *sham* have become accepted through continued usage, others disappear with time. Yesterday's *beatnik* is today's *hippie,* and tomorrow's who knows what? Last year's *super* is this year's *groovy,* and next year's who can tell?

Also, if you are not too familiar with the use of slang, and the listeners are, watch out! You can easily use a word in the wrong way and look foolish. On the other hand, if you know the meaning of the word and you are not sure that your audience understands, you are in trouble again. You either lose half your audience, or have to explain what you mean.

Clichés

Instead of depending on slang or old, well-worn figures of speech, try to think of simpler ways of saying things. Never "advise" someone of something, "tell" them. Never say "after all is said and done," when a simple "after all" would do. Don't be "at a loss for words," be "speechless." If possible, you might occasionally devise a more original way of putting a shopworn phrase, such as: "brave as a college dean" instead of "brave as a lion"; "brown as a California beach" instead of "brown as a berry"; "clear as the Hope diamond" instead of "clear as crystal"; "green as a Saint Patrick's Day tie" instead of "green as grass"; "mad as a hatter" instead of "mad as a wet hen"; and "red as Chairman Mao" instead of "red as a rose" or "red as a beet."

Common Errors

There is no need to give a detailed course in grammar here, but there are some common errors that frequently turn up in speeches. One is the dangling particple.

A participle is used to modify a noun or pronoun. When it gets separated from its noun or pronoun, it is said to "dangle." For instance: "Chugging and whistling, I watched the train pull into the station." This is confusing. Who was chugging and whistling, the man or the train? It would sound better if it were put: "I watched the chugging and whistling train pull into the station."

As most people know, "It's me," while often used in informal conversation, is not really correct, and should be "It's I." However, they become so self-conscious about the use of *I* instead of *me*, that you often hear public speakers say, "They spoke to my friend and I." Or "It pleased my wife and I." Or "It was considered by my associate and I." None of these is correct, and it would be obvious if you just removed the extra words *my friend and*, *my wife and*, or *my associate and*. No one would think of saying, "It pleased I," or "They spoke to I," or "It was considered by I."

Another common error is the addition of *ly* to the word *bad*. Someone must have thought it sounded more refined to say, "I feel badly," or "The garbage smells badly," or "The music sounds badly." You wouldn't say, "I feel goodly," or "The perfume smells goodly," or "The stereo sounds goodly." So, if you want to express regret, say, "I feel bad." If you want to express happiness, say, "I feel good." Unfortunately, to complicate things, you are supposed to say, "I feel well," to indicate good health.

A fourth error is the misuse of the words *us* and *we*. You are wrong if you say: "Us salesmen went to lunch"; "Some of we club members played golf"; and "The change in rules affects some of we players." It should be "*We* salesmen went to lunch"; "Some of *us* club members played golf"; and "The change in rules affects some of *us* players." If you eliminate the words *salesmen*, *club members*, and *players*, you will immediately see that you would never say, "Us went to lunch," or "Some of we played golf," or "The change in rules affects some of we."

Finally, there is the use of *who* instead of *whom* (or vice versa). Since they are used interchangeably in informal, spoken English, there is no need to worry about them too much. If there are any speech purists in your audience, they'll be in the minority, so forget it!

Say What You Mean

Ideally, a sentence is a series of words which conveys a complete and clear meaning. If a sentence in your speech seems fuzzy, strip it down to essential words and see if it still makes sense. For instance, "The speed of the small sports car equals the more expensive limousine."

This is not quite clear. So strip it down by dropping the phrase "of the small sports car," and the description "more expensive." You then have "The speed equals the limousine."

No wonder it wasn't clear. What you wanted to say was "The speed *reached by* the small sports car equals *that of* the more expensive limousine." This sentence still makes sense after being stripped to "The speed reached equals that of the limousine."

Don't Omit Essentials

Sometimes, just because a collection of words is long, it seems as though it makes a sentence, but it doesn't because some necessary words were omitted. This kind of thing is used by comic masters of doubletalk to get a laugh. But when it happens by accident, the result is confusion. Take this example: "The member was a new resident who, coming from another part of the state, with little knowledge of our area, but eager to make friends." What was intended was "The member was a new resident who, coming from another part of the state, *had* little knowledge of our area, but *was* eager to make friends."

Another instance is "The computers used by the Navy are different than the Army." This, of course, should be "The computers used by the Navy are different *from those used by* the Army."

Never use doubletalk, unless you want to be another Pat Paulson.

Match Your Parallels

Matching your parallels means that those parts of a sentence which are alike in thought should be alike in structure. The following are examples of mismatched sentences:

"Flying is a faster way to get there than to drive."
"Women have two aims, of which the first is to marry money; in the second place they want to have a happy love life."
"Other colleges provide education of ininferior quality and have higher yearly tuition fees."

These are examples of matched sentences:

"*Flying* is a faster way to get there than *driving*."
"Women have two aims, of which the first is to marry money and the second to have a happy love life."
"Other colleges provide education of inferior quality and higher yearly tuition fees."

Split Construction

It is important to keep related parts of a sentence close together for clarity. This can be done by avoiding such split constructions as "We have, in spite of many setbacks, achieved our goal of fifty thousand dollars." Say instead: "We have achieved our goal of fifty thousand dollars, in spite of many setbacks," or "In spite of many setbacks, we have achieved our goal of fifty thousand dollars."

Another split construction is "With a good education you can have a successful career, with hard work." This would sound better: "With a good education and hard work, you can have a successful career."

Have Something to Say

No matter how you say it, the important factor is to have something to say. You should choose a subject on which you have good basic information. Then you can enlarge upon this by intelligent use of the public library. There the *Subject Guide to Books in Print* will tell you the books available on the subject you have chosen. The *Reader's Guide to Periodical Literature* will tell you about articles in magazines that will be helpful to you.

Pamphlets and bulletins on various subjects can be obtained from the U.S. Government Printing Office in Washington, D.C., and from organizations interested in those subjects. The American Cancer Society and American Heart Association will help you with smoking information. The Gaines Dog Food Company will supply you with material on dogs. The Weyerhaeuser Company will give you information on forestry. The American Association of Retired Persons has material on geriatrics. The American Medical Association has a fund of booklets on health matters.

You can sound like an authority on any subject if you make use of these sources of information, and translate that information into clear, simple language.

7 Delivery

THE ART of speaking can be developed by the use of elaborate vocal exercises to increase resonance, range, and flexible movements of the organs of speech. This takes time, however, and may only make you self-conscious. It is easier to concentrate on more simple ways to develop your delivery.

Pace

The novice speaker usually talks twice as fast as he imagines he does. Because delivering a speech makes him uneasy, he is anxious to get it over with as quickly as possible. Such a speedy delivery makes it hard to grasp what you are trying to say. Since the listener can't keep up with you, he may become bored or irritated.

You should consciously slow yourself down when you start to speak. This can be done by pausing between sentences and enunciating each word clearly. Don't overdo this, either. Practice should lead you to a middle course.

Pitch

In the excitement of the moment, an inexperienced speaker has a tendency to pitch his voice too high. As tension increases, he begins to sound like Tiny Tim. Women are especially plagued by this problem. The late Eleanor Roosevelt overcame this tendency, as most women must, by practicing speaking several notes below normal.

One cannot talk at the same pitch all the time without becoming monotonous. A speaker's voice should range from a few notes below natural pitch to a few notes above it. You can discover your natural pitch by comparing your voice to notes on the piano. The best pitch for you will be found by locating the highest and lowest notes you can produce and aiming at a sound that is about one-fourth the distance from your lowest note. If you don't have a musical instrument handy, you can test your proper pitch by humming down the scale as far as you can go easily. Call this note "do" and sing up the scale to "so." This should be your best pitch.

Volume

A speaker must talk loud enough to be heard by those beyond the first few rows in his audience. The amateur, besides talking too fast and too high, may also speak too low. Don't shout, but put a little force and energy behind your words. If there is a microphone, don't rely on it to do all the work.

A good way to get the right kind of volume is to breathe deeply, hold your breath for a few seconds, and then exhale fully before facing your audience. You have seen the baseball pitcher on the mound do this to relax, and relaxation is one of the secrets of good speech delivery.

Variation

It has often been said of an actor like Richard Burton or a spellbinder like Billy Graham that he could recite the telephone book and make it sound dramatic. The secret is variety in tones of voice. Even a series of meaningless names and numbers can sound interesting if they are rendered in a meaningful way. Since you will have something more profound to communicate than telephone listings, you can certainly add to the effectiveness of your delivery by making the tone of voice suit the words.

You can speak in a tone that is sympathetic or antagonistic, smooth or rough, dominating or beguiling, controlled or outgoing, according to the idea you are trying to put across. You can use a musical tone when you are trying to be persuasive, a throaty tone when you want to be threatening, or a stage whisper when you are speaking confidentially. The tone of your voice can supplement the meaning of what you are saying.

Emphasis

A good way to put punch into your speech is to emphasize those words that actually carry your message. In John F. Kennedy's last address to the General Assembly of the United Nations, he opened with the following paragraph. If some words had not been emphasized, the talk would have been flat:

"But man does not live by *bread* alone, and members of this organization are committed by the *Charter* to promote and respect *human rights.* Those *rights* are not respected when a Buddhist priest is driven from his *pagoda,* when a synagogue is shut *down,* when a Protestant church cannot open a *mission,* when a cardinal is forced into *hiding,* or when a crowded church is *bombed.*"

There are no strict rules as to where the emphasis should be placed. That is up to the indiivdual and the effect he wants to create. One could create an entirely different emphasis by stressing different words in Kennedy's address:

"But man does not *live* by bread alone, and members of this organization are *committed* by the Charter to *promote* and *respect* human rights. Those rights are not *respected* when a Buddhist priest is *driven* from his pagoda, when a synagogue is *shut* down, when a Protestant church cannot *open* a mission, when a cardinal is *forced* into hiding, or when a crowded church is *bombed*."

You will note that the final word of the paragraph is accented in both examples, since (no pun intended) it is the most explosive word in that sentence.

Articulation

An obvious rule for good articulation is to open your mouth when you speak. Don't talk through immovable lips like a ventriloquist. Avoid swallowing your consonants. They carry your meaning. You could leave out the vowels in many sentences and still make sense, as in the old days when swear words weren't allowed on the printed page. Everyone knew what was meant by h-ll, d-mn, b-st-rd, or b-tch; but they'd have had some problems figuring out -e--, -a--, -a--a--, or -i---.

Vowels have their place, too. If they are slurred or mispronounced, they reveal your geographic origins and make you an easy subject for mimics, as Lyndon B. Johnson was with his "Mah fella Amurricans." New Yorkers are likely to give themselves away by pronouncing their hometown "Noo Yawk," instead of "Nieu York." Bostonians will say, "Haahvid," instead of "Harvard."

The various aspects of my life and background—from New York to Hollywood—can be heard in my speech. I don't try to be anything other than myself, and I don't suggest that you try to become a purist in using English diction either.

Be yourself. Try to enunciate correctly; but don't become affected and say "cahnt" when "kant" is more natural, or "tomahto" when you grew up on "tomayto." You're sure to slip up somewhere and make yourself look foolish.

Pronunciation

If you are not sure of the correct pronunciation, it is a good idea to check with the dictionary. You may find that you have been mispronouncing some common word all your life. It is an embarrassing discovery, but not nearly as embarrassing as finding it out after you have delivered a speech.

Some words like *im*potent, *o*rator, *v*ehement, *spat*ula, and su*per*fluous are presently pronounced as indicated here. Others, because they have been so often mispronounced, have had these mistakes included in the dictionary. Thus the word *data* can now be pronounced dayta, dahta, or datta. Take your choice. And *incognito* may now be pronounced either in*cog*nito or incog*nee*to.

Sometimes you know the correct place to put the accent in a word, but you unconsciously omit either a consonant or a vowel, as in *un'erstan'* for *understand, reg'lar* for *regular.* This is not only incorrect, it is sloppy. Some of the words and letters we have to watch are

Arctic	History
Auxiliary	Landlord
Boundary	Literature
Contempt	Mathematics
Consumption	Miniature
Delivery	Temperature
Different	Victory

Another common mistake is the addition of a vowel or a consonant to a word, as in *singger* for *singer, sawr* for *saw, athaletic* for *athletic,* or *beauteeful* for *beautiful.* Some people have the bad habit, also, of reversing the letters in words, as in *larniks* for *larnyx, bronikal* for *bronchial,* or *modren* for *modern.*

How You Sound

Most of us are not aware of how we sound to others until we play back our voices on a dictating machine or recording tape. It is usually a surprise. An easy way to discover immediately how you sound is to cup your hands behind your ears and push the ears forward. Since you probably don't want to go around rehearsing your speech in that undignified position, it is best to borrow, buy, or rent a tape recorder.

Read your speech directly from manuscript, notes, or cards, and deliver it exactly as you plan to do before a real audience. Then play it back, five or ten minutes at a time, and look for flaws, such as *er-er's, ahem's, you know's,* mispronunciations, poor pitch, too fast or too slow a pace, throat clearings, and other unpleasant vocal mannerisms. Finally, go through the entire taped speech, making notes on your original draft to warn you where to watch out for mistakes.

If your voice gets hoarse as your speech progresses, that indicates you are forcing yourself. The solution to this problem is to bring up your words from deeper inside you, instead of overworking the throat muscles. Try to project your voice from your diaphragm.

Squeakiness at the start of a speech is due to a nervous tightening of the vocal cords and the diaphragm. Usually, as the speech advances, the speaker relaxes, and the voice returns to normal. This is a common complaint, so don't let it bother you too much. Try taking a few good, deep breaths before you start your next speech rehearsal.

How You Look

Some modern courses on public speaking provide their students with video-taped recordings of their performance. This enables you to see yourself as others do. There is another, more commonplace, bit of equipment that performs this same function—the mirror. After you have dictated your speech into the tape recorder, try delivering it on your feet in front of a looking glass. This will help you correct your posture, gestures, and facial expressions. You will find yourself straightening up, avoiding nervous movements, and composing your features.

You may also find that your hair, face, and clothing do not look as well as you would like. Remember this. By the day of the speech have your hair trim and neat. Have your clothing fresh from the cleaner. Clothes should be comfortable for ease of movement and conservative enough so that your dress does not detract attention from what you have to say.

Good carriage gives you self-confidence and impresses the audience better than a slumped, insecure posture. Stand erect, but not stiff, with arms and hands hanging loosely at your sides. If it makes you feel more relaxed to put one hand in a pocket or on the lectern, that's all right. Look directly at the audience, with head held naturally. Don't freeze in your original position, but move your head and hands spontaneously to emphasize your points.

Doing What Comes Naturally

The more you do something, the more it becomes second nature to you. This is certainly true of public speaking. You won't want to bore your family and friends with repeated rehearsals of your speeches, but you might get them to help you practice speaking aloud.

Ask your librarian to choose some book for you that is lively, but suitable for the entire family. You can spend one night a week taking turns at reading from it to one another. It will be good for all of you.

An amusing way to have a different kind of evening with friends would be to choose some play, either current or classical, and assign the principal parts to each of your guests and yourself. A play read with feeling can be fun, and it can help you all in the art of oral expression, whether the choice is Shakespeare, O'Neill, or George Bernard Shaw. Once you have played Hamlet or Henry Higgins (or Ophelia or Liza Doolittle) before a group, you will find that the mere delivery of a speech will seem like child's play.

You will also discover something else, which you may never have thought about before. That is, that the same part is played very differently, depending upon who plays it. Classic parts are played at different times and places by many different people. There have been as many interpretations of Hamlet as there have been actors who have played him, from Booth to Burton.

So it is with the delivery of a speech. The speech is more than just words. Two people could make the same speech and each deliver it equally well, but with entirely different effect, for each puts upon it the impress of his own personality. A cardinal rule of speechmaking is, therefore, never to imitate anyone else's delivery. Take advantage of your own individuality by being yourself. Would Dustin Hoffman imitate Marlon Brando? Would Jane Fonda imitate Anne Bancroft? Would George Burns imitate Jack Benny?

Practice Counts

Although practice alone, or among family and friends, is helpful to the speaker, there is nothing that will improve his speaking delivery more than actually delivering speeches. Each new time you should find yourself doing better than the last. Every speaker has a certain amount of stage fright and nervous tension, but this becomes less and less bothersome with practice.

You will learn from experience to talk at the right speed, pitch, and volume, with sufficient variation in tone and emphasis. Proper articulation and pronunciation will become automatic, along with stance and gesture. You can't learn to swim if you don't go in the water. You'll never become a skier by spending your time by the fire in the lodge. The more invitations to speak you accept, the more you will enjoy speaking, and the more your audiences will enjoy listening to you.

8 How To Conclude

THE CONCLUSION of a speech is like the last course of a meal. It should be short, sweet, and leave a good taste in the mouth. Make your final words count and don't rush through them. They will be the last impression your audience will carry away.

Your closing comments should answer the question, "What do I want them to bear in mind as they leave?" Pick out and plant in their minds the particular parts of your speech you most want your listeners to remember. In making up your manuscript, notes, or reminder cards for your speech, be sure to have some notations as to the ending. Don't leave it up to chance or you may forget an important point.

Simple Repetition

A simple, narrative speech, like a talk on flower arrangement, or a descriptive tour of a building, or a travelogue, does not require a punchy ending, but merely a repetition, in different words, of your opening exposition, and an expression of thanks for the listeners' attention. You might pay the audience a compliment, or end up with a light remark that will send them away feeling good.

Summarize

If your talk is intended to influence your audience in one way or another, however, your ending must be stronger. You should go back and restate the main points of the speech. Such a repetition helps the listener retain the thoughts you have been trying to get across.

This may be done in an itemized, point-by-point restatement; in a short digest of the important material; or in a repetition of the central idea or proposal.

Restatement

The late Martin Luther King did this most eloquently in his famous "I have a dream" speech, whose last paragraphs begin as follows:

1. "I have a dream that one day on the red hills of Georgia. . . .
2. "I have a dream that one day even in the State of Mississippi. . . .
3. "I have a dream that my four little children. . . .
4. "I have a dream that one day in Alabama. . . .
5. "I have a dream that one day every valley shall be exalted. . . .
6. "This is our hope. . . ."

Digest

When David E. Lilienthal was made head of the atomic energy program, he answered a question from the Joint Congressional Committee on Atomic Energy with a talk on the rights of an individual that has been called an "American Credo." It was summarized in his final digest paragraph like this:

"Whether by administrative agencies acting arbitrarily against business organizations, or whether by investigating activities of legislative branches, whenever those principles fail, those principles of the protection of an individual and his good name against besmirchment by gossip, hearsay, and the statements of witnesses who are not subject to cross-examination—then, too, we have failed in carrying forward our ideals in respect to democracy."

Repetition of an Idea

Owen D. Young, former chairman of General Electric, illustrated the method of repeating an idea when he spoke on culture at Hendrix College in Arkansas.

In his first paragraph, he said, "Culture does not exist in the form of powder, a mere mass of incoherent particles." In the middle of the speech, he said, "You must fuse at white heat the several particles of your learning into an element so ductile and so strong that nothing can destroy it without destroying you." At the end, he repeated, "My point is that it is not enough for you to study economics in an insulated compartment and history and government and the languages and the sciences. It is not enough to gather them up as separate particles into a powder which you carry out with your diploma. They must be fused and integrated."

Pointing Up with a Final Question

A final question on the issue you have been discussing will send your audience home attempting to answer that question and giving it the desired consideration. If your talk, for instance, has been on the subject of pollution, you may give your listeners something to think about by saying, "Unless you do something about it at once, the air you breathe, the land you walk on, and the water in which you can no longer swim will become so fouled that life will be insupportable. Do you want your children to inherit such a world?"

Looking Forward

Whether your talk is on pollution, poverty, peace, or any other serious subject, you can always end your speech with a reference to the future. Such things are continuing problems, and people can be aroused about them by a prediction of dire events to come, or they can be stimulated by the hope for a satisfactory solution.

Governor John B. Connally of Texas closed one of his speeches with such a hope for the future:

"This country has always found itself engaged in crucial debates and inner contests. We have gone through tremendous economic and social crises. We have written and spoken for the poor and the degraded, for the rich and the powerful . . . and what has happened is that the American people have hammered out a democracy with a spirit of freedom in a form quite unlike its original conception.

"This is a democratic process. It has been growing and gaining strength steadily for two centuries, and each of us who has eyes to see and a heart with which to feel knows that we are still progressing, and that the democratic spirit itself, though attacked and criticized, has survived and grown.

"I believe we still have the courage and the dignity to fight for the democratic spirit which has given us our rights, our liberties. and our freedom, if each of us will contribute his part to the fight in order that we might maintain a nation in which the democratic spirit is vibrant and alive."

Appeal for Action

If you want your audience to act on the subject under consideration, instead of just thinking about it, you should conclude your speech with a call for action, such as, "So I will ask you to bombard your state representatives with letters of complaint against the proposed cutback in aid to localities for poverty problems, job opportunities, and special education," or "I urge you to write at once to the President and your senator concerning this problem."

David Rockefeller, president of the Chase Manhattan Bank in New York, ended his address on "Gold, the Dollar, and the Free World," with a strong call for action:

"There is more here, then, than a gold outflow or payments deficit to challenge us. These matters challenge our wisdom, our patience, and the sense of common purpose binding all free peoples.

"We can never respond by retreat, for isolation means evasion. We can never respond by panic, for no strength is born of fear. We can respond only by acting—ourselves and with our allies—in a manner both mature and imaginative to show the world the capacity of free nations to think anew and act together."

In Quotes

Perhaps someone else has already stated the theme of your talk in more effective words than you, yourself, can employ. A quotation that is appropriate to the occasion will end the speech with a flourish. General Douglas MacArthur knew this when he spoke to Congress after being relieved of his commands, as he said:

"The world has turned over many times since I took the oath on the plain at West Point, and the hopes and dreams have long since vanished; but I still remember the refrain of one of the most popular barracks ballads of that day which proclaimed most proudly that old soldiers never die; they just fade away."

Governor George Romney closed an address on "The Excess Concentration of Political, Social, and Economic Power," with a quote from James Russell Lowell:

"Keep this in mind: politicians, public officials, in the main, follow; they do not lead.

"The two stanzas from a poem by James Russell Lowell express a thought I want to leave with you. They go something like this:

> Then to side with truth is noble
> When we share her wretched crust,
> Ere her cause bring fame and fortune,
> And 'tis prosperous to be just;
> Then it is the brave man chooses,
> While the coward stands aside,
> Doubting in his abject spirit
> Till his Lord is crucified."

Leave 'Em Laughing

In this book, you will find humorous quotes for nearly every possible occasion that I have been able to think of, and I hope you will find them useful. You can give your talk a final lift with a humorous remark, such as one of the following:

"Bankers are just like anybody else, except richer."

—Ogden Nash

"Woman's virtue is man's greatest invention."

—Cornelia Otis Skinner

"Your public servants serve you right."

—Adlai E. Stevenson

"I say it's spinach, and I say the hell with it."

—E. B. White

"I want to know not his earning power but his yearning power."

—David McCord

"Baloney is flattery so thick it cannot be true, and blarney is flattery so thin we like it."

—Bishop Fulton J. Sheen

You may close with a story that illustrates the message you have been trying to convey. Be sure, however, to choose a story that is closely related to your subject, so that it serves two purposes—to illustrate your point and get a laugh. Then the size of the laugh it produces doesn't matter, since the story has performed an additional function besides being funny.

The beautiful red-headed movie star Arlene Dahl, who is also a syndicated columnist and vice president of a major advertising agency, addressed a group of fashion experts on the trend toward masculinization of women's clothes, of which she disapproves. She concluded by reminding her audience, "She who wears his pants will never wear his mink."

Planning Ahead

You have probably seen the little gag sign that says
Plan Ahe
a
d

A public speaker should keep that sign in front of him to remind him not to put all his effort in the start of the speech—letting go with the big guns, then running down in the middle, and falling away to a whisper at the end. A successful speaker, when first preparing his speech, gets his general material down in the rough, but polishes up the ending so that it is just the way he wants it. Then, when he is reworking the main part of the speech, he knows just exactly where he is heading and can build up carefully toward that end.

Don't let yourself reach the end, discover you have nothing more to say, and have to confess to the audience, "That's all there is. There isn't any more." Their mental reaction is likely to be a disappointed "So, what?"

Even worse than the speaker who suddenly finds he has run out of words is the poor guy who can't figure out how to stop. He keeps going on and on, long after he has put across his message, with no idea of how to get out of it all gracefully. When he has finally halted with a lame "Thank you," his audience has usually reached the yawning point.

Concrete Examples

The conclusion of a speech is often emphasized by ending with a concrete and specific illustration. For instance, a person delivering a talk on the harmful effects of cigarette smoking and the need for mature people to set an example for youth could end with the story of actor Tony Curtis, whose father had a lung removed because of cancer. The film star consumed a pack a day until he quit at age thirty-five. He joined the crusade against smoking when he became chairman of an American Cancer Society drive called I.Q. (I quit). Curtis recalled how movie stars once strewed packs of certain brands of cigarettes around the movie sets in exchange for free cartons for themselves. Now he, like many others, is taping Cancer Society commercials and spreading the word that quitting the habit makes your breath sweeter, your tongue less coated, your body odor pleasanter, and even has a favorable effect on your sex life.

Illustrative Anecdotes

Russell Conwell ended his famous lecture about opportunity, *Acres of Diamonds*, with an illustrative anecdote showing that you may have a title on the door and a fancy carpet on the floor, but you also need something on the ball to live up to the title. He told about an official who had been elected without any previous political experience and was a complete flop on the job, because he assumed that greatness was conferred automatically with the office.

Doctor You Chan Yang, when he was Korean Ambassador to the United States, used an anecdote to illustrate the fact that we all need courage and endurance:

"During one of the coldest days in a terrible winter in Korea, an old schoolteacher was sitting cross-legged on the floor of his ruined straw-thatched cottage. A young United Nations soldier rode by, and when he saw the old man sitting there blue with the cold, he stopped and called out to him: 'My poor old man, how cold you must be, with no fire, and the winter wind whistling into your house!'

"And the proud old schoolteacher raised his eyes and called

back, 'My good young man,' he said, 'it is not so bad. Do you not observe that as fast as the wind blows in through one window, it blows out at the other?' "

Personal Conclusions

Some speeches can be concluded with offers of service to the audience on the part of the speaker or his organization. This is particularly appropriate at the end of business or political speeches.

In some instances, a speech may be ended with personal leave-takings or expressions of gratitude. A formal farewell speech calls for this. And a speech at a convention could include thanks to the persons responsible for the occasion or to the officials of the host city.

Make It Relevant

Whatever the ending you choose, make it relevant and make it strong. Never admit to any doubts about your convictions or about your ability to put them across. People take you at your own valuation. They will believe in your ideas and in you, if you express sufficient confidence.

An action speech will conclude with instructions to join, contribute, vote, write, buy, investigate, exercise, beautify, pray, or whatever. A narrative speech will end with the hope that the members of audience will contemplate, read, view, or otherwise improve themselves. A provocative ending should send them away thinking, discussing, and planning for the future. A quotation ending should inspire them. A humorous ending should put them in a receptive mood so that your ideas can take hold. A story at the end should leave a picture in their minds that illustrates what you have been attempting to put across. It should not only relate to the subject, but add something to what you have already said.

Some Famous Conclusions

John F. Kennedy closed a speech on our need for strength to combat opposing forces by saying:

"For I am convinced that we in this country and in the Free World possess the necessary resources and the skill and the added strength that come from a belief in the freedom of man.

"And I am equally convinced that history will record the fact that this bitter struggle reached its climax in the late 1950s and early 1960s.

"Let me then make clear as the President of the United States that I am determined upon our system's survival and success, regardless of the cost and regardless of the peril."

Clare Boothe Luce closed a speech on "What's Wrong with the American Press?" as follows:

"Let us watch then, with hope, for the signs of a new, vigorous, masculine leadership in the American press. For if you fail, must not America also fail in its great and unique mission, which is also yours: to lead the world toward life, liberty, and the pursuit of enlightenment, so that it may achieve happiness? It is that goal which the American press must seize afresh—creatively, purposefully, energetically, and with a zeal that holds a double promise: The promise of success and the promise of enlightenment."

When Rabbi Stephen S. Wise delivered one of his great addresses in Springfield, Illinois, under the auspices of the Lincoln Centennial Association, it concluded:

"But the first word spoken after the death of Lincoln is truest and best—the word of Secretary of War Stanton, standing by the side of that scene of peace—'Now he belongs to the ages.' It was verdict and prophecy alike, for Lincoln is not America's, he is the world's; he belongs not to our age, but to the ages; and yet, though he belongs to all time and to all peoples, he is our own, for he was an American."

Impromptu, Incidental, and Special-Occasion Speeches

A PERSON who gets around very much in business and social life is certain to be called upon occasionally to "say a few words" for which he has not made any formal preparation. If you don't want to be caught completely unaware, you might make it a habit to collect your thoughts beforehand on subjects that will be likely to arise. You might also make a few penciled notes on three-by-five cards while others are speaking.

All-Purpose Stories

If you have a number of favorite stories that you can tell well, it can get you off to a good start. Choose a story that relates to the interests of your listeners and the reasons they are gathered together at this particular time and place. Give credit to the other speakers and the ideas they have presented. If you have formulated your views earlier, then you need only put them into words.

The Duplicate Speech

Occasionally, when there are a number of speakers on a program, you may discover to your dismay that the speaker preceding you has pre-empted most of your ideas. This requires a quick reshuffling of your speech to elaborate upon the portions your predecessor has not covered and to cut short the parts that are a duplication. The first time this happens, you may be almost at a loss for words; but as time goes on you will find that experience teaches you to make your speech flexible enough to adapt to any possible situation.

Be Orderly

Your impromptu speech will be made more easily if you plan a method of presentation that will fit nearly all possible situations, such as:

1. A problem occurs to you—state the problem briefly and offer a possible solution.
2. A question arises in your mind—state the question, suggest an answer, solicit answers from others.
3. You have an idea—state the idea, illustrate it, and give reasons for it.
4. You advocate action—state the reasons, illustrate them, and relate the illustration to the present problem.

Question Periods

One kind of impromptu speaking is that which results when there is a question period at the end of your formal talk. If you have watched official news conferences on TV, you know what this can be like. The President (or governor or mayor) reports on the accomplishments of his administration in certain areas. He explains certain courses of action that the government plans to take. Then the members of the press ask their questions, some of them eager for more information, others looking for flaws in the President's reasoning, and still others frankly antagonistic.

You will note that he does not attempt to answer a question unless he has an adequate reply to it. He says he will have to give it further study, or he can't comment at this time. You, in a similar situation, can say simply, "I don't know."

When you do know the answer, again follow the presidential example. Don't make a speech in reply. For one thing, you've already made your speech. For another, you want to give everyone a chance. So answer briefly and directly.

Question Period Etiquette

Cover the entire room with your eyes, so that no one who cares to speak may be overlooked. When two or more persons raise their hands at once, recognize the first one you see, but make a note to come back to the others. Indicate recognition with a nod of the head, a gesture of the hand, or a repetition of the name if you happen to know it. Try to give everyone a chance to ask a first question before giving anyone a second round. Don't let over-eager persons keep the center of attention. Tell them something like, "Just a moment please, but I believe the gentleman (or lady) behind you is next."

Every question should be repeated before being answered, so that the subject of your reply is evident to all. It may be that the original question was not stated loudly enough for everyone to hear, or with sufficient clarity. If you restate the question, preface your restatement with "As I understand it, you are asking. . . ."

Do not allow yourself to be drawn into an extended conversation with some one member of the audience to the exclusion of the others. Like the President, try to remain courteous during the question period, no matter how doubtful or critical your questioner may be. Hecklers can be a problem. You can be curt to them if they are persistent. If you can turn them off with a humorous remark, so much the better.

Written questions should be screened by someone else, if possible, to eliminate those that are irrelevant or difficult to read. Read the question to yourself before reading it aloud, so that you can restate it if necessary.

Conclude the question session while it is still lively and interesting. Don't wait for enthusiasm to die down. Express your appreciation of the questions, praise the audience for its intelligent interest, and thank them.

Announcements

One of the incidental speeches on many programs is the announcement. It consists of a brief statement about the success of a past event, or the hopes for a future event. The announcement of a past event is usually congratulatory, and that of a future event persuasive in order to encourage attendance. The function of the announcement is informative.

Past Event

1. Name and event, character, intent.
2. Time and place it occurred.
3. Planners, supervisors, participants.
4. Describe the value of event.
5. Refer to related activities.

Future Event

1. Name of event, character, intent.
2. Time and place it will occur.
3. Planners, supervisors, participants.
4. Urge attendance or support.
5. Suggest related activities, if any.

Anniversaries

An anniversary speech relates some happening of the past to the present and the future. It can celebrate a long period of

activity by an organization, or any date that has historical, cul-
tural, scientific, or religious significance.

Suppose you were making a speech on the Fiftieth Anniversary
of the League of Women Voters of the United States. A skeletal
outline for the speech would

1. Describe the event being celebrated
   The achievement of women's suffrage and the founding of
   the League of Women Voters as an institution of research
   and information.
2. Explain its significance
   To involve more citizens as enlightened participants in government.
3. Relate the past to the present
   In the past, it was women who were disenfranchised through
   their sex, now it is the inner city resident who fails to make
   use of his vote.
4. State present results of past event
   For fifty years the League has been helping strengthen our
   democratic form of government by providing information
   services, speakers, workshops, and educational pamphlets,
   and by backing progressive legislation.
5. State future hopes for duplication of past success
   An all-out attack on citizen frustration by making citizens
   aware of their own responsibility for international cooperation, for improved management of natural resources, and
   for revitalization of state and local governments by active
   political participation.

Dedications

A dedication speech is delivered at the opening of a public
building, bridge, monument, or the laying of a cornerstone. It
should not be too full of hot air and solemnity, but should present
a positive, sincere viewpoint on the importance of the structure.

Imagine yourself dedicating the Golden Gate Bridge. You would

1. Indicate steps leading to present occasion
   Construction begun in 1933 and completed in 1937.

2. Praise those who made this event possible
   J. B. Strauss, the chief engineer.
3. Indicate outstanding features of the structure, and its purpose
   Over-all length 9,266 feet; span of 4,200 feet.
   Crosses the Golden Gate from San Francisco to Marin
   County.
4. Look forward to the future
   Its practical use and enduring beauty.

Commencements

When making a commencement address, although you are ostensibly speaking to the students, you are actually trying to impress the parents, faculty, and alumni. The students couldn't care less what someone over thirty has to tell them.

However, for the sake of the few students who may be listening, you can deal with the part each of them has to play in the outside world of business, professions, society, and the arts. Your approach should be hopeful but realistic, stating their potential contributions and rewards, along with the problems they will have to face and the adjustments they must make. You can also attempt to stimulate and guide their thoughts, feelings, and behavior in the days to follow. This will be wasted on them, but it will make their parents feel good.

Farewells

A farewell speech should be brief but sincere, expressing warm emotions without exaggeration. It may be made by a politician resigning from office, a businessman making a change in his career, a doctor or lawyer retiring from his profession, or a king abdicating his kingdom.

King Edward VIII of Britain, later the Duke of Windsor, expressed in his farewell address:

1. Allegiance to his successor.

2. The reasons for his resignation.
3. Appreciation for the cooperation of his associates.
4. A reference to his future plans.
5. An invitation to continuance of cordial relations.
6. A wish for the happiness and prosperity of those being addressed.

No one could do better than that.

Presentation and Acceptance

The speech of presentation is addressed to the recipient of a gift or honor, but should also be of general interest:

1. Give the reason for presentation.
2. Name the recipient and applaud his services or contributions and his worthwhile qualities, or the services and purposes of the group he represents.
3. Express your pleasure in presenting the gift or award and describe it as you present it.

An acceptance speech should be short—merely an extended "Thank you" to the presenter and the group he represents. It should express appreciation and pleasure, give credit to the assistance of others, and affirm faith in the future of their common aims.

Opportunities Unlimited

Once you gain a reputation for making a good speech, you will find yourself called upon with greater frequency. There are over sixteen thousand national associations in this country just waiting to get good speakers. You can see how many local groups there are by looking in your yellow pages under the "Associations" listing. Some of these associations want speakers to address them; others send speakers out to spread their own message, whatever it may be. There are over three hundred thousand churches in the United States, most of which have clubs meeting regularly. They will welcome a competent speaker. Women's associations and clubs are always anxious to have people address their groups or represent them to outsiders. Health and medical organizations, trade associations and commercial firms, as well as men's service clubs like Lions, Rotary, and Kiwanis are all in need of speakers.

Become a good speaker and the world is your oyster, or clam, or shrimp, or herring, or whatever they're serving at speaker's tables these days!

PART

II

Humorous Stories and Jokes for Every Occasion

Advice

Mr. Smith was very stubborn. He would never wear rubbers when it rained or put on an extra sweater on a chilly night. Mrs. Smith became peeved at his obstinacy.

"You never take any good advice," she complained.

"Darn good thing for you I don't," he retorted, "or you'd still be an old maid."

*

The grouchy, short-tempered doctor glared at the new patient.

"Have you been to a doctor," he asked, "before you came to me?"

"No, sir," replied the meek patient. "I went to a pharmacist."

"That shows how much sense some people have," the doctor growled. "And what sort of idiotic advice did he give you?"

"He told me to come to see you."

*

A young soldier new to battle went to his captain and asked: "Is there anything in particular I can do to keep from being shot?"

"Yes," replied the officer, "don't remain stationary on the battle-field. Zigzag—just zigzag."

After the battle, the captain, visiting the wounded at a nearby field hospital, noticed the young soldier who had spoken to him.

"I see that you are wounded," said the captain. "Didn't you do as I told you?"

"I did," replied the soldier, "but I guess I must have zigged when I should have zagged."

*

"Doctor, I'm always worried about my baby," said the young mother to the psychiatrist. "I'm afraid to leave him alone for even a minute. For example, I'm even afraid to leave him in the bedroom for fear I won't hear him if he falls out of his crib."

"Well, you can remedy that easily," said the doctor. "Just take the carpet off the floor."

*

A doctor diagnosed a patient's run-down condition as being caused by worry over money matters.

"Relax," he ordered. "Just two weeks ago I had another fellow here in a dither because he couldn't pay his tailor bills. I told him to forget about them and now he feels great."

"I know," said the patient glumly, "I'm his tailor."

*

An old Texas politician gave this advice to his son: "Be careful what you say in front of newspaper reporters. If you don't, some day they'll dig up something you said in the past, compare it with what you just said, and then claim you're a liar."

"Father, have they ever claimed that about you?" asked the son.

"Heck no," spluttered the father, "they proved it."

*

"My wife's away and things at home are in such a mess," moaned Bill. "Wish she'd hurry back."

"Why don't you do what I did? She'll be right back," his smiling friend said.

"Anything—I'll do anything."

"My wife was visiting her relatives for a couple of weeks and wouldn't pay attention to my letters," said the friend. "So I just sent her a copy of the local paper with one item clipped out."

Age

Jack Brown returned from a long-anticipated trip to Paris and was greeted by a friend.

"And how was Paris?" inquired the friend.

"Wonderful," replied Jack. "I just wish I could have made the trip twenty years ago."

"When Paris was really Paris, eh?" remarked the friend.

"No, when Jack Brown was really Jack Brown."

*

Three elderly gentlemen were discussing the effects of advancing age. The first, who was seventy years old, said, "My hearing is going. People have to shout at me to make themselves understood. I can't even hear when a girl whispers 'yes,'" he added, smiling.

The second man, seventy-five, said: "It's my eyes that are affected. I can't always recognize faces and so I can't flirt with pretty girls."

The third man, eighty, said: "My trouble is worse than either of yours. The other night I wanted to make love to my wife, and she said we just had. The trouble with me, gentlemen, is that my memory is slipping."

Airplanes

The trans-Atlantic jet had reached cruising altitude and the passengers were settling themselves for the flight from New York to London. From the pilot's compartment emerged a distinguished looking, uniformed man. Stopping at each row of passengers, he introduced himself as the navigator and thoughtfully made some small remark about the flight.

Seated at the rear of the plane were two young Navy lieutenants on their first crossing. One read a newspaper; the other was trying to assume a comfortable position for a nap. Wearing a smile of assurance and radiating that feeling of confidence peculiar to all airline personnel, the navigator approached the two young sailors with a cheerful, "Good evening, I'm your navigator. Where are you boys headed?"

The lieutenant engrossed in the newspaper lowered it slowly. With a startled expression on his face, he replied, "Good Lord—you mean *you* don't know?"

*

A European passenger on a trans-Atlantic flight was carrying on a conversation with the stewardess for the obvious purpose of impressing his fellow passengers with his English. He asked the stewardess, "How high is this plane?"

"Nineteen thousand feet," she answered.

He nodded solemnly, thought for a moment, then called to the stewardess again: "How wide is it?"

Animals

The biggest elephant in the Berlin Zoo expired of old age, and his trainer was inconsolable. Finally the zoo superintendent told him: "It's ridiculous to carry on that way about the loss of one elephant. We expect to replace him, you know."

"It's easy enough for you to talk," wailed the trainer. "Just remember who has to dig the grave!"

*

The orchestra manager looked up at the applicant. He observed the man's dark clothes and his carefully trimmed mustache.

"And what was your previous occupation?" he asked.

"I was an organist," the applicant boomed in a rich, baritone voice.

"Why did you give that up?" the manager continued.

"The monkey died," replied the applicant.

*

In an effort to teach his parrot to talk, the bird owner would say "Good morning!" to it each day upon arising. This went on for several months, but the parrot refused to cooperate and said absolutely nothing.

Then one morning the man, being out of sorts, walked right by the bird without his customary greeting.

The parrot eyed him coldly and said: "Well! What's the matter with you this morning?"

*

A family who moved from town to the suburbs decided they

needed a watchdog to guard the house at night. So they bought the largest dog they could find at a local kennel. Not long afterwards burglars broke into the house. The dog slept through the robbery. The furious head of the house went to the dealer and complained.

"Well," explained the dealer, "what you need now is a little dog to wake up the big dog."

*

A mild-mannered minister accepted the call to a church in a town where many of the church members bred horses and sometimes raced them. After a few weeks he was asked to invite the prayers of the congregation for Mary Hill. Willingly and gladly he did so for three weeks. On the fourth Sunday one of the deacons told him that the prayers were no longer needed.

"Why?" asked the good minister with an anxious look. "Is she dead?"

"Oh, no," replied the deacon. "She won the Kentucky Derby."

*

Two horses, born and bred in the same stable, met again one day. One of them, looking healthy, sleek, and well groomed, was on his way to the National Horse Show in New York City. The other was pulling a small cart and looked like nothing on earth—ribby, dusty, badly shod, and very hairy round the hoof. They exchanged life histories.

The first had had the good luck to be purchased by a horse-loving millionaire. He had an air-conditioned stall, squads of grooms to look after him, and little to do except haul his master's kids about in a small cart occasionally.

"You are lucky!" said the second horse. "I've been having a hell of a life. I was bought by a dealer in old junk and I hardly ever get groomed or even fed. What's more, he's never so happy as when he's walloping me, and I work at least eighteen hours a day."

"Why stand for that sort of thing?" asked his sleek friend. "If I were you I'd write to the S.P.C.A. about it."

"Don't be silly," replied the run-down one. "If the boss knew I could write he'd make me keep his books, too."

*

A woman went into a yarn shop and said she wanted to knit a sweater for her dog.

"What size?" asked the salesgirl.

"Oh, I really don't know," replied the woman. "I have him out in the car."

"Well, why don't you bring him in here so we can measure him," suggested the girl.

"My goodness, I couldn't do that," replied the horrified customer. "You see, it's going to be a surprise!"

*

A girl who lived alone in New York asked her boy friend to buy her a pet for company. He found her a beautiful canary which sang light opera but unfortunately had only one leg. The girl loved the bird's voice, but couldn't bear to look at the poor thing standing on one leg. She asked her boy friend to trade it in for a whole bird. Next day the young man told the pet shop owner that his girl loved the bird, but couldn't bear to see the pathetic creature on only one leg.

"If you don't mind," he said, "I'd like to trade this one in for a bird with two legs."

"Whaddya want," asked the owner scornfully, "a singer or a dancer?"

*

A customer walked into a pet shop and asked for a canary. The owner said: "I have just the bird for you. He can sing 'It Had To Be You,' 'Stormy Weather,' and 'Old Black Magic.'"

The customer became infuriated: "Don't try to palm off a phony on me," he screamed. "For my money I want a bird that can knock out original tunes!"

*

Two dog owners were talking about the intelligence of their pets.

"The brightest dog I ever owned," said one, "was a Great Dane that used to play cards. He was a whiz at poker, but finally a friend complained about him and I had him shot."

"You had him shot, a bright dog like that? A dog like that would be worth a million dollars."

"Had to," said the ex-owner. "We caught him using marked cards."

*

A valuable dachshund, owned by a wealthy woman, was run over. The policeman detailed a man to tell the woman of her misfortune. "But break the news gently," he said. "She thinks a lot of this dog."

The man rapped on the mansion door and when the woman appeared he said: "Sorry, lady, but part of your dog has been run over."

*

A woman wanted to spend a month at a new resort hotel, but before packing her luggage, she took the precaution of writing the hotel manager to be sure that dogs were permitted in the hostelry. The manager had a couple of dogs he was very fond of himself. He sent her this letter:

"Dear Madam:

I have been in the hotel business for some twenty-eight years. Never in all that time have I had to call the police to eject a disorderly dog at four o'clock in the morning. Never once has a dog set the bedclothes afire by carelessly throwing away a lighted cigarette. Never has a dog stolen my towels, bedspreads, or silverware. Of course your dog is welcome at my hotel.

Sincerely,
The Manager

P.S. If the dog will vouch for you, you can come, too."

Apartments

"The owners of this apartment house insist upon absolute quiet from their tenants," explained the renting agent.

"Yes, I understand," said the apartment hunter.

"You don't have any children, do you?"

"No, we don't."

"Or any pets of any kind?"

"Oh, no."

Then, suddenly remembering something that would undoubtedly disqualify him as a tenant, he said sadly, "But I do have a fountain pen that scratches a little."

Bankers

A furrier dashed into his bank and rushed into the manager's office.

"Mr. Brown," he said, "my note for fifteen thousand dollars is due next Wednesday. Can you give me an extension of time?"

"Certainly not," came the curt reply. "Be sure to have that money here next Wednesday by noon sharp."

The furrier shouted angrily, "Were you ever in the fur business?"

"Certainly not," replied the bank official.

"Well," he said, "by next Wednesday at noon sharp you will be!"

*

At a large private dinner party, two strangers were seated next to each other and started talking.

"So you are an actor," said the first stranger, on learning the other's profession. "I'm a banker. I'm ashamed to admit it, but I haven't been to the theater in more than five years."

"Oh, don't feel bad about that," said the actor. "It's been much longer than that since I've been in a bank."

Bargains

"Yes," said the old man to his visitor, "I'm proud of my girls and I would like to see them comfortably married. I've made a little money, and they will not go penniless to their husbands. There is Mary, twenty-five years old and a good-looking girl. I'll give her a thousand dollars when she marries. Then comes Elizabeth, who won't see thirty-five again. I'll give her three thousand dollars. And the man who takes Kate, who is forty, will have five thousand dollars."

The visitor, a young man not averse to money, reflected a moment, then asked: "You haven't one about fifty, have you?"

*

Two friends met on a street in New York. The first said excitedly, "Max, I have the buy of a lifetime for you. I've got this full-grown elephant, and I can let you have him for fifty dollars."

Max looked at him and said, "Are you crazy? I live in a two-room apartment, a sixth-floor walkup with three kids. My wife would kill me. What kind of a deal is that?"

"Okay," said the first, "you drive a hard bargain. How about two for seventy-five dollars?"

"Now you're talking," said Max.

*

A dignified, middle-aged gentleman decided to take advantage of a special sale and buy his wife a pair of nylons. After waiting about an hour on the fringe of a screaming, pushing mob of women, he plunged toward the counter with both arms flying. Suddenly a shrill voice hollered, "Can't you act like a gentleman?"

"I've been acting like a gentleman for over an hour and it got me nowhere," he replied, still plowing toward the counter. "Now I'm going to act like a lady."

*

Winter had already put in its appearance the day that Weary Willie slouched into a pawnshop.

"How much will you give me for this overcoat?"

He produced a faded, but neatly mended, garment. The pawnbroker looked at it critically.

"Two dollars," he said.

"Why," cried Weary Willie, "that coat's worth ten dollars if it's worth a penny."

I wouldn't give you ten dollars for three overcoats like that," replied the second-hand clothing dealer. "Two dollars or nothing."

"Are you sure that's all it's worth?"

"Two dollars," repeated the man.

"Well, here's yer two dollars," said Weary Willie. "This overcoat was hangin' outside your store and I was wondering how much it was actually worth."

Bartenders

The bartender was breaking in a young man to take his place while he went on vacation. The replacement was friendly and very talkative; there seemed no end to his store of bright jokes and youthful wit. But his patter just wasn't going over with the customers. Finally the old barman called the youngster to one side and we overheard this bit of wisdom: "Listen, kid—listen— don't talk. If these guys wanted to listen, they'd have stayed home."

Bill-Collecting

"I thought that fellow was a little too smooth," a hotel clerk complained to the manager after telling him about a guest who had left without paying his bill.

"Well, I'll send a letter along to the address he left," the manager said, "but I don't suppose we'll get an answer."

The note that the manager sent was brief. It read, "Will you please send us the amount of your bill?"

To the manager's surprise, he received a reply in a few days.

"My dear sir," it read, "the amount of my bill is fifty dollars, but I really do think you people should keep track of those things."

*

"My good man," said Mr. Baldinger to the grocery store owner, "how is it you have not called on me for my account?"

"Oh, I never ask a gentleman for money."

"Indeed! But what do you do if he doesn't pay?"

"Why, after a certain time," said he, "I conclude he is not a gentleman, and then I ask him."

*

The young couple had just finished going over their monthly bills and were down to the last two.

"Gosh, honey," said the husband, "we're practically broke. I don't know which to pay—the electric company or the doctor."

"Oh, the electric company, of course," answered his wife. "After all, the doctor can't shut off your blood."

Bull

The mama bull, the papa bull, and the baby bull set out to go to the fair. After walking a mile, the mama bull became tired and sat down to rest. A mile later the papa bull got tired and he sat down to rest. But the baby bull walked all the way to the fair.

Now there's a moral to this story: "Sometimes a little bull goes a long way."

Bums

A panhandler collapsed on the street and immediately a large crowd gathered.

"Give the poor man a drink of whiskey," a little old lady suggested.

"Give him some air," said several men.

"Give him a drink of whiskey," said the little old lady.

"Call an ambulance," someone suggested.

"Give him a drink of whiskey," repeated the little old lady.

The babble continued until suddenly the victim sat up. "Will you all shut up," he said, "and listen to the little old lady."

*

"Buddy, can you spare a nickel for a cuppa coffee?" whined the panhandler as he held out a dirty palm.

The fatherly-looking gentleman gazed at him with tender pity and replied, "I'm sorry, young man, I have no money but I should like to give you a little advice."

At this, the panhandler blew up and screamed impatiently. "All the time I get advice, but no money. If you guys never have any money, how can you expect me to think your advice is worth anything?"

*

Two tramps sat with their backs against an old oak tree. Before them was a rippling stream. Although the day was delightful, one of them was disconsolate.

"You know, Jim," he mused, "this business of tramping your

way through life is not what it's cracked up to be. Think it over—nights on park benches or in a cold barn. Traveling on freight trains and always dodging the police. Being kicked from one town to another. Wondering where your next meal is coming from. Wandering unwanted, sneered at by your fellow men. . . ." His voice trailed off as he sighed heavily. His companion shifted his position.

"Well," observed the second tramp, "if that's the way you feel about it, why don't you find yourself a job?"

The first tramp sat up with a jerk. "What?" he exclaimed. "And admit I'm a failure!"

*

A very unattractive woman was approached by a man in rags.

"Could you spare a dime for something to eat?"

"Why are you begging—a big, strong man like you? I should think you'd be ashamed."

"Mademoiselle," he said, removing his hat and bowing low, "I'm an incurable romanticist. I have woven lovely dreams and the wind has swept them away. And so I have turned to this profession—the only one I know in which a gentleman can approach a beautiful young girl without being formally introduced."

He got a dollar.

*

He was desperate.

"Madam," he muttered between tight lips, "if I don't get a dollar before the sun goes down, I shall have to do something that I've dreaded doing."

She searched through her pocketbook frantically and came up with a crumpled bill. "Here," she said, offering him the dollar, "I hope this money will tide you over until you are able to find a job."

"That, lady," he informed her, "is the thing I've dreaded doing."

*

A beggar approached a man on the street.

"Mister, I've had nothing to eat for three days. Will you please give me a dollar?"

"Of course not!" said the man. "If you are that bad off, I should think you would be humble enough to ask for a quarter which, no doubt, you would be more likely to receive than a dollar."

"Give me a dollar or give me a quarter," said the beggar, "but please don't tell me how to run my business."

*

Two tramps too lazy to walk to the next town noticed an old motorcycle and side car in front of a nearby house. They jumped in and drove off.

After about half an hour the driver looked at his companion and jammed on the brakes.

The other tramp's face was red, his eyes were protruding, and he could hardly breathe.

"What's the matter?" asked the driver.

"What do you think?" answered his companion. "There's no bottom in this side car and I've had to run like mad all the way."

*

The conductor, making his rounds on the train, was surprised to find a little old man curled up under one of the seats. Caught in his hideout, the man pleaded.

"I'm a poor old man and haven't got the money for a ticket. But my daughter is being married and I must get there for the wedding. Please let me stay. I promise to be very quiet and not disturb any of the passengers."

The conductor was a kindly man and agreed. But under the very next seat he found another little old gent huddled up and looking badly frightened.

"And where are you going?" he asked.

The man answered timidly, "I'm the bridegroom."

Business

A New York dress manufacturer who was having a showing of his fall line for forty important buyers sent his assistant to Lindy's restaurant with the following instructions: "Bring me back one sandwich—but make sure it's the most expensive one."

"All right," said the puzzled assistant, "but you've got forty buyers coming. How are you going to feed them all with one sandwich?"

"Don't tell me my business," snapped the boss. "After you buy that sandwich across the street, take it down to Sam's delicatessen and tell him to knock off thirty-nine copies."

*

The head of a big advertising agency was lunching with a group of his top executives—all of whom had unlimited expense accounts. When the check appeared, everybody made a grab for it, but the boss won out.

"I'll take care of this, boys," he said firmly. "That's the one way I can be sure I'll pay for it just once."

*

The sales manager was going over one of his salesmen's expense accounts. "Just look at this!" he declared. "How can you spend nine dollars for food in a single day in Sandusky, Ohio?"

"It's easy," answered the salesman cheerfully. "You just skip breakfast."

*

The owner of one of New York's largest department stores was awakened at three in the morning in his home by a phone call. The voice at the other end identified himself: "I'm one of your customers. I bought a sofa in your store, and I want to tell you how beautiful it is."

The sleepy store owner replied, "I appreciate the compliment, but tell me, when did you buy this sofa from us?"

"I bought it from you four months ago."

"You mean you bought it from us four months ago, and you wake me up at three in the morning to tell me about it?"

"Of course—it just arrived!"

*

A visitor was impressed by the number of slogans on an office wall reading "Think," "Think Big," "Think Creatively," and so on in the same vein. When he commented on them to the head man, the boss shrugged and said, "Yes, they're a great gang for putting up mottoes."

"But that man over at the corner desk doesn't have any signs at all," the visitor noted. "How has he resisted conforming?"

"Well," sighed the boss, "somebody around here has to do the work."

*

Joe, the ineffectual but talkative worker, spent most of his time complaining that fortune seemed to smile at everyone else, but merely sneered at him. Another employee with less seniority had just been promoted. Joe headed for the boss's office.

"It's the same old story," he moaned. "Other guys get all the breaks, but my ship never comes in."

The boss looked up at Joe and said, "Maybe you haven't heard that steam has replaced wind."

*

The head of the store was passing through the packing room when he saw a boy lounging against a box and whistling cheerfully.

"How much do you get a week?" he asked.

"Ten dollars."

"Here's a week's pay—get out."

When he saw the foreman later in the day, he asked: "When did we hire that boy?"

"We didn't. He just brought in a package from another firm."

*

It had been a bad day for the foreman. Everything had gone wrong. He came to the end of his rope when he entered the shop to find the men loafing for the third time that day.

"Why is it," he exploded, "that whenever I come into this shop, I find you men idle?"

"Probably," muttered one of the culprits, "because you wear rubber heels."

*

The understanding employer was only too glad to give his clerk the rest of the day off, after the young man explained that his wife was going to have a baby. When the clerk came to work the following morning, the boss called him into his office to offer his congratulations and inquired, "Was it a boy or a girl?"

"Oh, it's much too soon to tell," the clerk replied. "We have to wait nine months to find that out."

*

"You just can't come in here like this and ask for a raise," the boss said to his newest employee. "You must work yourself up."

"But I did," the employee replied. "Look, I'm trembling all over."

*

An irate employee went to the company paymaster and carefully counted the money in his pay envelope.

"It's one dollar short! What's the meaning of this?"

The paymaster checked a record sheet and replied, "Last week

we overpaid you a dollar. You didn't complain about that mistake, did you?"

"An occasional mistake I can overlook," snapped the angry
man, "but not two in a row."

*

The self-made millionaire was addressing the graduating class
at the local university.

"All my success in life," he said, "I owe to one thing—pluck.
Pluck and more pluck."

But he hadn't reckoned with the present generation of youth
in turmoil.

"That's great, sir," said one bright student, "but will you please
tell us something about who to pluck and how?"

*

"Oh, yes, there's one more thing," said the sick man to his lawyer,
who was writing out the will. "I want these men to be my pall-
bearers."

The lawyer looked at the list of names and could not recognize
one of them as a good friend of the sick man. Naturally he asked
why they were the ones chosen.

"They're my creditors," the sick man explained. "They've been
carrying me most of my life, so they might as well finish the job."

*

Two businessmen vacationing at Miami Beach were comparing
notes. One said, "I'm here on insurance money, I collected fifty
thousand dollars for fire damage."

"Me, too," said the other man. "I got one hundred thousand
dollars for flood damage."

There was a long, thoughtful pause. Then the first man asked,
"Tell me, how do you start a flood?"

*

At a kosher Catskill resort, a vacationer encountered a frail, rabbinical old man who identified himself as the head dietician. His job was making sure that meat and milk were not served at the same meal. In February, the vacationer went to Miami where he met the same old man.

"What brings you south?" he asked. "The sun?"

"No, same thing as in the Catskills," replied the old man. "I'm in charge of the dietary laws here."

In June, the vacationer took a trip to Israel, and in Tel Aviv he ran into the old man for the third time.

"I suppose you're still taking charge of the dietary laws?" he said.

"Oh, no," the old man answered. "Here I'm the golf pro."

*

An office clerk was selected for jury duty, and the first morning he reported for service, he asked the judge to excuse him.

"We're very busy at the office now," he explained, "and I ought to be there."

"So you think your boss can't get along without you, eh?" queried the judge.

"No, Your Honor," replied the clerk, "I know he can, but I don't want him to find out."

*

A young graduate from the Harvard School of Business Administration got a job as a bus driver and was assigned to the Canal Street line. When he returned to the garage after his first day's work he handed the foreman sixty-five dollars.

"Sixty-five dollars! That's wonderful," declared the foreman. "You know, we've had this line running for years and years and nobody ever brought in over ten dollars. There's no business on the Canal Street line. How did you do it?"

"Simple," said the Harvard graduate. "When there was no business on Canal Street, I merely took the bus over to Broadway."

*

It was the weekly bowling session for the office gang and Harry, the new worker, was asked to fill in for one of the regulars who couldn't make it. Anxious to do well, but extremely nervous over bowling with a group of older men, the young man inadvertently used the boss's ball, smoked two cigarettes the old fellow had lighted, and mistakenly drank his beer.

"Young man," thundered the boss, "it's a good thing you don't know where I live."

*

The office boy was rather nervous the first day on his new job. Summoning up courage, he approached his employer and said, "Please sir, I think you're wanted on the phone."

The employer, busy with his problems, snapped: "You think? What's the good of thinking?"

"Well, sir," the office boy said, "the voice at the other end said, 'Hello, is that you, you idiot?'"

*

A junior executive complained to his wife of aches and pains. This went on for two weeks. One day he returned home feeling better.

"I found out what was wrong," he told his wife. "We got some ultramodern office furniture two weeks ago, and I just learned that I've been sitting in a wastebasket."

*

The boss had his assistant on the carpet.

"Billings," he said, "I understand that after the office party yesterday, you pushed a wheelbarrow down Madison Avenue. Don't you realize the company could lose prestige by such actions?"

"I never gave it a thought," said Billings, "since you were in the wheelbarrow!"

*

At the conclusion of a concert, two ushers were applauding

harder than anybody else. People seated nearby smiled appreciatively at the two music lovers—until one of them stopped applauding and the other one was heard to say, "Keep clapping, you dope. One more encore and we're on overtime."

*

Two insurance agents—an American and an Englishman—were talking about their rival methods. The Britisher was holding forth on the system of prompt payment carried out by his company: no trouble, no fuss, no attempt to wriggle out of payment.

"If a man died tonight," he explained, "his widow would receive her money by the first post tomorrow."

"You don't say?" said the American. "But if you want an example of prompt payment, listen to this. Our office is on the sixth floor of a building sixty-nine stories high. One of our clients had his office on the forty-ninth story. One day he fell out of his window. We handed him his check as he passed our floor."

*

A professor of physics was crossing the border into Mexico at Tia Juana to see the bullfights one Sunday afternoon. The Mexican guard who stopped his car asked the usual questions. After the professor gave his name and address, the guard asked: "What business are you in, please?"

"Physics," replied the professor.

A few moments elapsed while the Mexican guard pondered this development. Then he inquired, "Wholesale or retail?"

*

"Papa, what does it mean—business ethics?" asked junior.

"Well," said papa, "it's like this. A man comes into the store and makes a purchase. He gives me a crisp new five dollar bill, which is just the right amount. As I turn to the cash register, I discover it is not one but two five dollar bills stuck together. Now comes the business ethics. Should I tell my partner?"

*

It was Sam's wedding anniversary, and he bought a five thousand dollar diamond ring for his wife. His partner Harry became enchanted with the ring and insisted that Sam sell it to him at a profit of five hundred dollars, which Sam did. But then Sam had misgivings and pleaded with Harry to sell the ring back for six thousand dollars.

The ring passed back and forth between these two partners until the cost had skyrocketed to ten thousand dollars. Harry left with the prized ring. The following day Harry told his partner that he had run into an old friend on the way home. The old friend had admired the ring and purchased it for twelve thousand dollars.

"Harry," said Sam pleadingly. "Why did you do a stupid thing like that? We were both making such a fine living from that ring."

*

A new bride asked the butcher the price of his hamburger meat.

"Eighty-nine cents a pound," he told her.

She complained that she could get it down the street for sixty-nine cents a pound. He asked why she didn't.

"They're out of it today," she said.

"When I'm out of it," the butcher replied, "I sell it for twenty cents a pound."

*

Two businessmen were discussing a competitor who had once been an employee of one of them. His ex-boss said, "I happen to know that fellow is a sharpie. He's not above lying and stealing when it's to his advantage."

"Do you know him personally?" asked the other businessman.

"Know him! Why, I taught him everything he knows."

*

A young man, tired of working for others, went into business for himself. A few months later, a friend asked him how it was to be his own boss.

"I don't know," he replied. "The police won't let me park in front of my own place of business; tax collectors tell me how to keep books; my banker tells me how much balance I must maintain; freight agents tell me how my goods must be packed; federal, state, county, and local agencies tell me how to keep records; the union tells me who I can employ and how and when; and on top of that, I just got married."

*

"Boss," the bookkeeper said as he entered the manager's office with a broad grin on his face, "you remember that big Christmas order we got from the Palace Company?"

"Of course I do," replied the manager. "What about it?"

"That was the order that finally put us in the black," the bookkeeper announced proudly.

"Wonderful," beamed the manager. "Now you can throw out that cursed bottle of red ink and run out and get a bottle of black."

"I'm afraid that wouldn't do," said the bookkeeper meekly. "If I went out and bought a bottle of black ink, we would be in the red again."

*

An auto manufacturer, proud of his assembly lines, advertised that in a test one of his cars had been put together in exactly six minutes.

The next day he received a phone call. "Is that advertisement about assembling a car in six minutes true?" a man's voice asked politely.

"Yes, sir!" the manufacturer assured him. "An auto was actually turned out in precisely that time."

"Well, I just wanted to know," the voice said. "I think I'm the owner of that car."

*

The circus proprietor looked more worried than usual as he faced the troupe on Friday.

"Gentlemen," he began, "as you all know, business is very bad just now. Last week I could only manage to pay you all half wages. This week things have been even worse."

He stopped for a moment and looked with growing anxiety at the angry faces around him. Then, wiping his damp forehead, he went on: "I've gone carefully into the matter and find there is enough cash in hand to pay—er—three of you this week. The lucky three are Hercules, the strong man; Dave Dauntless, the lion tamer; and Strangler Sam, the champion wrestler."

*

Sales had been going down, down, down, until finally the manager summoned all salesmen to come to the home office for a meeting. "All right," he shouted at them, "we're going to have a sales contest—and the man who wins it keeps his job!"

*

The small traveler from another planet had a cone-shaped head, square eyes, and rabbit ears. He landed on the lower East Side of Manhattan, where a vegetable peddler asked him to mind his pushcart for a few minutes. A little girl passing by stared at the stranger from outer space and said to her mother, "Ma, isn't that a crazy-looking vegetable peddler?"

The mother shrugged and said, "Maybe he looks crazy, but he's getting forty-nine cents a pound for tomatoes."

*

An American businessman was touring the Far East. In Taiwan, he was entertained at a luncheon by the local equivalent of the chamber of commerce. At the end of the meal, he was asked to "say a few words."

His address was to be translated by an interpreter.

"Well," he began, "I just want all you fellows to know that I'm tickled to death to be here."

A look of agony appeared on the interpreter's face. "This poor man," he said in halting Chinese, "scratches himself until he dies, only to be with you."

*

A large company was reclassifying all jobs by sending out a questionnaire to employees. When the elevator operator received his, he had no trouble answering all the questions except one: "How much time do you spend at each of your duties?"

The operator gave the question much thought and then wrote: "Up fifty per cent, down fifty per cent."

*

A man waiting for his car in a garage watched as a mechanic working on another car changed the oil without spilling a drop, checked the water level, lowered the hood carefully and locked it, cleaned the windshield, wiped all the greasy finger marks away, checked the battery, and after washing his hands, drove the car slowly out to the street.

"Now, there's a real mechanic," remarked the man, turning to the shop foreman. "How careful he is of that car."

The foreman nodded knowingly, and replied, "It's his."

*

A man had a business appointment in one of those ultra-modern windowless office buildings. When he left, he took the wrong corridor and lost his way. Finally, he spotted a secretary typing away at a desk. "How do I get outside?" he asked.

Without looking up, she replied, "Dial nine."

*

An ad man who went to heaven was stopped at the gate. "Sorry," he was told, "but we've filled our quota for your profession. In order for you to get in, you'll have to convince one of the others to leave."

"Fair enough," replied our man. "Give me twenty-four hours."

By the end of the day, every one of the advertising angels had departed. Asked by the stunned gatekeeper how he had managed it, the advertising man answered: "It was easy—I started a rumor that the devil was looking for a new agency. Incidentally, I'm not staying either. You never can tell about those rumors."

*

A lady came into a drugstore and bought two packages of invisible hairpins. As she paid for them, she asked the clerk, "Now, are you sure these hairpins are really invisible?"

"Lady, I'll tell you how invisible they are," the clerk said. "I've sold four bucks worth of those pins today, and we've been out of them for weeks."

*

An indignant customer marched resolutely into the butcher shop and plunked a piece of metal down on the counter.

"See that?" he demanded.

"Uh-huh," replied the butcher, "looks like a piece of tin."

"It does," said the customer, breathing fire, "and I found it in one of those sausages you sold me yesterday."

The butcher picked it up and inspected it thoroughly. "I think I can explain it," he said.

"You can bet your life you will," snarled the customer.

"Well," mused the butcher, "it looks very much as if I had forgotten to remove the license tag."

Country People

The elderly farm couple sat in their rocking chairs in front of the fireplace one wintry night in Iowa.

"The years are passing us by, Sarah," said the old man.

"Yes," she agreed.

"We're getting older," he said, "and pretty soon only one of us will be left."

"That's right," she said, "and when that happens, I'm moving to California."

*

The county desperado had broken out of the local jail and the entire police force was alerted. One of them was ordered to go to the railroad station and keep close watch.

"The roads are all blocked," the sheriff said, "so his only means of escape is the railroad."

Two hours later the deputy was back.

"What are you doing here?" barked the sheriff. "I told you to watch the railroad station."

The deputy grinned. "He can't get away. I tore up all the train tickets."

*

Tom and a friend were walking hurriedly through the woods one dismal afternoon, trying to reach home before the storm broke. They didn't make it. There was a deafening crash from the heavens, and the two men made for the nearest tree.

"Say," said Tom's friend, "I wonder why it is that lightning never strikes twice in the same place?"

"Probably," answered Tom, "because after its hits a place once, the same place ain't there any more."

*

The farmer and his wife had been to the big town for a few days of sightseeing. When they checked out of the hotel the proprietor handed them a bill for thirty dollars. The old farmer declared that he would pay only fifteen dollars of it, as he had not eaten any meals at the hotel.

"But they were here for you," insisted the hotel proprietor, "and you offer to pay me only half of my bill?"

"Yes," retorted the farmer shrewdly, "and you kissed my wife while we were here."

"I did nothing of the kind," was the angry retort of the hotel man.

"Well," the farmer blandly replied, "it was here for you."

*

A tough old mountaineer had been missing for five days, and his wife finally decided to look for him. She found him in a thick clump of bushes, looking rather peaked.

"Suppertime, Paw," she ventured.

"Yep," agreed the mountaineer.

"Well then," she continued, "ain't ye comin' home?"

"Nope," said he.

"Why not?" said she.

"Becuz," he said with finality, "I'm standin' in a bear trap."

*

Two farmhands were sitting under a tree having their lunch. One farmhand asked the other: "See that train crossing over yonder?"

"Yes," said the second farmhand.

"If you saw a train coming seventy miles an hour down the track, and the crossing signal wasn't working, and you saw a car coming around the bend doing sixty and not able to see the train, what would you do?"

"I'd call my cousin Eustice," said the second farmhand. "He's never seen a really big wreck."

*

Once upon a time there were two old men who were very stubborn. Somehow they were always encountering each other in situations that required one to give in. But since neither would, the matter usually had to be settled by a third party. One day each man was driving a large load of hay in a different direction along a narrow country lane. Each saw the other approaching and determined that he would not move out of the way. They drew closer and closer together, but neither would give an inch. Finally, one said to the other: "I'm prepared to stay here as long as you want to wait."

He took out his newspaper and began to read. The other filled his pipe and puffed contentedly. After half an hour of silence, he leaned out of his high seat and called over to his neighbor: "Would you mind lettin' me read that paper when you're through?"

*

A tourist spending the night in a small Vermont town joined several men sitting on the porch of the general store. They were a tight-lipped bunch, and after several futile attempts to start a conversation, he finally asked: "Is there a law against talking in this town?"

"There's no law against it," answered one of the men, "but there's an understanding. No one talks unless he can improve on the silence."

*

A small town shoemaker left the gas turned on in his shop one night. When he arrived the next morning, he struck a match to light the stove. There was a terrific explosion, and the shoemaker was blown out through the door into the middle of the street.

A friend rushed to his assistance, helped him up, and inquired if he was hurt.

The old fellow gazed at his shop, which was now burning quite briskly, and said, "No, I ain't hurt. But I got out jest in time, by cracky."

*

The bus was crowded, and a lanky mountaineer was crushed into a seat with a pretty girl whose mini-skirt kept creeping up. She fought a constant, though losing, battle because she no sooner would pull it down, then it would slide up again.

In desperation she gave it one hard yank and then looked up to meet the eyes of her traveling companion.

"Don't rip your calico, sister," he said comfortingly. "My weakness is liquor."

*

A ranch-reared city dweller was determined that his son know life in the saddle, so he farmed out the boy to an old rancher friend. After the boy had been at the ranch for a couple of months, his father inquired about his progress.

"Well," replied the rancher, "he's a good worker and already he speaks cow language. But," said the old cowman dubiously, "he ain't learned to think like a cow yet."

*

A newspaper editor remarked one morning to his landlady, "I think we'll have a good potato crop this year."

She took issue with him, replying firmly, "I think the crop will be poor."

When he got to the office, the editor had this information printed: "An excellent potato crop is expected this fall."

To his delight, that night the landlady said apologetically, "I was wrong about the potato crop. I saw in the paper that the crop will be excellent."

*

"Any big men born around here?" a tourist asked in a condescending tone.

"Nope," responded the native, "best we can do is babies. Different in the city, I suppose."

*

A tourist stopped at a combination service station and general store in the back country. While his car was being serviced, he noticed an old-timer basking in the sun and holding a piece of rope.

The tourist walked over to him and asked, "What have you there?"

"This is a weather gauge, sonny," he said.

"How can you possibly predict the weather with a piece of rope?" the tourist wanted to know.

"It's simple, sonny," was the answer. "When the rope swings back and forth, it's windy—and when it gits wet, it's raining."

*

The Yankee visitor was in Louisville, Kentucky, for the Derby. On the eve of that racing classic, he was going along with the happy local custom of doping the race over a few bourbons.

"Bartender," said the Yankee at last, "it is true that Kentuckians are very bibulous?"

The bartender thought carefully and then measured out another bourbon as he answered, "No, suh. Ah don't reckon there are mo' than a few dozen Bibles in the whole state."

*

A family had just moved to a small town in New England. After they had settled into their new home, the woman of the family began familiarizing herself with the local stores. Determined to get some meat for her family's evening meal, she entered the only meat market in the village. She was quite surprised to find only two trays of meat in the showcase. Upon closer examination, she found that the meat in each case looked exactly alike.

"How much is this meat?" she asked, pointing to one of the cases.

"Fifty cents a pound," replied the old butcher.

"And that?" she asked, pointing to the other tray.

"One dollar a pound."

"What's the difference?" she asked.

"No difference," grunted the butcher. "Some people like to pay fifty cents a pound and some like to pay a dollar."

*

A farmer had twenty employees on his farm and, as they were not as energetic as the farmer thought they should be, he hit upon a plan that would cure them of their lazy habits.

"Men," he said one morning, "I have a nice, easy job for the laziest man on the farm. Will the laziest man step forward?"

Instantly nineteen of the men stepped forward.

"Why don't you step to the front with the rest?" inquired the farmer of the remaining one.

"Too much trouble," came the reply.

Credit

A young man applied to a finance agency for a job, but he had no experience. He was so intense that the manager gave him an account to collect with the promise that if he collected it, he would give him a job.

"He'll never collect it," he told his secretary. "It's that mechanic down the street who's owed us that money for three years."

Much to his surprise, the young man came back with the entire sum. "This is amazing!" said the manager. "Just how did you do it?"

"Easy," replied the youngster. "I told him if he didn't pay up, I'd tell all his other creditors he had paid us."

*

The man had barely paid off his mortgage on the house when he mortgaged it again to buy a car, and not too long after borrowed money to build a garage. His banker hesitated, and said, "If I do make this new loan, how will you buy gas for the car?"

"It seems to me," the man replied curtly, "that a fellow who owns a big house, a car, and a garage should be able to get credit for gas."

Criminals

A condemned prisoner awaiting execution was granted the usual privilege of choosing the dishes he wanted to eat for his last meal.

He ordered a large plate of mushrooms.

"Why all the mushrooms and nothing else?" inquired the guard.

"Well," replied the prisoner, "I always wanted to try them, but I was always afraid to eat them before."

*

Two expert pickpockets were strolling along the road together. Every now and then one of them would stop, take out his watch, and look at it. His companion began to get annoyed.

"I say, Jim," he said, "what's up with you? Why d'yer keep looking at your ticker? Ain't it going or something?"

"I'm not looking at it to see the time," said the other. "I'm looking at it to make sure that it's still there."

*

When a certain New England bank was having trouble gaining new depositors, the vice-president hired an attractive young lady as a teller. He was sure she would stimulate business.

It was a few days later when the vice-president walked into the bank just as a young man walked out with a broad smile on his face. The vice-president hurried over to the new teller.

"That's how I like to see our customers walk out of here," he said. "Did he make a deposit?"

"Make a deposit?" gasped the young lady. "He just robbed the bank."

*

A couple of bank robbers hit a small country bank one lazy afternoon when the staff was small, and herded everyone into the vault at gunpoint. They gagged the teller, however, bound him hand and foot, and forced him to the floor of the cashier's cage.

Suddenly the teller began to squirm, at the same time gesturing with his head to make it evident he wanted to say something. After stuffing the money into sacks, the robbers leaned over the helpless figure on the floor and shifted the gag.

"Give a guy a break, fellows, will you?" he begged. "Take these books along with you. I'm almost three thousand dollars short."

*

Two burly assassins waited in ambush for the King. They had hidden themselves behind a bush on the path of the palace grounds which His Majesty passed every day, precisely at noon. Noon came and went. Another hour went by and still another, but the intended victim didn't appear. The killers grew impatient.

"I can't understand why he doesn't come," muttered one.

"Neither can I," whispered the other. "I hope nothing's happened to him."

Courtship

During a lull in the doings at a discotheque, the young girl impulsively said, "Let's get married, George. I don't want to wait around until I'm thirty-five and have wrinkles, bags under my eyes, and a pot belly."

"Well," George replied, "if that's the way you're going to look at thirty-five, let's forget it."

*

He was exceedingly brave and eloquent as he told her how much he loved her.

"There's nothing in this world I wouldn't do for you, sweetheart," he said. "Why, I would even face death for you."

At that moment a bull snorted and charged. The young man took off like a shot.

"But darling," she called after him, "you just said you'd face death for me."

"Sure, sure," he replied over a fast-disappearing shoulder, "but he ain't dead yet."

*

Among her many admirers was an extremely fat man. Even though he knew he didn't have a chance, he persisted in his attentions. One evening, while they were sitting on the living-room sofa, he proposed. He became so wrought up that he dropped to his knees and pleaded for a "yes" to his offer of marriage.

When she made it crystal clear that she was not among those who could love a fat man, he sighed heavily and dropped his head in sorrow.

"Well, at least," he said, holding out his hand, "help me get up."

*

She was very rich and he was poor but honest. She liked him, but that was all, and he knew it. One night he had been a little more tender than usual.

"You are very rich," he ventured.

"Yes," she replied frankly. "I'm worth about one million dollars."

"Will you marry me?" he asked.

"No."

"I didn't think you would."

"Then why did you ask me?"

"Oh, I just wanted to see how a man feels when he loses a million dollars."

*

A college freshman fell in love with a town girl and gave her his fraternity pin. Then he heard rumors that she was going out with another boy. One night he was watching when she came down the street with a senior. As they reached her door, the senior put his arms around her and kissed her good night.

The freshman came charging out of the shadows and shouted, "Fickle woman, now I know everything!"

"Don't brag," she remarked calmly. "When was the Battle of Gettysburg?"

Divorce

The flighty young blonde had just told her luncheon companion that she was divorcing her husband.

"By the way," queried the other girl after a while, "how much is that lawyer going to charge you for handling your divorce suit?"

"Oh, he's not charging me a thing," gushed the blonde. "You see, he's an old friend of my husband's and he's doing this as a favor to him."

*

The attorney for the complainant in the divorce case put his client on the stand.

"Now, as I understand it," he said sympathetically, "every night when you came home from work you found a different man hiding in the closet?"

"Yes, that's right."

"And this, of course, caused you untold anguish, heartaches, and suffering, did it not?"

"It sure did! I never had any place to hang up my coat."

*

"I'd like to know if I can get a divorce from my husband," said the delicate young thing.

"What has your husband done?" inquired the lawyer.

"Is that information necessary?" she asked.

"Of course, we must make some charge against him. State what he's done."

"Well, as a matter of fact, he hasn't done anything. I haven't got a husband, but I'm engaged to a man and I just wanted to see how easily I could get a divorce if I needed one."

*

A beautiful blonde passed two men on the street.

"There goes my ex-wife," said one. "Wonderful little housekeeper."

"Doesn't look it," remarked the other. "Not the type."

"She is though," insisted the first. "Divorced three times and kept the house each time."

*

He was groggy from lack of sleep. His friend urged him to buck up.

"I know your wife left you," he sympathized, "but you mustn't let it get you down. You've just got to get some sleep. Why don't you try counting sheep?"

"I don't have time," he said. "I'm too busy counting my lucky stars!"

Doctors

A fellow called by the draft board was examined by his family doctor who happened to be on the board. He passed easily and was inducted immediately. Furious, he returned to see the doctor.

"You're a fine doctor," he raged. "It's funny you always found something the matter with me when I was paying you ten dollars a visit!"

*

A tramp was walking along a street in London and was met by a brother hobo, who reproached him for his ragged trousers.

"Why, you ought to be ashamed of yourself," he said.

"But how am I to get a pair of trousers?" the ragged tramp asked. "They don't grow on trees."

"Well, just go into the first house that looks like the folks might have an extra pair of trousers and ask for an old pair," the second hobo advised.

The ragged tramp took his friend's advice, and seeing a doctor's sign across the street, he went up to the door and lifted the knocker. A lady answered the summons and he asked her if the doctor whose name appeared on the door was in. She answered in the affirmative.

"Then," said the tramp, "will you be kind enough to ask the doctor if he has an old pair of pants he could let me have?"

The woman replied that she was afraid they would not do.

"Oh," the tramp assured her, "I don't mind if they are very old."

But the lady informed him, "That isn't the problem, my good man. You see, I am the doctor!"

*

The lecturer on medical economics was addressing the senior medical class.

"You men will soon be in practice," he stated, "and you must weigh the cost of your medical education against the number of productive hours you will have in practice. That's what I did and soon it proved I had to obtain the prestige of specialization and the fees that go with it."

The seniors listened attentively.

"And so today," continued the professor, "I charge fifty dollars for a house call after six o'clock in the evening, twenty-five dollars for an office consultation, and ten dollars if my advice is sought over the phone."

A hand was raised in the front row.

"How much do you charge, Professor," asked the senior, "for passing a patient on the street?"

*

A woman went to her doctor to have a prescription renewed. She sat in the crowded waiting room and became engrossed in a magazine. When the nurse called her name, she found her leg had gone to sleep and she limped awkwardly into the doctor's office. The doctor wrote a new prescription and two minutes later the woman walked briskly out into the waiting room again.

As she put on her coat, she noticed another patient staring at her in astonishment. The surprised patient poked her companion and whispered excitedly, "See Myrtle? I told you he is the best doctor in town."

*

Tension reigned in the operating room as an obstetrician and a surgeon delivered a baby by Caesarean section in a particularly difficult maternity case.

Later, the danger past, the anesthetist inquired, "What was it, a boy or a girl?"

"I don't know," replied the surgeon.

"Neither do I," said the obstetrician.

A student nurse standing nearby spoke up shyly: "Let me see the baby—I can tell."

*

The telephone in the doctor's home rang at three in the morning.

"What do you charge for a house call?" the woman at the other end of the line asked.

"Ten dollars," the doctor mumbled sleepily.

"And how much for an office visit?"

"Five dollars."

"All right," the woman said quickly. "I'll meet you at your office in ten minutes."

*

This nurse was new on the job and anxious to make a good impression on the doctor's patients. Therefore she turned on her most charming smile when the new patient entered the office.

"What kind of a guy is this doctor?" asked the patient.

"The best doctor in the city," replied the nurse, laying it on thick.

"Is he the kind of a guy who cuts you open at the drop of a hat?"

"Oh," she reassured him, "not this doctor. He never operates unless it's absolutely necessary. In fact, if he doesn't need the money, he won't lay a hand on you."

*

"You're nothing but a quack," the irate patient shouted at the doctor. "For months you've had me come back for needless treatments. You have robbed me blind without helping me. You've gotten rich on my case alone!"

The doctor shook his head sadly. "That's gratitude," he said. "And to think that I just named my new yacht after you."

*

The lady was a well-known hypochondriac and inclined to describe her symptoms at length to anyone who would listen. So her friends were astonished one night when she sat through a dinner party without saying a word.

"What's wrong, dear?" asked the hostess when the meal was over. "Are you too ill even to talk?"

"Oh, no," replied the woman sadly. "But I went to a new doctor and he cured all my topics of conversation."

*

A little old lady had some false teeth made. Three days later she returned to the dentist's office.

"You know those teeth you made for me?" she asked. "They're no good. They don't fit."

"Well," the dentist replied, "that's not too unusual. Let's take a bite test and see what the trouble is."

So she took a bite test, and the dentist could see that they fit fine.

"I'm not talking about my mouth," the woman insisted. "They don't fit in the glass."

*

A hostess invited her doctor to a party and in return received a note written in a typically illegible doctor's scrawl.

"I just have to know if he's coming to the party," she told a friend, "but I can't read a word he's written."

"That's easy," said the friend. "Take the note down to the drugstore. Druggists can always read a doctor's writing."

At the pharmacy, the hostess handed over the note and the druggist disappeared into the back room. After a few minutes, he came back.

"Here you are, ma'am," he said, giving her a bottle of pills. "That will be two dollars and fifty cents."

*

An actor who needed an expensive operation went to the best doctor in town. The operation was a success. When he received a bill for two thousand dollars, he explained that he couldn't afford that much. The doctor agreed to cut the fee in half, and the actor confessed that he couldn't afford that either. After much discussion, the doctor agreed to take two hundred dollars for his fee. Then he said, "For that price you might as well have it for nothing."

"Thanks, Doc," said the actor. "I was hoping you'd say that."

"Tell me," said the doctor, "if you knew you couldn't afford my fee, why did you come to the most expensive doctor in town?"

"Where my health is concerned," said the actor, "money is no object."

*

Doctor Jones had worked hard to put his boy through medical school. When his son graduated, the old doctor turned over his medical practice to the boy and took a well-earned vacation.

Upon his return he was greeted by his son at the station. The son said, "Father, I've made some marvelous cures. I've even cured Mrs. Smith's stomach trouble after you had treated her for years."

"What?" said the father. "I'll have you know that Mrs. Smith's stomach put you through college!"

*

A young doctor returned to the village of his birth and called upon the old family physician.

"I suppose you intend to specialize," remarked the elder.

"Oh, yes," replied the youth, "in the diseases of the nose. The ears and throat are too complicated to be combined with the nose for purposes of study and treatment."

Thereupon the family physician inquired, "Which nostril are you concentrating on?"

*

The two specialists conferring at the patient's bedside differed in their diagnosis.

"My dear colleague," said the first specialist, "it would appear the lady has rheumatism."

The patient looked up and said, "How right you are."

The second specialist shook his head. "I think it's arthritis."

The patient smiled wanly. "How right you are."

The patient's husband was peeved. "You both can't be right."

The patient looked at her husband. "How right you are."

*

A famous lung specialist from New York City was taking a vacation in Florida. One warm, sunny afternoon he was lying on the beach with another doctor, and both of them were lost in thought as they admired the shapely young females who cavorted around in their bikinis. Finally, the Florida doctor turned to his New York friend and, with a twinkle in his eye, said, "Doctor, the girls at these Florida beaches certainly have beautiful legs, don't they?"

"I hadn't noticed," was the reply. "Don't forget I'm a chest man."

*

A man accidentally swallowed a ping-pong ball, and he was rushed to surgery for its removal. The patient insisted on having a local anesthetic so he could watch the operation. He winced a little as the first incision was made, but he didn't actually feel it; nor did he feel the next cut, nor the next. He did become a little alarmed at the number of incisions, however, as the surgeon cut here and there, in what seemed a rather random manner.

"Why do you have to cut in so many places?" he asked. "They don't seem to be consistent."

"Well," replied the surgeon, cutting away, "that's the way the ball bounces."

*

A physician we know always insists on the presence of a third party in the room whenever he examines a female patient.

Near the close of a busy afternoon, he wearily motioned a couple into the examining room. The woman complained of pains in her lower abdomen and submitted to examination reluctantly. The man looked on with unfeigned interest.

When he had finished, the doctor prescribed some medicine. The woman jumped up from the table, dressed hurriedly, and ran out of the room.

"Your wife's certainly lively," commented the doctor. "She'll be all right in a few days."

"My wife?" said the man. "I never saw her before, Doc. I was wondering why you called me in here with her."

*

A man went to the doctor.

"Doctor," he said, "I have been feeling steadily worse. I'm here for a checkup."

"Well," said the doctor, "let me see. What are your eating habits?"

"Well," said the man, "in the morning I have a little grape juice, a little orange juice, a little prune juice, and then a little cereal (not more than two cupfuls). After that I have eight, maybe ten rolls. Then I have about seven eggs, and a little more grape juice, and a cup of coffee. For lunch, I have a little chopped chicken liver (two plates at the most), a bowl of soup, a piece of duck, some cabbage salad, seven rolls, and a cup of coffee. At supper, I start off with a little bit of lobster, and then some meat balls, then some chicken and a little stew, about twelve slices of bread, a little orange juice, and maybe pie with a little ice cream (no more than two scoops), and a cup of coffee. What I'd like to know, Doctor, am I drinking too much coffee?"

*

The lady patient said to the doctor's nurse, "I would have been here sooner, but I have sitter trouble."

The nurse raised her eyebrows. "Sitter trouble? You must be

in the wrong office. This doctor is an eye specialist. You want a proctologist."

*

Fresh out of medical school, the young doctor opened his office in a small town and waited for his first patient. Finally, in walked a man covered all over with a purple rash.

The young practitioner rifled through the pages of his medical books but could find nothing even remotely resembling the symptom.

"Did you ever have anything like this before?" he eventually asked the patient.

"Shore thing, Doc. It plumb had me down six times last year."

"Well," diagnosed the young doctor, "you've plumb got it again."

Drivers

A man and his family had just returned from their vacation.

"Did you enjoy your trip?" a neighbor asked him.

"Very much," he replied. "My wife did all the driving."

"Then you had a chance to enjoy the scenery."

"Yes, indeed," said the husband, "all I had to do was hold the wheel."

*

An insurance claim agent was teaching his wife to drive, when the brakes failed on a steep grade.

"I can't stop," she screamed. "What should I do?"

"Brace yourself," advised her husband, "and try to hit something cheap."

*

Lady driver: "Do you charge batteries here?"

Attendant: "Sure do."

Lady driver: "Then put a new one in this car and charge it to my husband."

*

A woman in a handsome new car pulled up to a spot where there were three empty parking spaces. She backed in until she hit the car behind her with a loud bang. Then she pulled forward and smacked into the car ahead. The crash attracted the attention of the policeman on the corner. The woman realized that he was watching her. She leaned out of the window and called cheerfully, "Did I park all right, Officer?"

"I suppose so, lady," he snapped, "but do you always park by ear?"

*

"But I did so give a left-turn signal," cried the indignant lady driver.

"Lady," wearily replied the unlucky male who had been following and subsequently hit her car, "your arm was out, I'll admit. But first it was up, then down, then into circles, then straight out. That's a left-turn signal?"

"Silly," came her reply, "the first two might have been wrong but didn't you see me erase them and give you the right one?"

*

On a crowded street, a motorist stopped suddenly for a red light and had his rear bumper bashed by the car behind. The driver got out, looked over the damage, glared at the woman driving the other car, and took off.

At the next light, the same thing happened. Finally, after the third bump, the woman got out of her car and came over, holding out a driver's license and other credentials.

"Look, madam," said the victim helplessly, "never mind all that stuff. All I want from you is a five-minute head start."

*

One of those little foreign cars was doing about fifty miles an hour on one of our main highways. Every fifty feet or so the little machine would hop up in the air about five feet. A state trooper finally overtook the midget-motor and brought it to a stop.

"What's the big idea of driving a car that jumps that way?" asked the cop.

The driver answered: "Why, officer, there's nothing wrong with the car. You see, I've got—hic—hiccups."

*

The brakes of the approaching car squealed in protest as the unwary pedestrian stepped into its path. The driver glared.

"Why don't you look where you're going?" he shrieked. "You pedestrians cross a street like you own it!"

"Well, young man," replied the unperturbed pedestrian, patting the tax receipt in his pocket, "I've made more payments on this street than you have on your car."

*

A husband went for a drive with his wife, a typical back-seat driver. With every turn of the wheel she gave directions. "Go to the left!" "Go to the right!" "Look out for that truck!" "Slow down!" "Step on the gas!" She drove her husband crazy.

They came to a railroad crossing. A train was approaching in the distance. The husband drove halfway across the tracks and stopped.

He jumped out of the car.

"I got my end over," he shouted. "What are you going to do with yours?"

*

A wife, just learning to drive the family car, had traffic hope-lessly snarled as she tried to make a left turn. Excitedly, she turned to her husband and screamed, "What do I do now?"

"I don't know," he replied calmly, "but I'm sure if you'll just climb into the back seat, you can figure it out."

Drunks

A confirmed drunkard had at long last been cured of the bottle, and his psychiatrist was about to test him to see if the cure was complete.

"Now, then," he said, "what does the name Gordon convey to you?"

The ex-drunkard thought. "Wasn't that the name of a famous general?" he said.

"Very good," said the psychiatrist. "And what does the name Haig mean?"

"He was a noted earl," was the reply.

"Excellent," said the psychiatrist. "And now for the supreme test. What does Vat 69 mean to you?"

The man sat deep in thought. At last he looked up and asked, "Isn't that the Pope's telephone number?"

*

A customer watched as a man came into a bar and ordered a martini. When the drink arrived the newcomer carefully removed the olive and placed it in an empty jar. Then he downed the martini in one gulp and ordered another. He removed the olive and dropped it into the jar before downing the second drink. He repeated this process for nearly an hour. When the jar was full of olives and he was full of martinis he staggered out of the door.

"That's the strangest thing I've ever seen," said another customer.

"What's so strange about it?" asked the bartender. "Didn't your wife ever send you out for a jar of olives?"

*

Late one evening at a convention in Las Vegas, the night club doorman assisted four happy delegates into a taxi and told the driver: "This one goes to the Thunderbird, these two go to the Sahara, and the one with the hiccups goes to El Rancho."

In a few minutes the taxi was back. Beckoning to the doorman the driver asked: "Would you mind sorting these fellows out again? I hit a bump."

*

Two men planned to go hunting.

"I'll bring all the hunting paraphernalia," said one, "and you bring the provisions."

The provisions man arrived with one loaf of bread and four bottles of whiskey.

"Fine thing," snapped the other. "I leave it to you and what happens! You bring a loaf of bread and four bottles of whiskey. Now what are we going to do with all that bread?"

*

A midwesterner on his first trip to New York City managed to hit all the bars in Times Square before he stumbled down a stairway leading to the subway.

Emerging a half hour later, he met a friend who had been searching for him.

"Where in the world have you been?" the friend demanded.

"Down in some guy's cellar," the drunk replied, glassy-eyed. "And, boy, has he got a set of trains!"

*

Strolling into a saloon, the drunk lugged a cardboard carton perforated for ventilation. With elaborate care he placed it on the bar. "What have you got there, Mac?" asked the bartender.

"Ssshhh," hissed the drunk. "When I have too many drinks, I see snakes. So I've taken to carrying a mongoose to chase away the snakes."

"Yeah," said the bartender, "but they're imaginary snakes."

"I know," confided the drunk in a whisper. "But this is an imaginary mongoose."

*

Two men who were fond of sports arrived at their favorite tavern one evening to watch the prizefights on television and enjoy each other's company.

They had a few drinks and watched the preliminaries on the large TV screen in back of the bar. The action picked up during the semi-main event, and it was in the second round of the main event that one of the men suddenly stood up, gazed at his friend with unseeing eyes for a long moment, and then fell to the floor.

His pal looked at him solemnly for a minute and turned to face the bartender.

"That's one good thing about Bill," he said. "He always knows when to stop."

*

A man was told by his doctor that he must stop drinking. To overcome the craving, the doctor advised him to eat something every time he felt like taking a drink. He tried it, and found that it worked rather well.

One night, however, while stopping at a hotel, he heard a strange sound in the next room and climbed on a chair to look through the transom. Imagine his consternation when he saw a man just about to hang himself.

He rushed from the room, charged down the stairs three steps at a time, and grabbed hold of the hotel clerk.

"S-a-say," he stammered, "there's a f-f-feller in the next room, the room next—next to mine. He's hanging himself. I saw him. For gosh sakes, give me a plate of ham and eggs!"

*

The defense attorney was carefully building up the case for his client who had been arrested for drunkenness.

"Your Honor," he reasoned, "just because a man is in the middle of the road on his hands and knees at midnight is no sure sign that he is drunk."

But the arresting officer wasn't having any of the defense lawyer's tricks.

"What the attorney says, Your Honor, is quite true," he conceded, "but the defendant was trying to roll up the white line."

*

A merchant seaman would make the rounds of the numerous waterfront bars as soon as his ship landed in New York, and invariably would end up at the bar of justice. After the most recent bender, he appeared before a judge who had tried to straighten him out on previous occasions.

"You here again?" moaned the judge. "I thought I told you I didn't want you to appear before me again."

"That you did, Your Honor," replied the sailor, "and I told this policeman that, but he wouldn't believe me."

*

A man and his wife drove through a red light and were stopped by a policeman. The man's replies to the officer's questions were somewhat surly. His wife, realizing he was becoming more involved every minute and thinking to help her husband out of the difficulty, spoke up and said, "Don't mind him, Officer, he's drunk."

*

A man telephoned a police station one night and excitedly reported that the steering wheel, brake pedal, accelerator, clutch pedal, and dashboard had been stolen from his car. A sergeant promised to investigate. But soon the telephone rang again. "Don't bother," said the same voice—this time with a hiccup. "I got into the back seat by mistake."

*

A husband came home drunk every night and every time he did, his wife would bawl him out.

"Why do you do that?" a neighbor asked the wife. "Don't call attention to his drinking. Be kind to him. I'll tell you what you do. When he comes home tonight give him a kiss."

That night when the husband again staggered home, his wife puckered her lips.

"Darling," she said, "give me a kiss."

So he puckered his lips, staggered, and kissed her on the forehead. He tried again, but missed and kissed her on the ear. He staggered back and started over again. This time he kissed her on the nose. She pointed to her mouth.

"You bum," she yelled. "If this was a saloon you'd find it!"

*

The doctor was fed up. The patient was always getting blind drunk, feeling terrible, and turning up for treatment.

"What do you think I should do, Doctor? I'm feeling worse than ever," he moaned one morning, as he held his aching head.

Solemnly the doctor suggested: "Why not try and get some blood into your alcohol stream?"

*

Mr. Murphy had been imbibing heavily. He lurched gracelessly down the avenue and ran into his priest.

"Father," he moaned unhappily, "I'm so sorry."

"So am I, Patrick," the priest replied. "How much have you had to put you in this condition?"

"Only eight glasses of beer and three of whiskey," hiccuped Murphy.

"Good heavens!" gasped the priest. "I can't even drink four glasses of water."

"And neither can I," said Pat.

*

The clergyman had a certain truculent woman parishioner noted for her fondness for a drop of gin. One day she went to church hiccuping loudly. The clergyman bore it for a few moments. Then looking at the sexton, he exclaimed publicly: "Smith, kindly remove that person from the church."

Smith rose reluctantly to obey. The congregation held its breath, expecting a scene, but to their relief the woman rose and left without a murmur. After the service the clergyman congratulated the sexton on the tactful way in which he removed the culprit. "How did you manage it?" he asked.

"Well," replied the sexton, "I just went to her and whispered, 'Come on, Ma. Come out and have one with me.'"

*

A fellow dressed as a Roman senator in the finest linen toga and crowned with a laurel wreath walked to the bar and announced, "I'll have a martinus."

"Don't you mean a martini?" asked the bartender.

"When I want two, I'll ask for them."

*

They promised to meet in the same bar at the same time, ten years later.

So ten years later one of them walked in diffidently and sure enough there was his pal on a stool.

"I never thought," he said, "that day when we left this bar that I'd really see you here today."

"Who left?" hiccuped his pal.

*

A drunk was relating his adventures in the jungle: "All the ammunition, food, and whiskey had run out," he said, "and we were all parched with thirst."

A friend asked, "But wasn't there any water?"

"Sure," said the drunk, "but it was no time to be thinking of cleanliness."

*

Two brave firemen, choking and gasping, made their way through a smoke-filled bedroom. They were able to detect the faint shape of a man slumped in a burning bed. As they grew nearer, they realized the man was drunk. Pulling the drunk out of the room, the firemen yelled, "You darned fool, that'll teach you not to smoke in bed."

The drunk answered, "I wasn't smoking in bed. It was on fire when I got in."

*

The lush tottered into a candy shop.

"Hey," he asked the girl, "you have them candies with liquor in the middle?"

"Yes, sir," the girl said.

"Okay," the drunk said, hurriedly, "gimme a fifth of middles."

*

A young minister assigned to a rural parish had been doing his best to convert the town souse. But aside from inducing him to attend one service, he had been quite unsuccessful. One morning the parson met the drunk on the street, carrying his usual load of cheer.

"Frank," said the minister disgustedly, "how does an old inebriate like you ever expect to pass through the gates of heaven?"

"Oh, I'll just use the same system I did to get into speakeasies during prohibition," replied the drunk. "Rap three times and ask for Pete."

*

Two drunks in a midtown bar were discussing life.

"I had the darndest dream last night," said one. "I dreamed that suddenly about one thousand funny little men were dancing on top of my body. They had pink caps and green suits and funny red boots that curled up in front."

"Yes," agreed the other, "and there was a tinkly little bell at the toe of each of the boots."

"How do you know?" said the first one in surprise.

"There are a couple of them still sitting on your shoulder," said the other.

*

Late one night a doctor received an excited call from a woman.

"Doctor, come right away. I think my husband is dead in bed."

Knowing the man's drinking habits, the doctor suggested she stick her spouse with a pin and let him know if the man didn't move. In a short time she called back and said, "Doctor, can you meet me at the hospital?"

"Weren't you able to rouse your husband?" the doctor inquired.

"Oh, the pin worked all right," she said, "but he hit me in the mouth, and I think I'll need stitches."

Duels

Two Mexicans quarreled and decided to fight a duel. To do this without attracting too much attention, they took a train into the country. The first Mexican asked for a return ticket, but his opponent only took a single.

"Caramba!" laughed the first. "You expect not to come back, my friend? I always get a return."

"I never do," replied the other calmly. "I always take my adversary's return half."

Dumb

The speaker was getting tired of being interrupted. "We seem to have a great many fools here tonight," he said. "Wouldn't it be advisable to hear one at a time?"

"Yes," said a voice, "get on with your speech."

*

"How did you enjoy your vacation?" a neighbor asked the tanned, but weary, Mr. Jones.

"I'm afraid I need another one already," moaned Jones.

"How is that?" his neighbor wanted to know.

"I dunno, guess I'm still tired."

"Well, where did you go?"

"Atlantic City."

"Uh-huh. What hotel did you stop at?"

"The Benjamin Franklin."

"The Benjamin Franklin! That isn't in Atlantic City. It's in Philadelphia."

"Oh, no wonder I had so far to walk to the beach."

*

The Duke and Duchess of Windsor recently attended a performance of a hit Broadway musical. When the show was over, they were escorted backstage to meet the stars and greet the other members of the cast. As the celebrated couple departed, one chorus girl asked another if she had seen the Duchess close up.

"You bet," was the reply. "Not only did I see the Duchess, I also saw her husband, the Dutch."

*

Two wealthy real estate agents were discussing outer space, moon shots, and various planets.

"Everyone is trying to get to the moon," one said. "Why don't you and I do something spectacular? Why don't we build a space capsule and fly to the sun? We could look around for some good property."

"Are you crazy?" his friend asked. "Don't you know that if we came within five hundred miles of the sun, it would fry us to a crisp?"

"You jerk," said the first, "we'll fly at night."

*

Two young men were invited out to dinner by their employer. During the course of the meal the conversation drifted into channels that took the young friends into rather deep water.

"Do you care for Omar Khayyam?" asked their host at one point during dinner, thinking to discover the literary tastes of the young men.

"Pretty well," the one addressed replied, "but personally, I prefer port."

The subject was dropped, but on the way home the other said to his friend: "Why don't you simply say you don't know when you're asked something you don't understand? Omar Khayyam isn't a wine. It's a kind of cheese."

*

Dinner was a little late. A guest asked the hostess to play something. Seating herself at the piano, the good woman executed a Chopin nocturne with precision. She finished, and there was still an interval of waiting to be bridged. In the grim silence, she turned to a deaf old gentleman on her right side and said, "Would you like a sonata before going in to dinner?"

He gave a start of surprise and pleasure as he responded:

"Why, yes, thanks! I had a couple on my way here, but I could stand another."

Education

"Can you write?" the lawyer questioned the witness.

"Nope," the other replied.

"Can you read?"

"I can read figgers," was the reply, "but I can't understand writin'."

The lawyer was puzzled. "Would you please explain what you mean by that?" he asked.

"Well," the witness explained, "you know those signs posted along the road? I can read how far but not where to."

*

A teen-ager greeted the new high-school teacher, Mr. Smith, with, "Hey, Smitty."

The teacher grabbed the youth by his collar and snapped, "Don't ever say that again. For one thing, hay is for horses, and for another you should have the consideration and courtesy to address me as Mr. Smith." Seeing the bewilderment on the boy's face, he added, "Don't you know the words 'consideration' and 'courtesy'?"

"Consideration and courtesy?" the boy said. "I didn't even know hay was for horses!"

*

Two college freshmen were gloomily discussing what form of work would supply them with a livelihood after graduation.

"Well, I've always thought I'd like to be a doctor," said one. "Specialize in something or other—obstetrics, maybe."

"Obstetrics?" scoffed the other. "At the rate science is going, you'd no sooner learn all about it when—bingo—somebody would find a cure for it."

*

Two kindergarten pupils were standing in the school playground during recess when a jet flew over.

"Look at that," said one lad. "It's a BX50."

"No, a BX51," said the other. "You can tell by its wing sweep."

"You're right," the first youngster conceded. "It's not going more than seven hundred sixty miles per hour either, because it didn't break the sound barrier."

On this point they both agreed. "It's amazing the pressure that develops on those planes when they go into a dive," the second boy said. "Almost twelve hundred pounds per square inch."

At this point the bell called the children back to the classroom. The first boy turned to the second.

"There's the bell," he sighed. "Let's go back in and finish stringing those damn beads."

*

It seems the current system of school grading is designed to encourage parent and student. Even though Junior may be dumber than an ox, the idea is to hold out some hope.

The ultimate in strained encouragement came when one teacher added this note to what otherwise was a very poor report: "He contributes nicely to group singing by his helpful listening."

Embarrassing Moments

A famous orchestra conductor, who was young and handsome, had a date with a young lady that he wanted to keep a secret. He pulled up his coat collar, put on dark glasses, jammed his hat down over his ears, and then in a disguised voice told the driver of the cab the address he wanted.

Arriving at his destination, he paid the cab driver and began to look for the entrance to the girl's house. The driver watched him for a few minutes and then said, "If it's the same girl you visited last Tuesday, Maestro, she's two doors to the left."

*

An army officer had a young daughter who always introduced herself to others as "General Taylor's daughter."

Her mother thought this sounded snobbish and told her to refer to herself as Jill Taylor. So when she was asked, "You're General Taylor's little girl, aren't you?" she replied, "I thought I was but Mother says No."

*

A man decided to test a computer's accuracy.

"Where is my father?" he asked.

The machine answered: "Your father is in a Mexican prison."

Delighted at the mistake, the man responded, "Wrong! He's in Los Angeles working in a bank."

The computer's answer was: "Your mother's husband is in Los Angeles. Your father is in a Mexican prison."

*

A comely young matron stepped on the drugstore scales after devouring a giant sundae and was shocked at what she saw. She slipped off her coat and tried again. The results were still unflattering, so she slipped off her shoes. Then she discovered she was out of pennies. Without a moment's hesitation, the man behind the soda fountain stepped forward.

"Don't stop now," he volunteered. "I've got a handful of pennies and they're all yours."

*

When one of the two first-grade teachers at a posh suburban

school left on her two-week honeymoon, the other volunteered
to teach both classes in her absence. A few weeks later, at a
housewarming party given by the newlyweds, the guests were
somewhat taken aback as the groom introduced them to his wife's
colleague: "And this, ladies and gentlemen," announced the
grateful husband, "is the lovely lady who substituted for my wife
during our honeymoon."

*

Three gentlemen on Manhattan's lower East Side decided to stop
at a restaurant for a spot of tea. The waiter appeared with pad
and pencil. "I want a glass of weak tea," ordered one.

"I'd like tea, too," said the second, "but very strong, with two
pieces of lemon."

"And you?" queried the waiter of the third.

"Tea for me, too, please. But be sure the glass is absolutely
clean."

In a short time the waiter was back with the order. "Which
one," he asked, "gets the clean glass?"

*

A fellow entered a cafeteria. He got some custard pie and went
over to a table. He was about to sit down when he realized he
had forgotten to get coffee. So he put the pie down and went for
the coffee. When he returned to his table a man was sitting there.

"That's my seat," he said. "You've got my chair."

"What do you mean, your chair?" said the man. "How do you
know it's your chair?"

"Because you're sitting on my custard pie."

*

A waiter in a chic restaurant accidently stumbled and poured an
iced drink down a woman's back. She leaped to her feet with a
shriek, knocking over the table and spilling her escort's drink all
over him. With all eyes upon them, the two fled from the restaurant in wild confusion.

"Waiter!" called a nearby diner, "we'd like two of whatever they had."

*

A man finally took all his torn umbrellas to be repaired. The next day, on the bus that he took to work, he absent-mindedly picked up the umbrella which belonged to a woman beside him when he got up to leave. The woman cried out and rescued her umbrella. The man was covered with shame and confusion.

That evening, on his way home he stopped at the repair shop to pick up his mended umbrellas. When he entered the bus with the unwrapped umbrellas tucked under his arm, he was horrified to see the same lady of his morning adventure glaring at him. Her voice was charged with sarcasm as she said, "You had a good day, I see."

*

A young lady went into a drugstore and asked if it were possible to disguise castor oil. "It's horrid stuff to take," she shuddered.

"Why, certainly," said the druggist. At that moment another young lady sat down and ordered a chocolate ice-cream soda. The druggist asked the first patron if she would like one too. She accepted the invitation, and drank it with pleasure.

"Now, tell me, how would you disguise castor oil?"

The druggist beamed. "My dear young lady, I just gave you some—in the soda."

"Good heavens!" she shrieked, "I wanted it for my sister!"

*

The clergyman decided to offer the parents a little homily before he baptized their infant.

"Think of the future that may lie before this dear child," he said. "One day he may become a pastor like myself or perhaps a gallant airman or sea captain. Who knows, he may even become President. Think of the joy that will be yours in guarding and watching his career," he concluded. "Now what name did you say?"

Said the mother timidly, "Mary Jane."

*

The guests at the banquet were chatting in little groups of twos and threes and seemed to be having a good time.

The toastmaster turned to the first speaker and said, "Shall I let them enjoy themselves a little longer, or shall I introduce you?"

*

The manager of a ten-story office building was informed that a man was trapped in an elevator between the second and third floors. He rushed to the grillwork under the stalled car and called to the passenger: "Keep cool, sir. We'll have you out soon. I've phoned for the elevator mechanic."

There was a brief pause, then a tense voice answered, "I am the elevator mechanic."

*

One of the guests turned to a man by his side to criticize the singing of the woman who was trying to entertain them.

"What a terrible voice! Do you know who she is?"

"Yes," was the answer. "She's my wife."

"Oh, I beg your pardon. Of course, it isn't her voice really. It's the stuff she has to sing. I wonder who wrote that awful song?"

"I did," was the answer.

*

A woman slipped on a station escalator and started to tumble down to the bottom. Halfway down she collided with a man, knocking him down, and the two continued downward together.

After they had reached the bottom, the woman, still dazed, continued to sit on the man's chest.

Looking at her, he said politely, "I am sorry, madam, but this is as far as I go."

*

A man who was driving along a country road offered a stranger a lift. The stranger accepted. Shortly afterwards, the motorist noticed that his watch was missing.

Whipping out a revolver, which he happened to be carrying, he dug it into the other man's ribs and exclaimed, "Hand over that watch!"

The stranger meekly complied before allowing himself to be booted out of the car. When the motorist returned home, he was greeted by his wife.

"How did you get on without your watch?" she asked. "I suppose you know that you left it on your dressing table?"

*

It was an early morning fire, and the cub reporter, upon arriving at the scene, was lucky to get an account of it from one of the residents of the apartment house who had escaped.

"It was terrible," explained this man. "Imagine walls crumbling about you, the flames of the fire practically licking your cheek in whatever direction you turned, and the very iron of the banisters smoking under your hands. But in the midst of it all, I want you to know, I kept cool and calm."

"It's a shame, since you were so calm and cool," said the reporter, "that you didn't remember to put your pants on."

*

Henry Brown arrived late at the country club dance and discovered that in slipping on the icy pavement outside, he had torn one knee of his trousers.

"Let's go up to the ladies' dressing room, Henry," said his wife. "There's no one there and I'll pin it up for you."

The rip was too large to be pinned, so a maid furnished needle and thread. She was stationed outside the door to keep out intruders, while Brown removed his trousers. His wife then went to work on them.

Soon excited voices were heard at the door.

"We must come in," a woman was saying. "Mrs. Jones is ill. Quick, let us in."

"Here," said the resourceful Mrs. Brown to her horrified husband, "get into this closet for a minute."

She opened the door and pushed her husband through it just in time. Almost immediately, from the other side of the door, there came loud thumping and the agonized voice of Brown demanding that his wife open it at once.

"But the women are in here," Mrs. Brown objected.

"Oh, damn the women!" yelled Brown. "I'm out in the ballroom."

*

The actor hadn't worked in two years. Then one day an ad man took a liking to his face and signed him to do a lucrative season of live TV cigarette commercials.

During the first show, the actor smiled, got his cue, took a deep, satisfied draw of his cigarette, blew a ring of smoke, and sighed blissfully, "Man, that's real coffee."

*

The company president arose to give a "short speech" at an employees' banquet, and two hours later he was still going strong. One of the firm's promising young junior executives, fidgeting restlessly as the voice droned on and on, turned to an elderly woman seated next to him. "Long-winded old grouch, isn't he?" he whispered.

"Young man, do you know who I am?" asked the matron.

"Why, no," replied the young fellow, "I can't say that I do."

"My name is Mrs. Johnson," replied the dowager angrily, "and I happen to be the President's wife."

"Is that so?" replied the panic-stricken young executive. "And do you know who I am?"

"No, I don't," snapped the matron.

"Thank God!" sighed the man, as he headed for the nearest exit.

*

A young physician and his wife had considerable difficulty teaching a new maid to answer the telepone properly. In spite of repeated instructions, she persisted in answering "Hello," instead of "Dr. Jones's residence."

After many practice sessions, everything seemed to be all right. Then one morning the extension in the bedroom rang, and the maid, busy making the bed, grabbed the phone and blurted, "Dr. Jones's bedroom."

England

An Englishman visited the United States and liked it so much he decided to stay. Some years later he took out his citizenship papers and became a citizen. One day a friend came to visit him from England and was surprised to find he had become an American citizen.

"What did you gain by becoming an American citizen?" asked the visitor.

"Well, for one thing," was the reply, "I won the American Revolution."

Fishing

A new arrival was stopped at the pearly gates. "I'm sorry," explained Saint Peter, "but you told too many lies during your time on earth. I'm afraid you'll have to go you-know-where."

"Ah, come on now, Saint Peter," begged the newly arrived one. "Have a heart. After all, you were once a fisherman yourself."

Fog

Two men who had traveled abroad were comparing their opinions about foreign cities. "London," said one, "is certainly the foggiest place in the world."

"Oh, no, it's not," said the other. "I've been in a place much foggier than London."

"Where was that?" asked his friend.

"I don't know where it was," replied the second man. "It was too foggy to tell."

Friends

A New York tenderfoot was on his first camping trip in the West.

"What happens," he asked the cowboy, "if one of those rattlesnakes should bite me in the arm?"

"Don't worry, son, one of your friends will just cut open the fang-holes and suck out the poison."

"What happens if I get bitten on the leg?"

"Same thing, son."

"Suppose I should sit on one of them?"

"Son, that's when you'll find out who your real friends are."

Funeral

A funeral procession was wending its way to the cemetery. The business partner of the deceased was following behind the hearse until, just before they reached their destination, a big coal truck pulled out from a side road into an opening between the hearse and the first car.

Upon seeing the coal truck ahead of him, the partner said, "I knew where Bill was going, but I didn't think he had to supply his own fuel."

Gambling

A young man entered a book store and purchased two leather-bound Bibles.

"One of them," he explained, "is for myself. The other is for a guy at our shop who I'm trying to convert. Gambling is rampant there, and he is the ringleader."

As the clerk wrapped up the volumes, she remarked: "I hope you succeed in converting him."

"I do too," the purchaser replied. "They've bet me five to three I can't."

*

A notorious poker addict, always in a jam with his wife over his all-night poker sessions, was on his way home from the office the other night when he ran into an old flame. As she still looked mighty attractive to him, he invited her into a nearby cocktail lounge for a drink. What with one thing and another, time crept up on them, and it was well toward morning when he walked into his house and came face to face with his wife.

"Well," she snapped, "now what's your alibi?" There was an embarrassed pause. Then the man decided to give it to her straight.

"Honey, I'm sorry," he said, "but it was just one of those things. I ran into an old girl friend and we had a drink, and before we knew it, it was three in the morning. Well, I had to take her home, and—"

"Okay, okay!" interrupted his wife impatiently. "How much did you lose tonight?"

*

When the driller left the offshore rig, the first thing he did was head for a nearby gambling joint. At the dice table, he laid a hundred dollar bet. He shook the dice, but as he threw them a third cube fell from his sleeve.

The man was unruffled. He handed back two dice and pocketed the third, saying, "Okay, roll again. Your point is fifteen."

*

A famous psychologist had finished his lecture and was answering questions. A little man asked, "Did you say that a good poker player could hold down any kind of executive job?"

"That's right," answered the lecturer. "Does that raise a question in your mind?"

"Yes," replied the little man. "What would a good poker player want with a job?"

*

A wealthy Indian parked his Cadillac in front of a gambling place in Las Vegas, and entered the hotel carrying a satchel filled with five hundred thousand dollars. After making an inquiry at the desk, he was royally escorted to the roulette table.

After playing for two hours, the Indian lost all his money. He drove to the mountains and began to send a smoke signal.

"Please send me another five hundred thousand dollars."

Just at that moment, an atomic bomb explosion went off some miles behind him, the mushroom cloud billowing into the sky.

A few hours later, the Indian read the answering smoke signal in the distance. "The money is on the way, but don't holler."

*

A hatchet-faced lady tapped the keeper of the monkey house indignantly on the shoulder.

"Those wretched animals of yours appear to be engaged in shooting dice. I demand that you break up the game at once."

"Shucks," shrugged the keeper, "they're keeping strictly within the law, ma'am. They're only playing for peanuts."

*

A religious and charitable woman noticed a down-and-out sort of man standing at the corner of the street near her residence.

One morning she took pity on him, pressed a dollar into his hand, and whispered, "Never despair."

Next time she saw him he stopped her and handed her nine dollars.

"What does this mean?" she asked.

"It means, ma'am," said the man, "that Never Despair won at eight to one."

*

An inveterate gambler was entertaining an elderly uncle, a minister, and took him to a racetrack. Never having seen such a sight, the old minister was agog and finally became so interested that, despite his scruples, he bet five dollars on the nose of one of the entries. Much to his nephew's surprise, the horse won. He accompanied his uncle to the winner's window where the old man received several times the amount of his bet.

"Now, young man," the minister admonished the cashier at the window as he placed the folded bills in his wallet, "let this be a lesson to you."

*

A bookie handed over the money to the little old lady. "How did you manage to pick the winner?" he said.

"I just stuck a pin in the paper," she answered, "and there it was."

"But how come you knocked off four winners yesterday?"

"Oh," laughed the little old lady, "yesterday I cheated a little. I used a fork."

*

A racing fan was stopped by a cop for speeding. "I feel sick; that's why I was speeding," he said.

"That's a likely story," said the cop. "You're headed for the track, aren't you?"

"Yes," said the guy, "but with me it's a sickness."

*

A gambler was reminiscing. "For three nights straight, I dreamed about salami, bologna, and liverwurst. Is that a hunch, or isn't it? I go to the track and in one race three horses by the names of Salami, Bologna, and Liverwurst are running. So I bet on all three to win—"

At this point, a friend interrupted. "Which horse won?"

"A long shot by the name of Cold Cuts."

*

A poker player went insane from gambling and was sent to a mental institution. For years the poor fellow's keeper served him toast for breakfast.

The unfortunate man always snapped up the toast, peeked at it as he held it close to his chest, and then said, "I pass," after which he pushed it aside.

Fifteen years it went that way. Then one morning they served him raisin toast and it had just one raisin in the middle of the slice.

Looking at the slice of toast excitedly, he shouted, "I open."

*

The psychiatrist informed his patient: "You're cured. You are no longer a compulsive gambler. If you wish, you may call your wife and tell her the news. Use my phone or the one in the reception room."

The patient thought for a moment and then took a coin from his pocket, flipped it in the air, and said, "Heads or tails?"

Hippies

A tourist in New York City walked up to a resident who seemed to show some of the identifying marks of a hippie. The tourist asked, "How do I get to Carnegie Hall?"

The resident looked the tourist up and down, and then with a happy grin replied, "Practice, man, practice."

*

Three hippies were driving along the turnpike, doing about ninety miles an hour, when suddenly the one in the back seat noticed that his door was rattling, so he slammed it shut.

The driver glanced suspiciously into the rear-view mirror. "Hey, man," he asked, "who got in?"

*

Two hippies walking down the street met a Catholic priest with his arm in a sling.

"What happened to you?" inquired one of them.

"I fell in the bathtub and broke my arm," replied the priest.

The hippie turned to his friend, "Man, what's a bathtub?"

"How should I know?" replied the second one. "I'm not a Catholic."

Hobbies

A man went looking for a house the other day, and while he was in one model, he heard the agent explaining the value of the different rooms to a newly married couple.

"This is the hobby room," the agent explained as they entered one room. "Do you have a hobby?"

"Oh, yes," said the husband.

"And what is it?" asked the agent.

"Looking at model homes," was the reply.

Hollywood

An actor in Hollywood decided to dine in an Italian restaurant. The waiter handed him an elaborate menu. Without even glancing at it, the actor handed it back and said, "Order me the best dinner you can."

The dinner was excellent, and for the next three weeks he followed the same procedure at the restaurant, letting the waiter order for him.

Finally, when the actor was about to return to New York, he had a farewell dinner at the restaurant. He gave the waiter a large tip and thanked him for his help.

The waiter assured him, "It was no trouble, sir. I was very glad to help. If you have other friends who cannot read, send them to Giovanni. I will do my best."

*

Some TV producers just don't seem to realize that TV means big money. One fellow, operating on his usual shoestring, was interviewing a girl for the lead in a TV special.

"You're just right," he said. "Right face, right voice, right coloring, just what the script calls for. By the way, what's your salary?"

"Six hundred dollars a week," the girl said.

"Sorry," snapped the producer, "you're too tall."

*

An American film producer was selecting a chief for his scenario staff. The producer insisted that the successful applicant must be a college graduate. He looked with favor upon one applicant and asked if he had a college education. The answer was affirmative.

"Show me your diploma," demanded the producer.

The applicant tried to explain that it was not customary for college graduates to carry diplomas around with them.

"Well, then," demanded the producer, "say me a big word."

*

In Hollywood, the big stars lead a much different life from most people. Recently, a well-known actor approached his seven-year-old son and said, "I'm sorry, son, but tomorrow morning I have to use the chauffeur and limousine for business."

"But Daddy," objected the boy, "how will I get to school?"

"You'll get to school like every other kid in America," answered his father angrily. "You'll take a cab."

*

A new motion picture company was formed. It was decided that it would be called the Miracle Film Company.

"We'll get a big sign," said the boss. "We'll get the biggest sign in the world so it can be seen for miles. We'll spend five hundred thousand dollars for a slogan on it."

So, after half a million was spent on the sign, it read: If It's A Good Picture, It's A Miracle.

*

A Hollywood agent, usually in the best of spirits, sat despondently in one of the town's better night clubs.

"What's the sad look for?" asked one of his friends.

"It's that new client of mine," he answered. "Sings like Robert Goulet, has a build like Victor Mature, and acts like Marlon Brando."

"So what's the matter?" his friend laughed. "That's great, you'll make a million bucks on this guy."

"Guy, my foot," the agent cried. "It's a girl."

*

Two Hollywood film producers were making a war epic and decided to use armies of extras for the battle scenes—five thousand men on one side and four thousand on the other.

"That's colossal," said the first producer, "but when the shooting is finished, we have to pay nine thousand men. How about that?"

"A cinch," answered the second producer. "In the last battle we use real bullets."

*

"Take away Jane Fonda's hair and what have you got?" demanded a jealous wife.

Her husband lowered his paper and smiled dreamily. "Only the sexiest baldheaded girl in Hollywood."

*

A young actor with a name five syllables long won a big part in a new movie and promptly had his name changed to Lance Larde. The picture was a smash, and the actor won rave notices and a new contract. Ensconced in his new fourteen-room penthouse, he gave a great house-warming party and thoughtfully named his aged mother the guest of honor. Everybody showed up but mama, and the actor was frantic with worry. Finally, he went to the lobby to speak to the doorman.

"You didn't see a little old lady come in here at any time?" he asked anxiously.

"There was one," recalled the doorman. "She's been sitting patiently over in that corner for about three hours now."

It was mama all right. "Mama," he cried, "you've had me in a state! Why didn't you come up to my apartment?"

"I wanted to, my son," she told him with tears in her eyes, "but I couldn't remember your name."

*

This is a true story of a Hollywood writer who came home drunk one night. He could not negotiate his stairs to the second floor and passed out somewhere in the middle of the ascent. When he awoke, he heard his wife and two children in the kitchen. They couldn't have gotten there without passing his prostrate form, so he made it a point to ask them later why they didn't wake him up. The younger son's answer cleared things up.

"We thought," explained the eight-year-old, "that you was dead."

Hotels

After checking out of his hotel room, a guest discovered he had forgotten his umbrella. Meanwhile, his room had been rented to a young honeymoon couple. When he returned to the room he heard this conversation:

"Whose little hair is this?"

"All yours, honey."

"Whose little eyes are these?"

"All yours, honey."

"Whose little nose is this?"

"All yours, honey."

"And whose little mouth is this?"

"All yours, honey."

Unable to contain himself any longer he yelled in the door, "When you come to an umbrella, that's mine!"

*

The big city was crowded. Every hotel and rooming house was full. The young man was tired. He simply had to find a place to sleep that night.

"Anything will do," he said to the hotel clerk.

"I can let you have a cot in the ballroom," replied the clerk, "but there is a lady in the opposite corner. If you don't make any noise she'll be none the wiser."

"Fine," said the tired young man, and into the ballroom he went. Five minutes later he came running out to the clerk.

"Say," he cried, "that woman in there is dead!"

"I know," was the answer, "but how did you find out?"

Insanity

A psychiatrist informed his female patient, "You seem perfectly rational to me; in fact, I would say that you are just as sane as I am."

"Exactly," cried the girl happily. "But because I like apple dumplings, everyone thinks I'm crazy."

"That's absurd," retorted the psychiatrist. "Why, I like apple dumplings myself."

"You do?" squeaked the girl in sheer joy. "Well you must come over and try some of mine. I have closets full of them."

*

A man who climbed a flag pole and then began shouting at the top of his voice was arrested and charged with disturbing the peace. After hearing the charge, the magistrate peered over his glasses at the defendant.

"What have you got to say for yourself?" he demanded.

"Well, it's like this, Your Honor," replied the man sheepishly, "if I didn't do something crazy once in a while, I'd go nuts."

*

A guy went to see a psychiatrist, and the doctor asked what seemed to be troubling him. The fellow said that nothing was wrong, but his family thought he ought to come because he liked cotton socks.

The psychiatrist assured him that lots of people didn't like silk or nylon socks. "As a matter of fact," he said, "I like cotton socks myself."

"You do?" cried the guy in great excitement. "How do you like yours—with oil and vinegar, or just a squeeze of lemon?"

*

The psychiatrist came storming into the hospital director's office.

"Jones has shoved me to the limits of my patience," he screamed. "Being nuts is no excuse. This time he has heaped the final straw on me."

"What happened?" asked the director.

"He asked me if he could have a date with my wife," yelled the psychiatrist.

"Was that your wife who picked you up in a station wagon after work yesterday?" inquired the director.

"Yes."

"Then put Jones under close observation," ordered the director. "He's crazier than I thought."

*

A doctor came up to a patient in an insane asylum, slapped him on the back, and said, "Well, old man, you're all right. You can run along and write your folks that you'll be back home in two weeks as good as new."

The patient went off to write his letter. He had it finished and sealed, but when he was licking the stamp it slipped through his fingers to the floor, lighted on the back of a cockroach that was passing, and stuck. The patient didn't see the cockroach. What he did see was his escaped postage stamp zigzagging aimlessly up the wall and across the ceiling. In depressed silence he tore up the letter he had just written and dropped the pieces on the floor.

"Two weeks! Hell!" he said. "I won't be out of here in two years."

*

Mr. Harris, a prominent businessman, was especially interested in the rehabilitation of the insane. While on a visit to a local mental hospital, he happened upon a patient who was laying a new brick wall. Harris was amazed at the caliber of the work. He asked him, "How are you getting on here?"

"Oh, fine," the inmate replied. "The doctor says I should be able to leave soon."

"Well," Harris replied, "how would you like to work for me?"

The inmate enthusiastically said that he would. Harris said that he would arrange on Friday to hire him.

Harris had gotten only about thirty feet when a brick struck him a stunning blow on the head. As he painfully picked himself up, he heard the bricklayer shout, "You won't forget Friday, will you, Mr. Harris?"

*

When Castro came to inspect a Cuban insane asylum, the inmates were assembled in the hall. According to instructions, they shouted: "Long live our beloved leader, the great Castro"— all except one man, who was immediately accosted by an agent of the secret police.

"Why did you not greet our beloved Comrade Castro?" was the stern question.

"Because," the man answered, "I'm not insane. I'm the janitor."

*

A man went into a bar and ordered a glass of beer. He drank half of it and threw the rest over the bartender. Then he apologized profusely.

"It's a nervous compulsion I have. I'm terribly embarrassed by it," he explained.

"You'd better consult a psychiatrist," the bartender said.

Several months later the man came back to the bar and did the same thing. The bartender was naturally indignant.

"I thought you were going to see a psychiatrist," he said.

"I've been seeing one," said the man.

"It certainly hasn't done you much good."

"Oh, yes it has," the man replied. "I'm not embarrassed about it any more."

*

The psychiatrist informed a female patient: "It's taken us a long time, Mrs. Smith, but I think we've finally cured you of the fixation that you're Elizabeth Taylor."

The woman said, "That's wonderful! But just remember to send your statements to Richard; he pays all the bills."

*

A man was bitten by a dog and went to the doctor. After an examination, the doctor told him he had rabies. The man immediately took out a small pad from his coat pocket, and started writing.

"You don't have to start writing your will," said the doctor. "We'll get you healthy again."

"It's not my will," said the man. "It's just of list of people I'm going to bite."

*

Two inmates of the asylum were talking together.

"I've made up my mind," blurted one suddenly, with a look of decision on his face. "Tomorrow I order my legions to invade England. History will never say that Julius Caesar faltered in pursuing the Britannic campaigns."

"England, eh?" mused the other thoughtfully. "Well, Julius, if I were you—and, incidentally, I am—"

Italians

An Italian, having made his fortune in America, returned to his tiny native village. His father, who had never been out of the village, said to his son, "Luigi, they say they have instruments in American so you can talk to people over long distances."

"That's right, Papa. They call it the telephone."

"How does it work?"

"You pick up a thing like a trumpet in your left hand, then with your right hand you start to dial—"

"Both hands? You need both hand to work this machine?" asked his astonished Italian father. "Then how do you talk?"

Joint Return

The new bride took the couple's first joint income-tax return to an accountant for help in preparing it.

"May I deduct the cost of my birth-control pills as a medical expense?" she asked, blushingly.

"No, ma'am," answered the consultant. "But if they don't work, you can deduct them next year."

Kids

A four-year-old child was out for a walk with his father. He had quite a time trying to keep up with his father's grown-up strides.

"Am I walking too fast?" asked the father.

"No," panted the boy, "but I am!"

*

A snoopy social worker investigating conditions in an old tenement stopped a ragged, neglected-looking youngster and asked him where his mother lived.

"Ain't got no mother," replied the child.

"What about your father, then?"

"Ain't got none, lady."

"What, both your father and mother dead!" exclaimed the social worker.

"Nope, never had any."

"Good grief, but that's impossible, my boy"

"If you've gotta know, lady," said the urchin contemptuously, "some damned con man played a dirty trick on my aunt."

*

A census taker working on the lower East Side came to a tenement that was crowded with children. Observing a woman bending over a washtub, he addressed her: "Madam, I am the census taker. How many children have you?"

"Well, lemme see," replied the woman, as she straightened up and wiped her hands on her apron. "There's Mary and Ellen and Patsy and Nora and Kate and Tommy and Joseph and Eddie and Charlie and Frank and—"

"Madam," interrupted the census man, "if you could just give me the number—"

"Number!" she exclaimed indignantly. "I want you to understand that we ain't got to numberin' 'em yet. We ain't run out of names."

*

The little boy's favorite uncle was about to be married, and the child had not taken the news lightly. For many days he looked fearful and apprehensive each time the wedding was mentioned. But no one realized the extent of his misgivings until one day he came to his mother with a troubled frown.

"Mother," he said, "the last three days they give them everything they want to eat, don't they?"

*

A kindergarten teacher assigned her youngsters the task of drawing a picture of what they wanted to be when they grew up. Soon one child had drawn a cowboy, another a nurse, and so on. But one little girl was staring at a blank paper.

"What's wrong, Janie?" she asked.

"I don't know how to draw it," cried Janie. "I want to be married!"

*

A mother had sent her four-year-old son to a progressive camp. On visiting day, she found him very excited about having gone swimming in the camp pool.

"How did you do that?" she asked. "I forgot to pack your bathing trunks."

"I went in naked."

The mother asked, "Did the girls go in naked, too?"

"Oh, no," was the answer, "they wore bathing caps."

*

The science teacher was lecturing to some four-year-olds attending a preschool class sponsored by a museum. The subject was mammals.

"Mammals are warm blooded," she told them. "Mammals have fur, and mammals carry their babies inside their bodies."

A small boy spoke up immediately. "My mother must be a mammal," he announced.

"Oh-oh," thought the teacher, seeing trouble heading fast in her direction. She gathered her courage and decided to see the thing through.

"Why do you think your mother is a mammal?" she asked.

"Because," said the small boy, "she has a fur collar."

*

A little girl marched into a bank, handed the teller a dollar bill, and said, "Would you please change that to nickels?"

Taking her nickels to a table, she counted them carefully. Five minutes later she returned to the window. "Would you change these into dimes?" she asked.

A few minutes later back she came to get the dimes changed into quarters. When she returned with the quarters and asked for half dollars, the patient teller was finally moved to ask, "What in the world are you doing?"

"Learning to count money," she replied briskly, and left with her half dollars.

*

A bandleader asked his pianist to give piano lessons to his young son. At the first lesson, the pianist said to the boy, "Do you know the scale?"

"Yes, sir," the nine-year-old answered. "One hundred bucks a week for sidemen and double for the leader."

*

A new teacher took over her class. "What's your name?" she asked one little boy.

"Jule," he said.

"Not Jule. Nicknames are not allowed. Your name is Julius." She turned to the next boy. "What's your name?"

"Billious," came the reply.

*

Trying to rest after an exceedingly hard day at the office, a poor father was being bedeviled by a stream of unanswerable questions from little Willie.

"What do you do down at the office?" the youngster finally asked.

"Nothing!" shouted the father.

After a thoughtful pause, Willie inquired, "Pop, how do you know when you're finished?"

*

Four little boys were trying to decide which movie to attend one Saturday afternoon. Mike was holding out for a Western, but his three buddies would have none of it.

"It's got a lot of kissing scenes," they complained.

"That's all right," said Mike. "When the kissing scenes start, we can just close our eyes and pretend he's choking her."

*

Two young children dressed in ragged jeans offered to clean up a woman's yard for a quarter. The woman agreed and, seeing that the children were badly in need of haircuts, told them she would pay for their visit to the local barbershop.

By the time she got to the barbershop, the younger child was nearly through getting a crewcut.

"My, that haircut looks good on your brother," she said with pleasure.

"He ain't my brother, lady," said the elder child. "He's my sister."

*

For the third straight time, the little boy brought home a terrible report card. After reading it with a shudder, the lad's father signed it with an X.

"Why did you do that?" the boy asked.

"I don't want the teacher to think that anyone with marks like that has a father who can read and write," replied the father.

*

The professor asked his class, "Who is happier, the man with six million dollars or the man with six children?"

One of the students had an instant answer: "The man with the six kids."

"Why?" asked the professor.

"Because the guy with the six million always wants more."

*

"Mother," Dad said, "I'm going to find out what Tommy wants to be when he grows up. Watch."

He put a ten dollar bill on the table to represent a banker. Next to it he placed a brand new Bible, representing a clergyman. And beside the Bible he placed a bottle of whiskey, representing a bum.

Mother and Did hid where they could see the articles on the table. Tommy, whistling, entered the room and spied the objects. He looked around to see that he was alone. Satisfied, he picked up the bill, held it to the light, and replaced it. He fingered the pages of the new Bible. He looked around once more. Then he quickly uncorked the bottle and smelled the contents. And, in a motion, he stuffed the bill in his pocket, lodged the Bible under his arm, grabbed the bottle by the neck, and strolled out of the room, still whistling.

"My goodness, Mother," Dad exclaimed, "he's going to be a politician!"

*

The manager of a large New York theater was walking down the aisle one morning when he saw a boy of about ten sitting in the theater, watching the picture with rapt attention.

The man went over, tapped the boy on the shoulder, and asked, "Why aren't you in school?"

"It's okay, mister," the boy assured him. "I've got the measles."

*

The little girl was visiting her aunt. It was the first time she had been away from home. After the first two days, the novelty had worn off and she began to cry.

"You aren't homesick, are you?" her aunt chided gently.

"No," was the tearful response, "I'm here sick."

*

A six-year-old went into a bank and asked to see the president. The smiling clerk showed her into his private office. She explained solemnly that her girls' club was raising money, and asked him to please contribute.

The banker laid a dollar bill and a dime on the desk and said, "You take whichever one you want."

She picked up the dime and said, "My mother always taught me to take the smallest piece." Then picking up the dollar bill, too, she added, "But just to make sure I don't lose the dime, I'll take this piece of paper to wrap it in."

*

When the teacher asked his class to write an essay on what they would do if they had a million dollars, everyone except little Willie began writing immediately. When the teacher collected the papers, he discovered that Willie had handed in a blank sheet.

"What's this, Willie? Everyone else handed in two sheets or more—and you've done nothing!"

"Well," replied Willie, "that's what I'd do if I had a million dollars."

*

A salesman called a prospective customer, and the phone was answered by what was obviously a small boy. "Is your mother or father home?" the salesman asked. The child said No. "Well, is there anyone else there I can speak to?"

"My sister," the youngster piped. There was a rather long period of silence, then the salesman heard the boy's voice again.

"I can't lift her out of the playpen," he said.

*

At a country club, a member told the owner of a big metropolitan newspaper, "Say, I owe you a vote of thanks. Your paper proved to be just the thing to stop my two kids from raising the devil this morning."

Obviously pleased, the newspaper owner inquired, "What particular article did the trick?"

"No article at all," explained the father. "I just rolled up your paper and whacked them with it."

*

Eminent physicians had been called in for consultation. They had retired to another room to discuss the patient's condition. In a closet of that room, a small boy had been concealed by the patient to listen in to the consultation and to tell him what the doctors had decided.

"Well, Jimmy," said the patient, when the boy came to report, "what did they say?"

"I can't tell you that," said the boy. "I listened as hard as I could, but they used such big words I can't remember much of it. All I could catch was when one doctor said, 'Well, we'll find that out at the autopsy.'"

*

Two fathers were discussing their families.

"My three boys sure stick together," said one dad. "When one of them gets in trouble, the other two will never squeal on him."

"But how do you find out the guilty one so that you can punish him?"

"That's easy. All I do is send all three of them to bed without supper, and the next morning I thrash the one with the black eye."

*

The little girl's aunt visiting for the holidays was talking about Christmas. "What are you going to give your little brother for Christmas?" she asked.

"I don't know," the little girl said.

"Well," asked her aunt, "what did you give him for Christmas last year?"

"The whooping cough," said the little girl.

*

The usual crowd of small boys was gathered about the entrance of a circus tent in a small town one day, pushing each other and trying to get a glimpse of the interior. A man standing nearby watched them for a few minutes and then walked up to the ticket-taker. He said with an air of authority: "Let these boys in, and count them as they pass."

The gateman did as he was requested and, when the last one had gone in, he turned and said, "Twenty-eight, sir."

"Good," said the man, smiling as he walked away. "I thought I guessed right."

*

During a flood in a little Ohio town, a little girl was perched on top of a house with a small boy.

As they sat watching articles float along with the water, they noticed a derby hat float by. Presently, the hat turned and came back, then turned again and went downstream. After it went some distance, it again turned and came back.

The little girl said, "Do you see that derby? First it goes downstream, then turns and comes back."

"Oh, that's my father," the little boy replied. "This morning he said that, come hell or high water, he was going to cut the grass today."

*

The door-to-door salesman rang the bell in a suburban home and the door opened, revealing a nine-year-old boy who was puffing on a long, black cigar. Trying to cover his amazement, the salesman said, "Good morning, sonny. Is your mother in?"

The boy removed the cigar from his mouth, flicked off its ashes, and replied, "What do YOU think?"

*

Six-year-old Scott came into the house covered with mud after finishing a rough day at play.

"Mom," he shouted at the top of his voice, "if I fell out of a tree, would you rather I broke a leg or tore my pants?"

"What a silly question," his mother answered from the next room. "I'd rather you tore your pants."

"Well, I got news for you then," the boy replied triumphantly. "That's exactly what happened."

*

Meeting at lunch, two businessmen began to talk about world problems, high taxes, the cost of living, and, finally, their families.

"I have six boys," one of them said proudly.

"That's a nice family," sighed the other man. "I wish to heaven I had six children."

"Don't you have any children?" the proud father asked with a touch of sympathy in his voice.

"Oh, yes," sighed the second man, "twelve."

*

A little boy said to his teacher, "I ain't got no pencil."

She corrected him at once: "It's 'I don't have a pencil'—'I don't have a pencil.' 'You don't have a pencil.' 'We don't have any pencils.' 'They don't have any pencils.' Is that clear?"

"No," said the bewildered child. "What happened to all them pencils?"

The Law

A man charged with theft showed up in court without an attorney.

"Do you want me to assign you an attorney?" asked the presiding judge.

"No, sir," said the defendant.

"But you are entitled to an attorney and you might as well have the benefit of his services," said the jurist.

"If it's all the same to you," said the defendant, "I'd like to throw myself upon the ignorance of the court."

*

The police station had been quiet all that day and, for that matter, most of the week. The men were playing cards to pass the time.

"What a life," complained one of the officers. "No fights, no burglaries, no riots, no nuthin', not even a stabbing. If it stays this quiet, they'll reduce the force."

"Rest easy, Mike," said the captain, raising the ante. "Things will break soon. You've got to have faith in human nature."

*

A lady went to the governor of her state and said to him, "Governor, I want to get my husband out of prison."

The governor asked, "What is he in prison for?"

She replied, "For stealing a loaf of bread."

The governor asked, "Is he a good husband?"

She replied, "No, sir. He drinks, he beats the children, and he's no good."

The governor asked, "Then why do you want him out of jail?"

She replied, "The fact is that we're out of bread again."

*

Things looked gloomy for the swindler. There was so much evidence against him that the jury couldn't help but bring in a verdict of guilty.

After passing sentence, the judge spoke fervently about what he thought of swindlers.

"I think it is a reprehensible and contemptible thing to swindle people who have placed their confidence in you," he said.

The swindler looked up at the judge with a hurt expression.

"But, Your Honor," he pointed out rather logically, "they are the only ones I have any success with."

*

A policeman arrested two men and confiscated a pair of loaded dice. In court, each accused the other of owning the dice.

"Officer," said the magistrate, "did you seize these dice without a search warrant?" The policeman nodded sheepishly. "You had no right to," said the magistrate. "Give them back immediately."

One culprit stuck out his hand to retrieve the dice. The magistrate then sentenced him to three months and released the other.

*

An elderly man of convivial habits was hauled before a judge.

"You're charged with being intoxicated and disorderly," snapped the judge. "Have you anything to say?"

"Man's inhumanity to man makes thousands mourn," began the prisoner in a flight of oratory. "I am not so debased as Poe, so profligate as Byron, so ungrateful as Keats, so intemperate as Burns, so demented as Tennyson, so vulgar as Shakespeare—"

"That'll do," interrupted the judge. "Seven days. And Officer, make a list of the names he mentioned and round 'em all up. I think they're as bad as he is."

*

A reckless driver was hauled into court for speeding. After a lengthy sermon by the judge, the driver quipped, "Aren't you the eloquent one? I'll bet you can recite Lincoln's Gettysburg Address, too."

"I'm proud to say I can," admitted the judge. "And I hereby sentence you to fourscore and seven days in jail."

*

"A driver in a stolen car, no license, no lights, came down on the wrong side of the street, went through the red light, and smashed into my car."

"What happened then?"

"A cop came along and arrested me. I told him it wasn't my fault, but the cop said it was my fault, and when I asked why, he answered, 'His father is the Mayor, and his uncle is the Chief of Police, and I'm engaged to his daughter.'"

*

Two judges were arrested for speeding. When they arrived in court, no other judge was present, so they decided to try each other. The first judge went up on the bench and said, "You are charged with exceeding the speed limit. How do you plead?"

"Guilty," was the answer.

"You are hereby fined five dollars."

Then they exchanged places and again the plea was Guilty.

"H'mm," said the other judge, "these cases are becoming too common. This is the second case of this sort we've had this morning. I hereby fine you ten dollar or ten days in jail."

Lawyers

A lawyer went to a judge to complain that the client for whom he had just won a case refused to pay his fee.

"Did you present your request in writing?" asked the judge.

"Yes, I did, sir," replied the lawyer.

"What did he have to say?" continued the judge.

"He told me to go to the devil," answered the lawyer.

"Then what did you do?"

"I came straight to you, sir."

*

A lawyer's young secretary got married. She stayed on the job, though. About a month later, the lawyer telephoned the newly-weds' house and happened to get the secretary's husband.

"Would you please ask your wife if my briefs are ready?" asked the lawyer.

There was a pause at the other end of the wire. Finally, the husband inquired, "Do you mean she does your laundry, too?"

*

A couple of business partners had a serious quarrel, and one of them consulted a lawyer about dividing the business so that one could buy the other out. After several days, the attorney reported to his client: "I've finally talked your partner into seeing things your way and he has agreed to a settlement that is very fair to both of you."

"Fair to both of us!" exclaimed the businessman. "I could have done that myself. What do you think I hired a lawyer for?"

*

When a hostile witness preceded each answer with "I think," the lawyer lost his patience and insisted for the third time that the witness tell the court and jury "what you know, and not what you think."

Whereupon the witness quietly replied, "I'm not a lawyer; I can't talk without thinking."

*

It seems the gate broke down between heaven and hell. Saint Peter appeared on the scene and called out to the devil, "Hey, Satan. It's your turn to fix it this time."

"Sorry," replied the devil, "my men are too busy to worry about fixing a mere gate."

"Well, then," scowled Saint Peter, "I'll have to sue you for breaking our agreement."

"Oh, yeah," replied the devil. "Where are you going to get a lawyer?"

*

A lawyer whose sparkling eloquence had won an acquittal for his client, was anxious to learn the truth.

"Now, Joe," he said, "you can confide in me. Did you really steal that horse you were accused of stealing?"

"No, sir," replied the man, "I thought I had, but your speech to the jury convinced even me."

Lecturers

One of the things that disconcerts lecturers is the habit some people have of looking at their watches.

One speaker was asked if he were bothered by the practice.

"No," he replied, "I don't mind—until they start shaking them."

Logic

"Come, come," the smiling psychiatrist said to his sobbing patient. "You mustn't carry on like this. Cheer up! Be happy!"

"Be happy!" echoed the tearful woman. "How can I be happy? Sixteen children I've had by that husband of mine—and he doesn't even love me! What is there for me to be happy about?"

"Well," suggested the doctor, "imagine what it would have been like if he did love you."

*

"Yes," she admitted, "you love me now. That's only natural, I suppose. But will your love for me remain as strong after we are married?"

"Don't worry your pretty little head about that," he answered softly. "You know darned well it will. Haven't you often commented upon my fondness for married women?"

*

A businessman had grave doubts about his assistant's intelligence. Finally, he decided to put him to the test.

"Johnson," he called. The young assistant came over. "Yes, sir?"

"Johnson, how many pancakes can you eat on an empty stomach?"

The assistant pondered. "Oh, about six," he said finally, puzzled.

"Wrong," bellowed his boss. "You eat only one on an empty stomach. After that one, your stomach is no longer empty."

*

The teacher was lecturing to a class in science. "Now, then, Bill," he said, "name a poisonous substance."

Bill Smith, who was not gifted with an oversupply of intelligence, thought deeply. "Aviation," he said.

The class tittered with amusement, and the teacher looked sternly at the embarrassed pupil.

"Explain yourself, Bill," he demanded.

Responded Bill, "One drop will kill, sir."

*

At a dinner party, a self-made businessman was chatting with a pretty young woman.

"You know, I sometimes feel ashamed of my failure to keep abreast of modern science," he said. "Take the electric light, for example. I must confess I haven't the slightest idea of how it works."

The pretty young woman gave him a patronizing smile.

"Why, it's very simple, really," she replied. "You just turn a switch and the light comes on. That's all there is to it."

*

A Mississippi steamboat captain was interviewing a likely young pilot.

"Do you know where all the snags are in this river?" the captain asked.

"No, sir," replied the pilot—whose name happened to be Mark Twain. "I don't know where all the snags are. But I do know where they ain't—and that's where I aim to do my piloting."

*

A stranger walked into a restaurant, gave his hat to the hatcheck girl, and went in to eat. An hour later he came out, and the girl gave him his hat before he could even dig up his check.

"How did you know it was my hat?" he asked.

"I didn't, sir," she replied.

"Why did you give it to me, then?"

"Because you gave it to me."

Magician

The magician was describing his act to a booking agent. He declared, "I've got a new trick that will panic them. I saw a woman in half."

The agent said, "A new trick? Magicians have been sawing women in half for years."

The magician said, "Lengthwise?"

Marriage

Mrs. O'Reilly confronted her husband, Mike, and said she'd need money for a new cradle.

"What do you need a new cradle for?" asked Mike.

"Don't you know we've had fifteen children," she said, "and every one of them has been in the same little cradle and now it's rickety?"

"All right," consented Mike. "Here's some money for a new cradle. But, for heaven's sake, this time buy one that's gonna last."

*

Lefkowitz came home and told his wife that because it was their wedding anniversary they were going to celebrate. They would go to a nightclub, eat, drink, dance, and be merry.

"Honey, darling, sweetheart, maybe we'll go in a taxicab? My darling, honey, sweetheart," she said. "Or maybe you'll step out a bit and get a private car, my darling, sweetheart, honey?"

"Listen," said Lefkowitz, "we're going by subway and you can call me Stinky."

*

Old Man: "Doc, I need a blood test. I'm getting married."

Doctor: "You are? How old are you now, anyway?"

Old Man: "Going on eighty-five."

Doctor: "And how old is your bride-to-be?"

Old Man: "Just past twenty-one."

Doctor: "Why Mr. Jones, do you realize that such disparity in ages could prove fatal?"

Old Man: "Well, if she dies, she dies!"

*

A woman who plays cards one night a month with a group of friends was concerned because she always woke up her husband when she came home at about midnight. One night she decided to try not to disturb him. She undressed in the living-room and, handbag over her arm, tiptoed nude into the bedroom—only to find her husband sitting up in bed reading.

"Good Lord!" he exclaimed. "Did you lose everything?"

*

A student in an evening class protested to the instructor that, although he hadn't missed a class, a notice was posted to him stating that he had been absent for three nights. After checking the records, the instructor agreed that an error had been made and assured the student that he would put it right with the principal.

"It's not the principal I'm worried about," said the student. "Who's going to explain it to my wife?"

*

A group of visitors was being shown through a large lunatic asylum. The doctor who acted as guide paused before a cell in which a man sat nursing a large doll. The doll was dressed in the gay and gaudy costume of a modern young lady.

"This poor fellow," explained the doctor, "has a very sad history. See how he is bending over that doll and fondling it so tenderly. He spends most of his time like that. He was engaged to a girl with whom he was deeply in love. She jilted him and married another man, and this one lost his reason over the affair."

The visitors were much touched and uttered various expressions of sympathy.

They passed to the next cell, which was barred and thickly padded.

"And this," resumed the doctor, "is the other man."

*

There once lived a very courageous man who was a lion-tamer.

He was not afraid of the most vicious lions. This brave lion-tamer was married to a woman who did not like him to stay out late at night. One night he did stay out late. When he realized the lateness of the hour, he was frightened. Being afraid to go home, he crawled into the lion's cage and went to sleep with his head resting on the largest lion.

Early the next morning, his wife began to look for him. She looked all over town and, not finding him, she came to the menagerie where he worked. There she discovered him in the lion's cage. Looking at him contemptuously, she cried, "You coward!"

*

A young married man met a friend of his bachelor days and insisted on his coming home with him for lunch. His wife was unprepared for visitors. She took her husband aside, and told him she had only one dozen oysters and that when his friend had eaten his quota of four, he must not be offered any more. Despite the husband's promise to remember, when the guest had eaten his four, the host pressed him to take more. The wife looked distressed and the friend declined. The husband insisted, the wife looked on in agony, and the guest firmly refused to have the rest of the oysters brought from the kitchen.

Later, the wife said to her husband, "How could you urge him to have more oysters when I had explained to you that there weren't any more?"

"I'm sorry," said the penitent husband, "but I forgot all about it."

"Forget about it! Why do you suppose I was kicking you under the table?" asked his wife.

"You didn't kick me," said the husband.

*

The wife was always antagonized by her husband's going out at night. His departing words, which especially angered her, were always "Good night, mother of three."

One night, she could stand it no longer. As usual, he put on his hat and started out the door, calling cheerily, "Good night, mother of three."

She answered gaily, "Good night, father of one."

*

A husband telephoned his wife. "I'd like to bring Jim home to dinner tonight."

"To dinner tonight?" screamed his wife. "You know I have a cold, the baby is cutting his teeth, and the house is as hot as an oven because you can't afford air conditioning, and my household money is gone, so we'll have to eat hash again."

"I know all that, darling," he interrupted quietly. "That's why I want to bring him. The idiot is talking about getting married."

*

A lawyer was cross-examining the defendant.

"After you poisoned the coffee, your husband sat at the breakfast table with you and sipped it. Didn't you feel the slightest pity for him?"

"Yes," she answered. "There was just one moment when I felt sorry for him."

"When was that?" the lawyer inquired.

"When he asked for his second cup."

*

Two commuters missed their train, so they went into a nearby tavern to await the next one. They missed that one, too. And the next. And the next.

"I was reading in the paper today," said the first commuter over his umpteenth highball, "about a lie detector they used on a criminal that *proved* he was lying. Must be a wonderful thing. Did you ever see a lie detector?"

"See one?" said the other commuter. "I married one!"

*

John: "My wife has a terrible habit of staying up until one and two o'clock in the morning. I can't seem to break her of it."

Joe: "What on earth is she doing all that time?"

John: "Waiting for me to come home."

*

They brought their wives to the convention, but managed to sneak away for a meal at a fashionable restaurant.

"Shall I bring you a couple of demitasses?" asked the waiter at the end of the meal.

"Heavens, no," pleaded one of them. "It would be just our luck if our wives walked in."

*

One day at lunch, a businessman said to an associate, "Bill, how long have you been married?"

"Twenty-odd years," replied his companion.

The first man was puzzled. "Why do you say odd?" The reply was, "Wait till you see my wife."

*

George fell asleep to the steady drone of his wife's voice. The next thing he knew she was shaking him violently.

"Wake up," she shrieked. "You're talking in your sleep."

He shook his sleepy head and yawned. "For heaven's sake, you don't begrudge me those few words, do you?"

*

"My husband talks in his sleep," complained a woman to her family physician.

"That's easy enough to fix," he replied. "Just give him one of these pills every night before he retires, and he'll be cured in no time."

"But you don't understand!" she exclaimed. "I don't want to cure him. He's really very interesting. I want something to keep me awake."

*

A woman expecting her seventh child decided that the time had come to tell her children about the blessed event. Assembling them that night in the living-room, she broke the news.

"The stork," she said happily, "will be coming to pay us a visit!"

"A visit!" her husband said, looking up from his newspaper. "What do you mean visit? He lives here."

*

Turning to her husband after the last guest had departed, the wife exclaimed, "I simply can't understand you! Why do you always insist on sitting on the piano stool whenever we entertain? Everyone knows that you can't play a note."

"I know, dear. And as long as I'm sitting there, no one else can play either."

*

The minister asked for anyone who knew a truly perfect person to stand up. After a long pause, a meek-looking fellow in the back arose.

"Do you really know a perfect person?" the minister queried.

"Yes, sir, I do," answered the little man.

"Won't you please tell the congregation who the rare perfect person is?" asked the minister.

"Yes, sir. My wife's first husband."

*

On his way out of church, a young man stopped at the door for a few words with the minister.

"Would it be right," he asked, "for a person to profit from the mistakes of another?"

"Absolutely not!" replied the pastor.

"In that case," said the young man, "I wonder if you'd consider returning the ten dollars I paid you when you married my wife and me last August."

*

A pregnant woman told her husband he had better get her to the hospital. The harried husband immediately rushed to the phone and called the hospital. He said he was bringing his wife in and that they should notify everybody that she was going to have the baby.

"Is this her first baby?" he was asked.

"Of course not," was the answer. "This is her husband."

*

A rather fickle bachelor was telling a married friend about the talents and accomplishments of a girl he had just met. The married man listened quietly. He had heard him rave like this before.

"And you know," the bachelor enthused, "this girl has brains enough for two."

His companion's terse comment was: "Then you ought to marry her right away."

*

The hostess poured a cup of tea for a middle-aged man at her party and asked him if he took sugar.

"No," he said.

"Yes," said his wife brightly at the same moment. Then she turned accusingly to him. "But I always put sugar in your tea."

"I know," the man said ruefully. "I used to remind you not to. Now I just don't stir."

*

A bride's mother didn't know how to advise her on the facts of life. Her grandmother volunteered to give counsel which would assure a happy marriage. So grandmother began, but she was soon interrupted by the bride.

"Never mind all that. If you want me to have a happy marriage, teach me how to make potato pancakes the way you do."

*

A man died and went to heaven, where he saw two lines of men.

One appeared endless and the other had only one guy standing on it. A friendly angel explained that the long line was composed of henpecked husbands. The man went over to the fellow standing alone on the line and asked, "What are you doing here?"

"My wife," explained the guy, "told me to stand here."

*

A poor officeworker had saved for years to take a vacation in Italy with his wife. Finally, the day arrived when his big dream was about to come true.

"Are you going to visit Mount Vesuvius?" a coworker asked.

"Vesuvius?" he repeated. "What's that?"

"Oh, that's a big volcano that belches smoke and spits fire."

"What do you mean—visit?" he said forlornly. "I'm taking her with me."

*

A man from out of town was having breakfast in a restaurant. He gave the waitress the following order: "Bring me some warm orange juice, no ice, burn the toast to a crisp, put a couple of sloppy eggs fried in grease on a dirty plate, a cup of coffee that tastes like mud, and be sure to leave the grounds in the cup. Now bring my order just that way and don't change a thing."

The waitress complied and said, "Is there anything else I can do for you, mister?"

"Yeh," he grunted, "now sit down and nag me. I'm homesick!"

*

A young married woman went home to her mother. She complained that her husband stayed out too late at night having a good time with other women.

"Well, dear, it's too bad," replied her mother, "but I think if you started a big garden for your husband to work in, it'd keep him out of mischief."

"I doubt it," observed the daughter. "A big garden didn't do Adam much good."

*

He was reading a letter from his Mother, congratulating him on his engagement.

"My darling boy," wrote the mother, "what glorious news! Your father and I rejoice in your happiness. It has long been our greatest wish that you should marry some good woman. A good woman is heaven's most precious gift to man. She brings out all the best in him and helps him to suppress all that is evil."

Then there was a postscript in a different handwriting: "Your mother has gone for a stamp. Stay single, you young fool."

*

She was an unusual mother-in-law in that she loved her son-in-law almost as much as her daughter. So it was with deep regret that she stood by while they argued. During one particularly violent session she interceded.

"Now, children," she said, "can't you agree once in a while?"

"But we do agree, Mother," her daughter assured her. "We both want Tom's pay envelope."

*

A high-school student asked his father to help him write a composition on how wars start.

"Well, now, let's suppose we got into a quarrel with Canada," his father began.

"That's ridiculous," his mother interrupted. "Why should we quarrel with Canada?"

"That's beside the point," her husband said. "I was merely using an example—"

"If you had an ounce of brains you wouldn't make such stupid—"

"Who do you think you're talking to? I want to teach my son—"

"*Your* son! I suppose I had nothing to do with his being here. You just found him someplace—"

"Please, folks," the boy pleaded. "Forget it. I just figured it out for myself."

*

A wife returned unexpectedly from her vacation and caught her husband in the arms of another woman. The "other woman" wanted to have it out, so she said, "Now you know. I love your husband, and he loves me. Will you gamble for him? Play me a game of gin rummy for him?"

"Fair enough," replied the wife.

The cards were dealt and the other woman said to the wife: "Here are the rules of this game. If I lose, I'll never see your husband again—I'll get right out of his life. If you lose, I want you to divorce him so that I can marry him. Do you agree?"

"Yes—but how about playing for a penny a point just to make it interesting?"

*

Mr. Smith called up his doctor.

"Doctor Jones," he said, "please come over to my house right away."

"What's the matter?"

"My wife—appendicitis. Hurry up!"

"Oh, don't worry about it," replied the doctor. "I operated on your wife three years ago. I took out her appendix and I've never heard of anybody having two of them."

"Oh, yeah! Well, did you ever hear of anybody having two wives? She's my second."

*

A man was suffering from what appeared to be a case of shattered nerves. After a long spell of illness, he finally called in a doctor.

"You are in serious trouble," the doctor said. "You are living with some terrible evil thing, something that is possessing you from morning to night. We must find it and destroy it."

"Ssh, Doctor," said the man, "you are absolutely right, but don't say it so loud. She's sitting in the next room and she might hear you."

*

Two women were talking about their husbands.

Said one, "I'm more and more convinced that mine married me for my money."

Replied the other, "Then you have the satisfaction of knowing that he's not as stupid as he looks."

*

Paul, who was well over six feet, dated two girls quite frequently, then finally settled down and married the one who was just five feet tall.

"Why did you choose the short one?" asked Al.

"Decided to choose the lesser of two evils," Paul replied, grinning.

*

A beautiful blonde in a convertible pulled up to a service station. Immediately, four attendants swarmed over the car. But one attendant made no move. He just looked on with an amused smile.

"Aren't you going over to check something?" he was asked.

"I don't have to," he answered with a grin. "I'm her husband."

*

A long-married couple was sitting in the living-room. He was asleep in his easy chair and she was watching television. Suddenly a violent tornado struck the house. It ripped off the roof, picked the man and woman up, swirled them into the air, and deposited them a mile from home. The husband, seeing his wife sobbing, said, "Stop crying, can't you see we're safe?"

She whimpered, "I'm just crying because I'm so happy. This is the first time we've been out together in ten years."

*

"I remember my wedding day distinctly," the elderly bookkeeper told the young cashier. "I took my bride home to the little house I had bought. I carried her over the threshold and said, 'Honey, this is your world and this is my world.' "

"And I suppose you both have lived happily ever after?" said the younger man.

"Well, not exactly," the other replied grimly. "We've been fighting for the world's championship ever since."

*

The newlywed was being pumped by her inquisitive neighbors.

"Your husband doesn't speak harshly to you, does he?" they asked anxiously.

"Oh, no," she assured them, "he hasn't raised his voice to me yet."

"He doesn't expect you to obey him, does he?"

"Oh dear me, no," she laughed, "didn't you girls know he had been married before?"

*

A man complained to his friend that his wife was always nagging him for money. "Last week she wanted two hundred dollars. The day before yesterday, it was one hundred. And this morning she asked me for another one hundred and fifty dollars."

"That's awful," his friend replied. "What could she possibly do with all that money?"

"I don't know," said the husband, "I never give her any."

*

A commuter retired after forty years of catching the same early-morning train. The next morning he told his wife not to turn his fried eggs over because he didn't like them that way.

"My dear," she exclaimed, "why didn't you ever tell me before?"

He replied, "Frankly, I never had the time."

Military

The GI was competing in a rifle tournament. When his card was brought to him, it reflected such a poor performance that he involuntarily remarked to the captain, who was scrutinizing it: "After looking at my card, I feel like shooting myself."

To which the captain murmured, still looking at the card, "Better take two bullets."

*

A soldier joined the Israeli army. After three days, he asked for a three-day pass. The sergeant said, "You've got a lot of nerve. You're in the army for three days, and you want a three-day pass. You've got to do something important, something heroic, something valorous to get a three-day pass."

The next day, the recruit drove into the camp with a late-model Arab tank. A friend asked him how he did it.

"Easy," he said. "I took one of our tanks and drove it toward Jordan. I saw one of the Arab tanks approach. I put up a white flag, and he put up a white flag. I went out and spoke to him. I said, 'Listen, buddy, do you want a three-day pass?' He said, 'Sure.' So we exchanged tanks."

*

During World War II, Hans sent a letter from Germany to his friend in which he said that the Nazis couldn't win.

"We're short of ammunition," he wrote. "We haven't got enough to carry on."

The censors got hold of his letter and Hans was arrested and sentenced to die for spreading defeatism. But Hans didn't seem to care. In the morning when the guard came to execute him, Hans had one question: "Are you going to hang me or shoot me?"

"Hang you," said the guard.

"You see," laughed Hans. "I was right. "We're short of ammunition!"

*

A conservative British tailor was retained by a newly formed South American republic to design its military uniforms. The first request he received was for an outfit with a tightfitting green jacket, royal blue trousers with a red and gold stripe on the side, and a canary yellow cap with a white ostrich feather.

The tailor was amazed. "I assume this uniform is for the guards at the presidential palace."

"Not at all," said the military chief of staff. "It's for our secret service agents."

*

World War II ended and the GI was told he would soon be going home. So he decided to see the sights of Paris.

He went to a very large cathedral. A wedding party was passing into one part of it. The American lad turned to a nearby Frenchman and asked, "Who's the groom?"

The Frenchman shrugged his shoulders and said *"Je ne sais pas."*

The boy walked on and in another part of the cathedral saw a funeral procession going out. Turning to the ubiquitous native, he asked, "Who's dead?"

The Frenchman said, *"Je ne sais pas."*

And the GI observed, "Well, he sure didn't last long, did he?"

*

An American soldier in Vietnam picked up for dead turned out to be very much alive when brought into the field hospital.

"You must have been in pretty bad shape," commented the

doctor, as he began to look his man over for bullet wounds and fractures.

"I was, Doc," the battler agreed. "But do you know, I felt sure all the time that I wasn't really dead."

"What made you so sure?" asked the surgeon.

"Well, Doc, my feet were cold, and I was hungry. I figured that if I was in heaven I wouldn't be hungry, and if I wasn't *there* my feet sure as hell wouldn't be cold."

*

The sergeant, strained to the screaming point by a batch of thick rookies, halted their drill and placed his hands upon his hips. With perspiration streaming down his face, he spoke in a tense and tremulous voice.

"When I was a little boy," he began, "my mother gave me some wooden soldiers to play with. A few days later I lost them. She said, 'Never mind, son, you'll get them back again some day.' Boy! I never realized until now how right she was."

*

Americans have always prided themselves on the resourcefulness of their soldiers. One young draftee was driving a car for a bachelor major who had a keen eye for a pretty girl. This officer saw a beauty walking along the sidewalk in the opposite direction.

"Turn the car around," he ordered quickly, hoping to offer the girl a lift.

The driver clumsily killed the engine and then had so much trouble getting it started again that the girl was out of sight before he could get the car moving.

"Soldier," snapped the major in disgust, "you would be a total loss in an emergency."

"No, I wouldn't, sir," replied the soldier. "That was my girl."

*

Two soldiers arrested in Times Square and charged with disturbing the peace pleaded Not Guilty.

The judge was not too anxious to bring pressure on two of Uncle Sam's defenders. "What about the officer's claim that he found you two fighting?" he asked.

"A pure optical illusion," replied one of the accused. "There is no doubt that he thought we were fighting."

"But if you weren't fighting," asked the puzzled judge, "what were you doing?"

"Trying to separate each other, Your Honor," was the prompt reply.

*

A new army draftee was loafing behind the barracks when his sergeant appeared.

"What are you doing here?" barked the three-striper.

"I'm procrastinating," answered the recruit.

"Okay," said the sergeant, "just as long as you keep busy."

*

An army doctor was examing a prospective serviceman.

"Sit down in that chair," ordered the doctor.

The reluctant draftee obeyed.

"1-A," exclaimed the doctor. "Next."

"Why, you haven't even looked at me."

"Well," the doctor explained, "you heard me tell you to sit down, you saw the chair, and you had enough intelligence to carry out the order. Move on, soldier."

*

A soldier parked an army jeep and started walking down the street. A policeman called after him, "Hey, buddy, drop a nickel in that parking meter."

"Put one in yourself," the GI yelled back. "That jeep belongs to you as much as it does to me."

*

It was his first tour of guard duty and the young recruit was a bit nervous. His orders were to admit only those cars which had a special windshield sticker. As luck would have it, one of the first cars he halted at the gate was a chauffeur-driven staff car with a high-ranking officer in the back seat and no sticker on the windshield.

"Drive right on in," the officer instructed the driver.

"I'm sorry, sir," the recruit said meekly, "but since your car has no sticker, I can't let you pass."

"Drive right on in," the officer instructed the driver.

"Begging your pardon, sir," the recruit said quietly, "but I'm new at this. Who do I shoot, you or the driver?"

*

An army officer was making his first trip in a submarine as an observer during a shakedown cruise. Walking past the engine room, he was amazed to hear loud cursing and blasphemy. The Army officer marched indignantly to the captain of the submarine and said, "Captain, I never heard such language in my life. What in the world is the matter with your men?"

"Major," replied the captain grimly, "this submarine has just sprung a leak. That swearing you heard is coming from the men who are trying to keep our engines running. As long as they're pumping and swearing, you're all right. But if you hear them stop swearing and start praying—forget it!"

Miser

A miserly man was approached by a friend who did his best to persuade him to dress more in accordance with his station in life. "I'm surprised," said the friend, "that you should allow yourself to become shabby."

"But I'm not shabby," said the miser.

"Yes, you are," insisted his friend. "I remember your father. He was always neatly dressed. His clothes were always well tailored and of the best material. Why don't you dress like him?"

"But," cried the other triumphantly, "I do. These clothes I'm wearing are Father's!"

Mistaken Identity

A college boy boarded the train, entered a sleeper, and tipped the six-foot porter liberally to put him off at Podunk.

"I'm a very hard sleeper," said the young man, "so don't pay any attention to my protests. Grab me and put me out on the platform."

The next morning, he woke up to find himself still on the train, which was steaming into New York. Furious, he found the porter and began to bawl him out in strong language.

"Sir," replied the porter calmly, "you've got quite a temper, but it ain't nothin' compared with the young fellow I put out of the train at Podunk."

Money

A businessman who belonged to a gym paid his monthly bill with a check. A few days later, the gym manager sent for him.

"What's the matter? Did my check bounce?" he asked.

"Did it bounce?" answered the gym manager. "Why, the boys are playing handball with it right now."

*

The French novelist Honoré de Balzac loved the good life. So when an uncle who was old and stingy died and left him a sizable sum, Balzac informed his friends of the good news in these words: "Yesterday, at five in the morning, my uncle and I passed on to a better life."

*

A lawyer was summoned to the bedside of a dying man who wanted to make his will.

"To my son Jim, in fatherly love," the old man began, "I bequeath ten thousand dollars—"

"Hold on there," interrupted the lawyer. "Your estate isn't worth more than three thousand dollars. Just how do you suppose the beneficiaries are going to get the money?"

The old fellow reared up indignantly in his bed. "Git it?" he shouted. "Let 'em work for it, same as I had to do!"

*

A man was complaining about how bad things were when his listener remarked, "Now, wait a minute. It can't be as bad as all that. In fact, if you ask me, you're doing all right for yourself. I saw you sitting at a sidewalk cafe recently."

"Sidewalk cafe, nothing!" came the angry retort. "That was my furniture after I was evicted!"

*

A successful businessman on his way to his office each morning passed on old man who, for years, had stationed himself on a midtown corner and sold shoelaces. The tenderhearted business-man gave the old fellow a dime every morning but took no laces. This had gone on for years. Last Monday morning, how-ever, the daily gift of a dime was extended, but the shoelace seller spoke up with more than just his usual "Thank you." Instead, he said, "I'm terribly sorry, sir, but the price of laces has gone up to fifteen cents."

*

A moviegoer standing in line for nearly an hour finally reached the box office. "That'll be two dollars," said the girl behind the glass.

Glancing at the sign Popular Prices over the box office, the customer grumbled, "You call two dollars a popular price?"

"Well," said the girl sweetly, "we like it."

*

A wealthy man driving his Rolls-Royce onto the George Washington Bridge in New York City stopped to pay the toll. After fumbling in his pocket, he told the toll collector, "I have no change."

"It's fifty cents," the toll collector said. "You have to pay."

"I told you I have no change," the fellow in the Rolls-Royce said. "How much do you want for the bridge?"

*

The lady in mink stepped out of the convertible at a very expensive Miami resort hotel and gave firm instructions. She wanted all of her suitcases removed from the car with care. She wanted special attention paid to her hat boxes. And she wanted her son carried upstairs to his room.

The doorman looked at the boy, estimated his age to be about thirteen, and said, "But, Madam, can't the child walk?"

The lady in mink replied, "Of course, but with our money, he doesn't have to."

*

A man who had become very wealthy through his own efforts was asked by a friend how it all happened.

"A lot of credit goes to my wife," the millionaire informed him.

"How did she help you?" the friend asked.

"Well, to be perfectly frank," the wealthy man replied, "I was curious to see if there was any income beyond which she couldn't live."

*

Two men were boasting about their rich relatives. Said one, "My father has a big farm in Connecticut. It's so big that when he goes to the barn on Monday evening to milk the cows, he kisses us all goodbye, and doesn't get back until the following Saturday."

"Why does it take him so long?" the other man asked.

"Because the barn is so far away from the house."

"Well, that may be a pretty big farm, but compared to my father's farm in Pennsylvania, it's no bigger than a city lot."

"How big is your father's farm?"

"Well, it's so big that my father sends young married couples out to the barn to milk the cows, and the milk is brought back by their grandchildren."

*

The *nouveau riche* manufacturer and his wife were having difficulty adjusting to a life of elegance. After the first dinner in their new twenty-five-room mansion, the husband turned to his wife and asked, "Shall we have our after-dinner coffee in the library?"

"It's too late," she replied. "The library closes at six."

*

Two successful, self-made businessmen who hadn't seen each other since their poverty-stricken childhood met at a party. One of the men smugly began kidding the other about his humble origins.

"Remember when you only had one pair of shoes to your name, Harry?" he asked.

"I sure do," the second man replied. "You asked me what they were for."

Mother-in-Law

The boss called his timid bookkeeping clerk into his office.

"Dinwiddy," he thundered, "you lied to me. You took yesterday off from work to bury your mother-in-law, and today I met her on the street."

"You misunderstood me, sir," stammered the frightened little man, "I didn't say she was dead; I only told you I'd go to her funeral."

*

The lady bather had fallen off the sand bar and she couldn't swim. Neither could the young man at the end of the pier. But when she came up for the first time and he caught sight of her face, he began to shriek. A burly fisherman ran up to him.

"What's up?" he asked.

"There!" cried the young man. "My wife! Drowning! I can't swim. A hundred dollars if you save her."

In a flash the fisherman dove into the sea. He came out with the rescued lady. Eagerly, he approached the young man again.

"Well, what about the hundred dollars?" he asked.

But if the young man's face had been pale before, it was dead white now as he gazed upon the features of the rescued woman.

"Yes," he gasped, "but when I made the offer, I thought it was my wife who was drowning. And now—now it turns out to be my mother-in-law."

The fisherman's face fell.

"Just my luck!" he muttered, thrusting his hand into his pocket. "How much do I owe you?"

Natives

A missionary was captured by cannibals and placed in a pot to cook. The chief appeared and began to speak in perfect English—the result, he said, of his Harvard education. The missionary protested, "You're a Harvard man, but you still eat your fellow man."

The chief replied, "Yes, but now I use a knife and fork."

*

An African chieftain flew to New York for a visit and was interviewed at the airport by newsmen.

"Did you have a good flight?" one asked.

The chief made a series of queer noises—*honk, oink,* screech, whistle, *z-z-z*—then added in perfect English, "Yes, very pleasant, indeed."

"How long do you plan to stay?" he was then asked.

Again the string of odd noises and the chief said, "About three weeks."

'Tell me, Chief," inquired one baffled reporter, "where did you learn to speak such flawless English?"

After the usual screeches and whistles, the chief said, "Short-wave radio."

*

There once lived a famous Indian chief who possessed a fabulous memory and could recall even the most trivial details long since past. A newspaper reporter, doubting this, once asked him, "Chief, I'll bet you can't tell me what you had for breakfast on June third, 1934."

Without a moment's hesitation, the chief answered, "Sausages."

Two years later, the reporter again had occasion to visit the chief and, approaching him, greeted him, "How!"

Without batting an eye, the chief replied, "Broiled!"

*

When the government engineers were first laying out the vast installations at Los Alamos, an inspector was sent to New Mexico to check progress. The first day there he saw a remarkably pretty Indian girl walk past, and he noticed that several of the engineers looked up appreciatively, too.

About a year later, the same inspector went out to Los Alamos again for a progress check, and again he saw the same red-skinned beauty. This time, however, she had a papoose strapped to her back. Tipping his hat, the inspector smiled at the woman, "Hello, there," he said, "I see you have papoose. Him little Injun, eh?"

The mother looked at him impassively. "Him only half Injun. Other half injuneer."

Neighbors

Every time the man next door headed toward Robinson's house, Robinson knew he was coming to borrow something.

"He won't get away with it this time," muttered Robinson to his wife. "Watch this."

"Er, I wondered if you'd be using your power saw this morning," the neighbor began.

"Gee, I'm awfully sorry," said Robinson, with a smug look, "but the fact of the matter is, I'll be using it all day."

"In that case," beamed the neighbor, "you won't be using your golf clubs."

*

A man entered a big store and made his way to the gardening department. "I want three lawnmowers," he said.

The clerk stared hard at him.

"Three, sir?" he echoed. "You must have a big estate."

"Nothing of the sort," snapped the man grimly. "I have two neighbors."

Newlyweds

Two new husbands were comparing notes about their wives' cooking. "I tell you, Bob," said one, "I never tasted anything like it. It's so awful that I have to make some excuse each night so I can get out to a restaurant for a decent meal."

"You think that's bad?" said Bob. "My wife's cooking is so bad that pygmies come all the way from Africa just to dip their arrows in her soup."

*

They had been married just two weeks and he was going through a batch of mail that had arrived that morning.

"Honey," he said, "aren't these bills for the clothes you bought before we were married?"

"Yes, darling," she replied. "You're not upset about it, are you?"

"Well," he retorted, "don't you think it's unfair to ask a fish to pay for the bait he was caught with?"

*

A pair of newlyweds just arrived in Puerto Rico stepped into their hotel elevator.

"Hello, darling," murmured the pretty operator.

There was a chill silence all the way up, but when the couple reached their floor, the bride exploded.

"Who was that hussy?"

"Now, don't you start," the groom said worriedly. "I'm going to have trouble enough explaining you to her tomorrow."

*

A newlywed bride was showing a friend the kitchen of her new seven-room house.

"We furnished the kitchen with soap coupons," the bride said.

"With soap coupons!" the friend exclaimed. "What about the other six rooms?"

"Oh, them," the bride replied, "they're filled with soap."

*

A cheerful bachelor met a newly married friend and stopped to congratulate him. He said warmly, "Well, Jack, I hear you have a very pretty and accomplished wife."

The newlywed nodded. "Yes, my wife is at home in music, she's at home in art, she's at home in literature, she's at home in science, she's at home bowling, in short, she's at home everywhere except—" His voice trailed off.

"Except where?" demanded his friend eagerly.

Replied the doleful husband, "Except at home."

*

The young husband of a few weeks had had a really hard day at the office, and when he arrived home that evening, he looked worn out. His bride was sympathetic.

"Darling," she said, "you look so tired and hungry. How would you like a nice steak smothered with onions, a green vegetable, some French fried potatoes, and some delicious pie a la mode?"

"Not tonight, dear," was the weary husband's reply. "I'm too tired to go out."

Normal

An advertising executive visited a psychiatrist and told him, "Doctor, I have never had an ulcer and I've never lost an account. I've never even worn a gray flannel suit."

The headshrinker eyed him for a moment and said, "I don't understand; what seems to be your problem?"

"Tell me Doctor," the ad man pleaded, "am I normal?"

*

A bank robber went into a bank and handed the teller a note reading: "Hand Over All Your Money; Act Normal."

The teller, a young intellectual, considered the note a moment, then wrote at the bottom: "What do you mean by Normal?"

Operations

Mr. Smith had just undergone his tenth operation in as many years. He seemed quite cheerful, though, when a fellow office worker came to the hospital to visit him.

"I don't see how you can be so cheerful after all those operations," said the friend, admiringly. "Did this last one give you much trouble?"

"Not too much," replied Smith. "I suppose I'm beginning to get used to it by now. Anyway, I don't think I'm going to have much trouble any more."

"What makes you think that?"

"Instead of sewing me up, this time they used zippers."

Optimists and Pessimists

Once upon a time, an Honest Man found himself answering the medical examiner as the latter went through a long list of questions on his family history furnished by the insurance company.

He told about his mother's death at forty-three of tuberculosis. At what age did his father die? "A little past thirty-nine." And of what cause? "Cancer."

"Bad family record," said the doctor. "No use going further," and he tore up the entry blank.

Determined not to make the same mistake twice, the Honest Man applied for a policy at another company.

"What was your father's age at death?" he was asked.

"He was ninety-six."

"And what did he die from?"

"Father was thrown from a pony at a polo game."

"How old was your mother at death?"

"She was ninety-four."

"Cause of death?"

"Childbirth."

*

An optimist and pessimist went into business. Business boomed and after the first month the optimist said, "We've had a wonderful month. It's been one constant run of customers."

The pessimist said, "Yes, we've had some good business, but look at those front doors. If people keep shoving through them, the hinges will be off in a week."

*

Fred Smith may well be the all-time champion optimist. He was sitting on the roof of his house during a flood, watching the water flow past, when a neighbor who owned a boat rowed across to him.

"Hello, Fred!" said the man.

"Hello, Sam!" replied Fred pleasantly.

"All your fowl washed away this morning?"

"Yes, but the ducks can swim."

"Orange trees gone, too?"

"Yes, but everybody said the crop would be a failure."

"I see the river's reached above your windows, Fred."

"That's all right, Sam," was the reply. "Those windows needed washing."

Organizations

A businessman handed a dollar bill to his youthful visitor, and in return got a card marked Associate Member from a local boys' club. "Now that I'm a member," he asked, "exactly what are my rights and privileges?"

The boy thought it over and said with a grin, "I guess it gives you the right to contribute again next year."

*

Jones belonged to an organization with many social benefits. Each person in the club was asked to buy a cemetery plot at a reduced rate—sort of a group plan so that they would have a place to live when they died. When the organization found that it wasn't paying off too well, they asked the president to talk to the delinquent members. Jones was the first to be called.

"You bought a plot twenty-five years ago," the president began, "and you haven't paid for it yet."

"I didn't use it," Jones answered.

"Who stopped you?"

Parents

A father said to his daughter, "Your boy friend approached me and asked for your hand. I consented, dear."

"But, Father," cried the girl, "I don't wish to leave Mother."

"I understand, child," the father said, "only don't let me stand in the way of your happiness. Take your mother with you."

*

The out-of-town student's mother asked her spouse, "Aren't we due to get another letter from that son of ours?"

"Yes," he replied, "we've heard from him once since he returned to college."

"That's what I thought. When did we write him last?"

"On the fourth."

"Are you sure?"

"Positive," replied the father. "I looked it up in my checkbook this morning."

*

Two fathers of sons in college were comparing notes.

"My son's letters always send me to the dictionary," said one father.

"You're lucky," said the other. "My son's letters always send me to the bank."

*

A young father was pushing a baby carriage in which an infant was screaming. As he wheeled the howling baby along, he kept murmuring, "Easy now, Donald. Keep calm, Donald. Steady, boy. It's all right, Donald."

A mother passing by said, "You certainly know how to talk to an upset child—quietly and gently." Leaning over the carriage, she said, "What seems to be the trouble, Donald?"

"Oh, no," said the father. "He's Henry, I'm Donald."

*

A man asked his friend for a thousand dollar loan. "I need it for a dowry for my daughter. I promised the groom-to-be two thousand dollars," he explained, "and I only have one thousand."

Said the friend, "Why not give the groom your thousand now and tell him you'll give him the other grand later?"

Said the father, "The thousand for later I got; it's the thousand for now that I need."

*

"How does your daughter like America?" a woman refugee was asked by a friend.

"Vunnerful!" the woman replied enthusiastically. "She married an American boy—he helps her wit' the house, he vashes the dishes, he stays wit' the baby when she vants t' go out—everything for her he does!"

"And how's your son doing?" inquired the friend.

"Oh, the poor boy iss terrible!" she moaned. "He married an American girl—he has to help her wit' the house, an' vash the dishes, an' stay wit' the baby when she wants t' go out—everything for her he has t' do!"

*

An irate mother stormed into the principal's office. "I demand to know," she screamed, "why my son Jimmy was given a zero on his English examination."

"Now, don't get excited," the principal tried to soothe her. "We'll get your son's English teacher in here. I'm sure she has some explanation."

A few minutes later, the English teacher arrived.

"Why did you give my son Jimmy a zero on his English final?" the mother demanded.

The English teacher said, "I had no other choice. He handed in a blank paper, absolutely nothing on it."

The mother was stumped for only a second. "That's no excuse," she shouted. "You could at least have given him an A for neatness."

*

An anxious father had been pacing throughout the night in a little waiting room just outside the maternity ward of a hospital. At long last, his wife's doctor appeared.

"Everything went just fine," he said reassuringly. "I know you wanted a boy, but I'm sure you will be just as happy when you see your beautiful new daughter."

The new father flashed a weak smile and replied, "Oh, sure, Doc! That's okay by me. As a matter of fact, a girl was my second choice."

*

A woman was boasting to her neighbor about her highly successful son.

"He lives in a beautiful apartment and wears expensive suits and he goes to Europe every year," she gushed. "Not only that, he goes to a fancy doctor, lies on a couch, and talks for an hour. And he pays him twenty-five dollars a visit."

The friend was impressed. "Twenty-five dollars an hour? What on earth do they talk about."

"About *me!*" the mother replied proudly.

*

Mrs. Smith went to visit her friend Mrs. Brown. When she arrived, she found Mrs. Brown putting up new curtains, arranging vases of flowers, and generally brightening up the place.

"Oh, Mrs. Brown," said Mrs. Smith, "are you going to have a wedding anniversary or something?"

"No," said Mrs. Brown, "we're going to have a celebration. My two sons are coming home from the penitentiary tomorrow."

"Coming home tomorrow? I thought they got seven years apiece."

"They did, but they got two years off for good behavior."

"What a blessing it is," said Mrs. Smith, "to have two sons who are so good."

Politics

In a Warsaw schoolroom, little Janek was asked to give an example of a dependent clause.

"Our cat has a litter of ten kittens," he piped, "all of which are good communists."

Teacher, delighted with his grasp of grammar and party line, urged him to do as well when the government inspector made his annual visit.

Next week, with the inspector sternly observing, teacher confidently called on Janek.

"Our cat has a litter of ten kittens," Janek piped, "all of which are good Western democrats."

Teacher cried, "Why Janek! That is not what you said a week ago."

"Yes," replied Janek very seriously, "but my kittens' eyes are open now."

*

A twenty-first-century teacher in Hungary was examining a pupil.
"What system do we live under?" he asked.
"Communism."
"What preceded it?"
"Socialism."
"Which is better?"
"I don't know."
"Communism, of course! Under socialism, you had to wait in line to buy meat."
"What's meat?"

*

The surgeon claims: "The Bible says that Eve was made by carving a rib out of Adam."

An engineer insists: "An engineering job came before that. In six days the earth was created out of chaos. And that is an engineer's job."

However, a politician asks: "Yes, but who created chaos?"

*

An American manufacturer was showing his plant to a prospective customer from an Eastern European country. When the noon whistle blew, thousands of men stopped work and hustled out of sight. The amazed visitor cried, "They're all escaping! Can't you stop them?"

"Oh, never mind," the manufacturer replied, "they'll come back." When the starting whistle blew, the visitor was again amazed to see the workmen returning to work.

"Now," said the manufacturer, as he concluded the tour, "I hope you have decided to buy some of our machines."

"Well, we'll talk about that later," said the visitor. "First, how much do you want for that whistle?"

*

It was during a terrific downpour in Washington, D.C., that a busload of tourists on a sightseeing tour passed the grounds of a large government building. One passenger, noticing that a dozen or more sprinklers were in action spraying the rain-drenched lawn, called out to the guide, "What in the world are those things on for on a rainy day like this?"

"Mister," replied the guide, "this is Washington, D.C. Nothing makes sense here."

*

A Russian peasant visited a zoo in Moscow for the first time.

The thing that surprised him most was finding a big bear and a little lamb in the same cage.

"What's that?" the peasant asked.

"That," said the guide proudly, "is peaceful coexistence."

The peasant still looked doubtful.

"Of course," added the guide, "we have to put in a new lamb every morning."

*

A Russian father was discussing his three sons: "I'm very proud of them. One is a people's lawyer and one's a people's doctor. But I'm proudest of all of my son who's in America. He's unemployed and gets money from the government—and if it weren't for the few dollars he sends home, we'd all starve."

*

A commissar for the people was rolling along in his car in the country near Moscow. Suddenly he noticed a man kneeling at the edge of a field, his hands folded, his eyes closed, his face up-turned.

"Why aren't you working instead of doing that?"

"But, comrade, I am praying to God for our leader."

"That's something! I suppose in the old days you used to pray for the czar."

"Yes, comrade."

"Well, look what happened to the czar!"

"Exactly!"

*

The government of a small communist country had just put down another attempted revolution, and now the defeated revolutionary leader was led before the firing squad.

"Do you have any last request?" asked the officer in charge, placing a blindfold over the doomed man's eyes.

"Just one," the unhappy revolutionary replied. "Use blanks."

*

A Russian big shot, making a tour of his country's grade schools, was impressed by the answers he was getting from one bright sixth-grade boy.

"What can you tell me about the United States?" asked the man from the Kremlin.

The lad answered, "The United States is a country where a few rich men dominate millions of poor people, most of them downtrodden, illiterate, starving, and stupid."

"Ah," beamed the Russian leader, "very good. Now tell me, what is the goal of Russia?"

"To catch up with the United States," said the lad.

*

Two Iron Curtain mountain climbers were hanging from a dangerous cliff by a rope. One appeared very frightened. The other said, "You seem afraid of the cliff."

Said the first man, "No, not the cliff—the rope. My factory made it."

*

A small Russian boy was asked by his teacher, "What is the size of the Communist Party?"

"About five feet, two inches," he promptly replied.

"Idiot!" exploded the teacher. "I mean how many members does it have? How do you get five feet, two inches?"

"Well," replied the boy, "my father is six feet tall and every night he puts his hand to his chin and says, 'I've had the Communist Party, up to here!'"

*

The American, English, and Russian doctors were discussing difficult operations.

"Brain surgery is the most difficult," said the American.

"Heart surgery gives me the most trouble," said the Englishman.

"I," said the Russian, "think a tonsillectomy is more difficult than either."

"Tonsillectomy?" said the other two in amazement.

"Yes," said the Russian. "People in Russia have to keep their mouths shut, and we doctors have to perform the operation through the ear."

*

A group of reporters was waiting for an interview outside the office of a senator campaigning for re-election. Suddenly the door flew open.

"Quick!" the candidate shouted to his secretary. "Where's that list of people I call by their first names?"

*

The senator had injured his eye while on summer vacation. His doctor treated it and then made a patch for him to wear over the hurt eye.

"You'd better wear this patch whenever you are exposed to a strong wind," said the doctor.

"Guess you'd better put it on me now then," said the senator. "I'm due on the Senate floor right away."

*

A comedian was in need of a straight man and was interviewing a young man for the job.

"I need a man who can keep a straight face throughout my performance and who will under no circumstances allow a smile to show on his face no matter what I say or do. Now what are your qualifications for the job?"

"Well," replied the youth, "I used to be a page boy in the House of Representatives."

*

"Senator, your speech was superfluous, simply superfluous," a woman admirer said.

"I'm glad you liked it," he said. And then he added, intending it as a mild joke, "I hope to have it published posthumously."

"Wonderful, just wonderful!" she replied. "I hope it will be soon."

*

It was during Franklin Delano Roosevelt's third term that a grammar-school pupil was asked how he was getting along with his studies. He explained that he studied just hard enough to get passing grades.

"Oh, that will never do," said his shocked aunt. "Don't you know that if you don't study very hard you will never grow up to be President of the United States?"

"I don't expect to, anyway," replied the lad, with complete lack of ambition. "I'm a Republican."

*

During the Huey Long administration in Louisiana, a politically inclined school teacher carried her political partisanship into the third-grade classroom. Asking a pupil to rise, she inquired, "Who gave us this beautiful school?"

Knowing who buttered his report card, the pupil answered, "Huey Long."

"And who gave us the wonderful bridge over Bailey Creek?"

"Huey Long."

"Who gave us our wonderful roads?"

"Huey Long."

Satisfied, the teacher then asked, "And who makes the grass grow and the flowers bloom?"

"God," said the student.

From the back of the room, a voice said, "Throw the damn Republican out."

*

The politician's name had been bandied about quite frequently in the press, and he was complaining to a friend about it.

"But I don't see anything wrong in that," declared the friend. "You're getting a lot of publicity out of it."

The politician wouldn't see it. "But half of those lies they tell about me aren't true," he protested.

*

A certain nobleman had a valet violently opposed to the capitalistic system. He devoted most of his spare time to attending meetings where he would listen while communistic theories were expounded. Suddenly, the valet stopped going to meetings, and after several weeks the master became curious enough to ask why.

The valet said, "At the last meeting I attended, it was proved that if all the wealth in the country were divided equally among all, the share of each person would be two thousand francs."

"So what?" asked the master.

"Well, sir," retorted the good man, "I happen to have five thousand francs."

*

A distinguished Hungarian economist who had just returned from a visit to the United States met a friend in a cafe.

"What did you study in the United States?" asked his friend.

"I went to study the death of capitalism," replied the economist.

"How did you find it?"

The economist replied, "What a wonderful way to die."

*

One evening after dinner, three doctors began boasting of their prize accomplishments.

"I grafted a leg on a man, and he later became a champion runner," boasted the first.

"That's nothing," said the second. "I grafted an arm on a man and he became a champion golfer."

The third doctor thought for a minute. "Hell, I have you all beat," said he. "I grafted a smile on a jackass and he became a governor."

*

The newly elected mayor was holding his first press conference.

Asked one reporter, "Will you consult with the interests that control you before making any big decision?"

"Of course," he deftly replied, "but why bring my wife into this discussion?"

Psychiatrists

The man brought into the doctor's office was hysterical and on the verge of a nervous breakdown. He apparently was an alcoholic and was suffering from an acute attack of delirium tremens.

"Get those red and white snakes away from me!" he kept shouting. "They're going to bite me."

The doctor turned to his nurse and told her to watch the patient while he went into the other room to get something for the man.

Soon the doctor came back and found the man completely composed.

"Whatever happened?" he asked the nurse.

"I just found his glasses," she replied, "and now he thinks they're barber poles."

*

Two psychiatrists met at a convention and fell to discussing their cases.

"One of my patients has a split personality," Doctor Lewis informed his colleague.

"That's not a very unusual case," replied the other doctor.

"This one is," Doctor Lewis explained. "They both pay."

*

A fellow awoke one morning and discovered lilies growing right out of the top of his head. He ran straight down to his psychiatrist's office. The headshrinker stared at the flowers. He said, "Why, this is fantastic. Now where on earth do you suppose those flowers came from?"

The guy yelled, "Look at the card! See who sent them!"

*

"Yes," concluded the psychiatrist, "you'll just have to forget your imaginary illnesses. Devote yourself to your work. In fact, it might be a good idea if you completely lost yourself in your labors."

"Then, again, it might not be," the patient replied. "I'm a deep-sea diver."

*

A man visited a psychiatrist and said, "Every time I step out of my apartment, there's a lion waiting to jump me."

The psychiatrist gave the matter some thought and replied, "Your mind is playing tricks on you, and you need psychiatric care. I suggest you come in for consultation three times a week."

The man did as suggested and visited the psychiatrist several times, then missed a visit.

The psychiatrist phoned the patient's home and, when the wife answered the phone, asked, "How is your husband?"

"Haven't you heard?" she replied sorrowfully. "When he stepped out of the door this morning, a lion ate him."

*

Two psychiatrists, one thirty, one seventy, were riding down in an elevator on a hot, sticky day. The young psychiatrist looked really beat.

He said to his older colleague, who was looking calm, cool, and quite refreshed, "I don't see how you can listen to those terrible, harrowing, heart-rending personal histories that your patients recount all day and still be so relaxed."

The elder analyst shrugged. "Who listens?"

*

A woman visited a psychiatrist and said, "You must help my husband. He insists that I always wear a seat belt."

The psychiatrist said, "I see nothing abnormal about that. Statistics show that seat belts help prevent serious injuries."

The wife said, "In restaurants?"

*

A man dressed as Napoleon visited a psychiatrist and said, "You can see I have no problems. I have the greatest army in the world, all the money I will ever need, and every conceivable luxury you can imagine."

The psychiatrist asked, "Then what seems to be your problem?"

The man said, "It's my wife. She thinks she's Mrs. Levine."

*

A visiting psychiatrist, wandering through the wards of a state asylum, was particularly intrigued by a patient who sat huddled in a corner all by himself, scratching himself for hours on end.

"My good man," the doctor addressed the patient gently, "why do you stay huddled in a corner all by yourself, scratching yourself?"

"Because," replied the man wearily, "I'm the only person in the world who knows where I itch."

*

A husband raced into a psychiatrist's office and shouted, "Doc, you've got to help me. My wife thinks she's Brigitte Bardot."

The headshrinker thought for a moment, then told the fellow, "If you bring her in for treatments, I'm sure I can help her."

"That's wonderful, Doc," the man smiled, "but make sure your office is heated, because my wife always goes around in the nude, and I wouldn't want her to catch cold."

*

"I've lost all desire to go on," the man in the psychiatrist's office explained. "Life is just too fast, too hectic."

"Yes," the doctor sighed, "I understand. We all have problems. You'll need several years of treatments at fifty dollars an hour."

For a few moments there was complete silence, then the patient spoke: "Well, that solves your problem, Doc," he said. "Now what about mine?"

*

Two psychiatrists were comparing notes.

"The toughest case I ever had," said one, "was a man suffering from delusions of grandeur. For years, he had been telling everyone that he was waiting for some letters that would give him title to a diamond mine, an oil field, and a pearl bed.

"For five years I struggled through long and laborious daily sessions with him before he was cured. And then those damn letters started arriving!"

*

A man came to a psychiatrist and proceeded to unfold before the doctor his life story, covering his childhood experiences, his emotional life, his eating habits, his vocational problems, and everything else he could think of.

"Well," said the doctor, "it doesn't seem to me there is anything wrong with you. You seem as sane as I am."

"But Doctor," protested the patient, a note of horror creeping into his voice, "it's these butterflies. I can't stand them. They're all over me."

"For heaven's sake," cried the doctor, recoiling, "don't brush them off on me!"

∗

Two actors discussed their respective psychiatrists. One said, "My analyst is the strongest man in the world. He could destroy your analyst with one hand tied behind his back."

The second said, "That may be true—but my analyst can cure him of his obvious aggressions."

∗

A psychologist was giving a young man some personality tests. He drew a vertical line and asked, "What does this make you think of?"

"Sex," said the young man.

Next the psychologist drew a circle. "And what does this make you think of?"

"Sex," said the young man again.

The psychologist drew a star. "And this?" he asked.

"Why, sex, of course," the young man said.

The psychologist put down his pencil. "In my opinion," he said, "you have an obsession about sex."

"*I* have an obsession!" protested the young man. "Who's drawing all the dirty pictures?"

∗

The psychiatrist was trying to reassure a patient who became terrified during thunderstorms.

"You must try to analyze your fears," said the psychiatrist. "The chance of lightning hitting you is only one in thousands. Much of our fear of being hit is egotism! We think we are important enough for Nature to go out of its way to hit us."

Just then a big bolt hit close by, followed by a terrific crash. Both patient and psychiatrist ducked under the couch.

"See," quavered the psychiatrist, "that's Nature for you."

∗

A psychiatrist told a patient: "Ridiculous that you should still be frightened of thunder at your age. Thunder is a mere natural phenomenon. Now the next time it storms and you hear a couple of claps of thunder, just do as I do—put your head under a pillow and stuff your ears until the thunder goes away."

*

A woman visited a psychiatrist and said, "Doctor, you must help my husband. He thinks he's a steam radiator and sits under the living-room window all the time."

The psychiatrist said, "Bring him in tomorrow and I'll cure him."

The wife said, "No, Doctor, we need the heat. Just stop his pipes from rattling."

Psychology

A businessman had to go to New York to attend a conference. His wife stated her desire to accompany him.

"But I'll be tied up nearly all the time," he protested. "You wouldn't enjoy going at all."

"Oh, yes, I would," said his wife. "I'll spend my time buying clothes."

"What! Go all the way to New York for a few clothes? That's silly—you can buy everything you want right here at home!"

"Oh, good!" she cried. "That's just what I hoped you'd say!"

*

After the college boy delivered the telegram, the man at the door asked, "What is the usual tip for a delivery?"

"Well," replied the youth, "this is my first trip here, but the other fellows say that if I get a dime out of you, I'm doing great."

"Is that so?" snorted the man. "Well, just to show them how wrong they are, here's a dollar."

"Thanks," replied the messenger. "I'll put this in my school fund."

"What are you studying?" asked the man.

The lad smiled and said, "Applied psychology."

*

While the child psychologist was studying some reports, his small daughter played with the girl who lived next door.

Suddenly his daughter gave the girl a violent shove, and she fell to the floor. Before the psychologist could scold her, his daughter turned to him and asked innocently, "Tell me, Daddy, why did I do that?"

*

The senator needed a secretary. The interviewing psychologist invited him down to watch the examination of candidates for the job. The psychologist called in the first girl and asked, "What's two and two?" Her answer was prompt: "Four."

The second girl thought for a moment, suspecting a catch, and said, "Twenty-two."

The last applicant answered, "Four, but it could be twenty-two."

After they had gone, the psychologist said to the senator. "The tests were very revealing. The first girl had a conventional mind: To her, two and two is always four. The second girl has imagination: She realized it might be twenty-two. The third girl is a combination of both: She's practical and has imagination. Clearly she will make the best secretary. Now, which would you like?"

Without hesitation, the senator replied, "The one in the tight sweater."

*

The stylishly dressed girl in the waiting room nervously flipped through the fashion pages of the women's magazines, looking at the angular models and their exaggerated poses as they showed the new high-style gowns and coats.

"What seems to be your trouble?" asked the doctor, ushering her into his office.

"Well," she explained, "I went shopping for some new clothes and, to my surprise, everything fits me without alteration—just as the clothes looked on the models."

"So," said the doctor, "what's so wrong about that?"

"I know this sounds silly," she replied, "but what I worry about is this—am I deformed?"

$\mathcal{R}$*eligion*

One Sunday morning, an earnest clergyman was exhorting those who had troubled consciences to be sure and call on him for guidance and prayer.

"To show you, my brethren, the blessed results of such visits," said he proudly, "I may say to you that only yesterday a man of wealth called on me for counsel and instruction. And today, my friends, he sits among us, not only a Christian, but a happy husband and father."

A stifled whisper: "Pretty quick work!"

*

A Jewish boy who attended Notre Dame returned home for vacation and ran into his family's rabbi. They talked for a while and the rabbi asked, "They aren't trying to Catholicize you at Notre Dame, are they?"

"No, Father," said the student.

*

A widow consulted a medium, who put her into communication with her late husband.

"Peter," said the woman, "are you happy now?"

"I am very happy," replied the spirit of Peter.

"Are you happier than you were on earth with me?"

"Yes, I am far happier than I was on earth with you."

"Tell me, Peter, what is it like in heaven?" asked the woman.

"Heaven!" exclaimed Peter. "I'm not in heaven!"

*

An enthusiastic golfer died and found himself before the Pearly Gates. Being of a cautious disposition, he thought he would do some investigating before entering the Celestial City. He approached Saint Peter and inquired, "Do you have any links in heaven?"

Saint Peter shook his head. He seemed never to have heard of them.

"No links!" exclaimed the golfer. "You must surely have a golf course. Why, you're not up-to-date at all."

And he turned sadly away to try his luck in hell.

Coming to the domains ruled by Satan, he was welcomed by an imp.

"Do you have a golf course here?" he inquired.

"Certainly," the imp replied. "We have all the modern conveniences."

The golfer's face lit up. Here, evidently, was the abode for him. "Lead me to it," he urged.

"Yes, sir, right this way, sir," said the imp and led him to a distant part of hell. Before the golfer stretched a course more wonderful than any he had ever seen or dreamed of.

"Fine!" he exclaimed. "Now, son, get me some sticks and balls, and I'll have the game of my life."

"We haven't any," the imp replied.

"What?" exclaimed the golfer. "No clubs and balls with a fine course like this?"

"No, sir," replied the imp, grinning fiendishly, "that's the hell of it."

*

A man dreamed that he had died and had found himself in a vast expanse where he was exceedingly comfortable. He rested for a while and then, becoming bored, shouted out, "Is there anybody here?"

In a moment, a white-robed attendant appeared and asked, "What do you want?"

"What can I have?" was the answer.

"You can have anything you want," replied the attendant.

"Well, bring me something to eat."

"What do you want to eat?" asked the attendant. "You can have anything you want."

And so they brought him just what he wanted, and he ate and slept and had a glorious time. He went on getting everything he wanted whenever he asked for it, but at last he grew bored and summoned the attendant and said, "I want something to do."

"I am sorry, but that is the only thing we cannot give you here."

And the man said, "I am sick and tired of it all. I'd rather go to hell!"

"Where do you think you are?" exclaimed the attendant.

*

A clergyman was sitting on a park bench reading a book when a seedy-looking individual came up to him and, in a belligerent tone, said, "I don't believe in heaven. There is no such place."

The clergyman went right on reading his book. The nuisance tapped him on the shoulder. "I repeat," he said, "there is no such place as heaven."

"All right, all right," replied the clergyman. "Go to hell, then."

*

A man dreamed that he died and went to heaven. At six o'clock in the morning, they put him to work shining the Pearly Gates, the stars, cleaning up heaven right and left. He had to work till six o'clock at night. After several days of this, he could stand it no longer and asked if he could take a rest. He was given two days off. So he decided he'd visit purgatory and see what it was like down there. He wanted to know if they worked as hard as he did in heaven. He arrived at purgatory at nine o'clock in the morning, and everybody was just sitting around doing nothing.

"I don't get it," he said to an attendant. "I'm up in heaven. And what happens to me? They work me steady from six in the morning till six at night every day. And down here where things are supposed to be so much tougher, you're all sitting around at nine o'clock in the morning doing nothing."

"It's easy to explain," said the attendant. "You see, there are more of us down here, so we get finished sooner."

*

The bus overturned, killing all the women returning from the church workers' convention. An embarrassed Saint Peter greeted them at the Pearly Gates, explaining that heaven was full, and he'd have to put them up in hell until the new subdivision was completed.

Three weeks later, a frantic Satan called Peter, begging that he take the women back.

"But I'm still having housing troubles," Saint Peter replied.

"Troubles? You don't know what trouble is!" Satan roared. "With their cake bakes, rummage sales, and bazaars, do you know those women are only forty dollars short of air conditioning this place?"

*

When family prayers were over one evening, an earnest mother was confronted by her five-year-old son.

"What's eternal life?" he demanded.

So she sat down and tried to explain to him as simply as she could what eternal life means. Finally, she said, "Now do you understand?"

He drew a long breath. "No, Mother, I don't understand it, but to be on the safe side, I'll believe it."

*

Father O'Malley met one of his parishioners on the street one day. After exchanging greetings, the lady asked him, "Father, is it a sin for my husband to play golf on Sunday?"

With a twinkle in his eye, Father O'Malley answered without hesitation, "The kind of golf he plays is a sin any day of the week."

*

"I've been racking my brains, but I can't place you," one man said to another at a gathering. "And you look very much like somebody I have seen a lot—somebody I don't like, but I can't tell you why. Isn't that strange?"

"Nothing strange about it," the other man said. "You have seen me a lot and I know why you resent me. For two years, I passed the collection plate in your church."

*

The preacher was delivering his sermon, and it was a highly successful one. He had just read the last line of the next to last page, when he discovered that he had lost the last page. The last line he read had been: "So Adam said to Eve—"

He carefully searched for the lost page and repeated, "So Adam said to Eve—" Then, forgetting that the amplifying system would carry the barest whisper to the last pew, he muttered to himself, "Good heavens, there seems to be a leaf missing."

*

A wealthy farmer decided to go to church one Sunday. After services, he approached the preacher with much enthusiasm.

"Reverend, that was a damned good sermon you gave, damned good!"

The preacher said, "I'm satisfied that you liked it. But I wish you wouldn't use those terms in expressing yourself."

The farmer replied, "I can't help it, Reverend. I still think it was a damned good sermon, and I was so impressed that I put a hundred dollar bill in the collection basket."

"The hell you did!"

*

The seven-year-old girl was supposed to draw the Nativity scene for the class. She did a fine job, complete with Jesus, Mary, Joseph, and all the scenery. But in one corner was a short, fat man who didn't jibe with the original. Asked to explain him, the girl answered, "That's Round John Virgin."

*

Two partners in the men's clothing business are discussing vacations.

Max says, "I'm going to Rome to have an audience with the Pope."

When Max returns, his partner says, "Well, what kind of fellow is the Pope?"

Says Max, "A thirty-nine short."

*

A bishop wanted to see a lunatic who believed himself to be God. So the bishop was ushered into the presence of a tall, benevolent-appearing old gentleman with a long white beard. The inmate asked if there was anything he could do for the bishop.

"Yes, there is something," the bishop said. "One question has bothered me from my days in the seminary. When you said you created the world in six days, did you mean six days as we know them, or six ages, or six eons?"

"Bishop," replied the venerable inmate, "I make it a rule never to talk shop."

*

A missionary, lost in the jungle, was beset by a lion. The missionary knelt in prayer, then looked up to see the lion on his knees, too.

"Brother," said the relieved missionary, "how delightful it is to join you in prayer when I feared you were going to eat me."

"Don't interrupt," said the lion. "I'm saying grace."

*

The weary chaplain, having made a five-mile forced march with a battalion of infantry trainees, dropped gratefully into one of a group of chairs placed around a table standing beneath shade trees on the side of the road. He'd removed one boot when a jeep braked beside him and a young lieutenant hurried over and said, "Sorry, sir. The general will be along any moment to inspect these troops. These chairs are reserved for the general and his staff."

"Son," grunted the chaplain, pulling at the other stubborn boot, "I'm on God's staff. And until someone comes along superior to Him, I'll not be moving."

*

At a prison in Ohio, one Sunday morning a group of inmates were being shepherded to the Catholic and Protestant chapels. One prisoner did not enter either chapel, but continued walking toward the main gate. When a guard caught up with him and asked where he was going, the prisoner replied, "I was told I could go to the church of my choice, and it's in New York."

*

A new minister chanced to ask an old member of the congregation what he thought of his sermon last Sunday.

"Excellent, sir," enthused the old gentleman. "It really was a revelation. Why, do you know, sir, I feel that I can say without fear of successful contradiction that we didn't know what sin was until you came here."

*

Mr. Cohen had made millions in the bakery business. When in Rome, he went to see the Pope and made a huge donation to the Church.

The Pope was very pleased and said, "Mr. Cohen, is there anything I can do to show my appreciation?"

"Why, yes, you can, Your Holiness," answered Cohen. "Could you make a small change in the Lord's Prayer?"

The Pope frowned. "Oh, Mr. Cohen, I'm afraid that would hardly be possible. The Lord's Prayer is repeated daily by millions of Christians."

"I know," said Cohen, "but couldn't you make just a small change? Where it says 'Give us this day our daily bread,' make it, 'Give us this day Cohen's pumpernickel bread.'"

*

A minister traveling for the first time on a jet seemed a little nervous. The stewardess asked if he would care for a drink.

"No, thanks," he said. "We're too close to the head office."

*

The main figure of this story is one of those people who accepts everything that happens as a manifestation of divine power. He never questions the workings of providence.

All his life, misfortune had been his, yet never once did he complain. He married, and his wife ran away with the hired man. He had a daughter, and the daughter was deceived by a villain. He had a son, and the son was lynched. His barn burned down, a cyclone blew his home away, a hailstorm destroyed his crops, and the banker foreclosed on the mortgage, taking his farm. Yet at each fresh stroke of misfortune, he knelt and gave thanks to God Almighty for His everlasting mercy.

After a time, penniless, but still pious, he landed in the county poorhouse. One day the overseer sent him out to plow a potato field. A thunderstorm came up and, without warning, a bolt of lightning descended from the sky. It melted the plowshare, stripped away most of the man's clothing, singed the hair on his head, and hurled him through a barbed wire fence.

When he recovered consciousness, he rose slowly to his knees, clasped his hands, and raised his eyes toward heaven. Then, for the first time, he asserted himself. "Lord," he said, "this is gittin' to be plum ridiculous!"

*

The minister was discouraged. He just wasn't getting results in his little church and was about to tender his resignation. He decided, however, to preach one more sermon and to make it his best.

That Sunday morning, he illustrated a point in his sermon by remarking that some flowers require much sunshine, whereas others, such as begonias, thrive in shady places.

The service over, a beaming woman approached the pastor. "Oh, it was such a good sermon," she enthused. "I can't tell you how I appreciate it."

"Thank you, thank you!" exclaimed the minister. "I was beginning to think I was not doing so well."

"Oh, nonsense," said the woman. "Just imagine, I had no idea why my begonias weren't growing."

R estaurants

Grimacing in evident distaste, the customer dropped his fork and called for the waiter.

"What sort of trash do you serve here?" he demanded. "Why, this food is absolutely poisonous."

Then he looked again at the plate. "And such small portions," he complained.

Revenge

The business tycoon was dying, and the priest hadn't yet arrived.

"John," he gasped to his partner, who was sitting by the side of the bed. "I want to confess to you. I stole that seventy-four thousand dollars from the safe. And I'm the one who told your wife about your mistress. And John—I sold our secret patents to our rivals for two hundred thousand dollars. And John—"

"That's okay," John whispered. "I poisoned you."

*

A scientist invented a serum to bring inanimate objects to life. One night, he decided to try it on the statue of a general in the park. Sure enough, the general gave a quiver and climbed down from his pedestal. The scientists was overjoyed.

"Tell me, General," he said, "what is the first thing you're going to do in your new life?"

"That's easy," rasped the general, whipping a gun from his holster, "I'm going to shoot about two million of those damned pigeons!"

Salesmen

"George is so forgetful," the sales manager complained to his secretary, "it's a wonder he can sell anything. I asked him to pick up some cigarettes on his way back from lunch, and I'm not sure he'll even remember to come back."

Just then the door flew open and in came George. "You'll never guess what happened!" he shouted. "While I was at lunch, I met old man Brown. He hasn't bought anything from us for five years. Well, we got to talking and by the time we reached dessert, he gave me this half-million dollar order!"

"See," sighed the manager, "he forgot the cigarettes."

*

When the traveling salesman left the hotel, he said to the owner, "Pardon me, but what are your mattresses stuffed with?"

"Why," said the owner proudly, "with the best straw money can buy!"

"That," replied the salesman, "is very interesting. Now I know where the straw came from that broke the camel's back."

*

Two New York manufacturers from the garment center decided to try something different for their vacations, so they joined a safari going to Africa. Somehow they became separated from their party. Undaunted, they wandered in the thick underbrush hunting for game. Suddenly, one of them thought he heard an animal behind him and yelled to his friend: "Hey, Seymour, I'm afraid to turn around. What's behind me, a leopard or a tiger?"

Seymour yelled back: "What are you asking me for? I'm not a furrier."

*

A department store advertised one hundred hats for sale at a dollar each, and the millinery department was soon jammed with women.

One woman finally struggled through the mass of squirming bodies, reached a clerk, and handed over a dollar. In her other hand, she held a hat.

"Don't bother to wrap it," she said, "I'll wear it."

"Don't you want a bag for your old hat?" asked the girl.

"No, thanks," the beaming customer replied, "I just sold it."

*

No one could figure out why Jack had opened a shoeshine stand. Maybe he really wanted to start at the bottom. But business wasn't good, and soon his competitors had all but ruined him. One day, Jack had an inspiration, and soon the customers were flocking to his stand. His luck changed immediately when he advertised: "One shoe shined free."

*

The salesman couldn't seem to hold his client's attention long enough to make a sale. Finally, he inquired about his client's problem.

"I promised my wife a Pomeranian," he replied. "The best price I can get is one hundred fifty dollars and that's too much."

Seizing the perfect opportunity, the salesman said, "It's much too much. I can get you one for seventy-five dollars."

"Terrific," beamed his client. "When can you deliver?"

"Just a minute and I'll find out." The salesman dashed out to a phone booth and dialed his office. "Listen, I've just sold a guy a Pomeranian for seventy-five dollars. What the hell is a Pomeranian?"

*

A famous art collector was walking through Greenwich Village when he noticed a mangy old cat lapping milk from a saucer in front of a store. The collector did a double-take when he saw the saucer. It was very old and very valuable. He sauntered casually into the store and offered to buy the cat for two dollars.

"Sorry, mister," the proprietor said, "the cat isn't for sale."

"Please," said the collector, "I need a hungry old tom cat around the house to catch mice. I'll give you ten dollars for him!"

"Sold," said the owner, taking the ten dollars.

"I was wondering," added the collector, "if, for ten dollars, you might include that old saucer. The cat seems to be used to it. It'll save me a dish."

"Sorry, mister," was the firm reply. "That's my lucky saucer. So far this week I've sold sixty-eight cats."

*

Two suspender salesmen were raving about their merchandise. One bragged that "the rubber in our suspenders is so good that fifty men took hold of each end of a single pair and couldn't pull the suspenders apart."

"That's nothing," boasted the other. "I was wearing a pair of my company's suspenders when I was trying to catch a train for New York. They got caught in the waiting room door. It took me two hours to get to New York, but the suspenders pulled me back to Philadelphia in five minutes."

*

A man living in the suburbs of Los Angeles worked in the advertising department of a large newspaper. One thing he had never been able to figure out was the deferential attitude of the children on his block. Out for a stroll one day, he came upon a group of little boys discussing the newest space launch. When he stopped to say hello to the kids, suddenly everything became clear. One of the boys asked in awe, "Are you really a space salesman?"

*

Two partners who ran a prosperous garment center business hired a new model. She was a beautiful girl from the country and extremely innocent. The two partners became interested in the model.

"Look," one partner said to the other one day, "since she's so young and pretty and innocent, she might be taken advantage of by some fast-talking fellow. I think we should take it upon ourselves to teach her what's wrong and what's right."

"Good idea," the other partner said. "You teach her what's right."

*

"I want to exchange these snakeskin pumps," a woman in the crowded shoe store told the clerk. "They are imperfect—see those scratches?"

The clerk agreed that there were some tiny scratches and

brought out another pair. The lady examined them carefully. "These are marred, too."

A few minutes later, the clerk returned with eight pairs of shoes. The customer thought she detected some flaw in each pair. "They're all imperfect!" she exclaimed as she discarded the last one.

"Madam," the salesman said wearily, "I'm not perfect, you're not perfect. How can you expect a snake to be perfect?"

*

An insurance salesman was having no luck getting one of his clients interested in buying a life-insurance policy. He kept calling the prospect at the office and at home. The client kept stalling, talking around the subject, and being unavailable whenever the salesman phoned.

Finally, the salesman caught him with a late-evening call to his home.

"I don't want to frighten you into a hasty decision," he said. "Why don't you just sleep on it tonight. If you wake up tomorrow, call me."

*

A man who had just begun his career as a salesman wasn't doing too well. His boss asked him to obtain a large order from a well-known buyer. So the salesman went to the buyer's office. Before he could utter a word, the buyer looked up from his desk and growled, "Well, what are you selling?"

"N-nothing, sir," the salesman stammered, "and my boss is raising hell!"

*

A traveling salesman pulled up in front of the farm house, hopped out of his car, leaped onto the porch, and rang the doorbell. A moment later, a beautiful girl with long blonde hair and big blue eyes answered his ring.

"Boy, I'll bet you're the farmer's daughter!" exclaimed the salesman.

"No," said the girl, "I'm his mistress."

*

Two shoe salesmen went to Africa to open up new territories.

Three days after their arrival, the first salesman sent a cablegram: "Returning on next plane. Can't sell shoes here. Everybody goes barefoot."

Nothing was heard from the second salesman for about two weeks. Then came a fat air-mail envelope with this message for the home office: "Fifty orders enclosed. Prospects unlimited. Nobody here has shoes."

*

A persistent salesman refused to leave when the secretary told him the boss was out. An hour passed, then two. Finally, weary of being a prisoner in his own office, the boss admitted the salesman.

"My secretary told you I was out," said the puzzled boss. "How'd you know I was in?"

"Easy," explained the salesman. "Your secretary was working."

Secretaries

An advertising executive who was swamped with work called his secretary.

"Look, Miss Smith," he said, "don't put through any calls to me this morning. I'll be incommunicado."

"Well, all right," the girl replied doubtfully, "but in case anything very important comes up, hadn't you better let me have your phone number there?"

*

A visitor at a Washington cocktail party was introduced to a secretary who worked in the Pentagon.

"Do you get nervous when you work with high government officials?" he asked.

"No," said the secretary, "I just think of them as other women's husbands."

*

As his secretary just could not seem to make it in on time, the boss suggested she see a doctor.

Armed with the pills the doctor had prescribed, the secretary went home, got to bed early, slept well, and awoke at dawn, feeling much refreshed.

She walked into the office five minutes early, beamed at her boss, and said, "I had no trouble getting up this morning."

"That's good," he replied, "but where were you yesterday?"

*

"Miss Welinsky," a chap told his new secretary firmly, "always add a column of figures at least three times before you show me the result."

The next day she came in with a broad smile. "Mr. Michaels," she said, "I added these figures ten times."

"Good, I like a girl to be thorough."

"And here," she said, "are my ten answers."

*

A secretary, returning from a coffee break, found her boss gazing dumbfounded into the file drawer labeled T-Z.

"Miss Smith," exclaimed the puzzled man, "where on earth do you keep the Zimmerman correspondence? This file drawer is completely empty."

"Zimmerman?" asked the secretary. "Let's see now, is that a company or an individual?"

"What possible difference does that make?" demanded her employer.

"Well, I should say it makes a lot of difference," bristled the girl. "I don't know whether it would be filed under D for Dear Sir or under G for Gentlemen."

*

Donna, a cute seventeen-year-old, was about to apply for a secretarial job. Naturally, she asked her friend Cathy, a secretary for several years, for some advice. "What should I say," she inquired, "if they ask what my job qualifications are?"

"The truth," Cathy counseled. "Tell them you can type fifteen words a minute—if the wind is with you."

*

The president of the company was showing a friend through his offices. They went past a series of small private rooms in which young men were busily hammering away at typewriters.

"These are some of our junior executives," said the company president.

"But they're typing letters," said his friend.

"Of course," replied the president, "I'm not so dumb. I can get a junior executive today for half the price I have to pay a good typist."

*

A congressional administrative assistant, who prefers to remain anonymous, says he heard a congressman tell one of his secretaries: "You've been here two months now, and I'm happy to say that your typing has improved considerably. However, it hasn't gotten so good that you can stop wearing those tight sweaters yet."

*

One by one, the vice-presidents of a large corporation were called into the office of the president and questioned. Then the junior executives were summoned. Finally, the office boy was brought in.

"I want the truth," the boss bellowed. "Have you been going out with my secretary?"

"No, sir," the office boy stammered. "I—I'd never do anything like that, sir."

"That's wonderful," said the boss. "Then you fire her."

Show Biz

A no-talent actor trying to get into a Broadway play for years had become a terrible pest. Finally, a kind-hearted producer told him, "I'll give you a one-line part in my next play, but promise me you won't hang around the theater. Don't come to rehearsal at all. Just come the night of the opening."

Thrilled, the actor went home and rehearsed his part over and over again. In his sleep he was saying: "Hark, I hear the cannon's roar."

Finally, the night the play opened, he went to the theater and with great anticipation got ready to go on. Then came his big moment. The stage manager pushed him onto the stage. He stood there motionless. Suddenly the cannon went off with a boom. The actor turned and exclaimed, "Hey! What the hell was that?"

*

An American comedian made such a hit in London that he was summoned for a command performance before the Queen. A palace aide spent a full day with him explaining the niceties of protocol. Even so, as the hour for the performance approached, the comedian seemed much too nervous.

"What's the matter?" asked the aide. "Surely you remember the few little things I told you?"

"I remember them all right," moaned the comedian, "but now I've forgotten my act."

*

A theatrical agent phoned an unemployed actor at his hotel and offered him a thousand dollars a week to play the lead in a TV series.

"Not on your life," replied the actor. "I won't do it for less than two thousand a week."

"Come down and we'll talk it over," urged the agent.

"What," shouted the actor, "and take a chance of being locked out of my room?"

*

A man met an actor just returned from a national tour with a stock company. He asked the actor how the tour had gone. The actor replied, "Not so good. When we played tragedy, the box office was a farce; when we played a farce, the box office was a tragedy."

*

An American tenor was nervous about making his debut in Italy. But when he finished his first song, he was gratified to hear the audience shout, "Again, again." So he sang it once more. Once more the audience shouted, "Again, again."

After singing the aria at least ten times, the tenor addressed the audience.

"It's a wonderful song, but haven't you heard it enough?"

A voice from the orchestra shouted, "Keep singing it until you get it right."

*

A press agent arranged for an audition with a well-known TV producer for his client, a talking dog.

The dog started with a joke or two, then went into an amusing political satire. The producer was really impressed. But the agent pointed out that his client actually wanted to be a singer. After several songs, the producer was convinced that he had found a gold mine.

Just then, a huge, ugly dog burst in, grabbed the little dog by the neck, and bounded out of the audition room.

The producer was wild. He demanded an explanation.

"That was his mother," the agent said dejectedly. "She wants him to be a doctor."

*

The master of ceremonies was trying to introduce a singer at a noisy teamster's convention, but he couldn't get it quiet. Finally, one of the men, obviously in authority, shouted, "Okay you guys, shut up. Let the man work."

Everyone quieted down. Suddenly the singer came from a side entrance singing at the top of his lungs. Without warning, a fist crashed into his face and an indignant trucker said, "You heard the boss. Shut up."

*

A man with a ragged coat and soup-stained whiskers applied to the manager of the dime museum for employment as a freak, and the following conversation took place:

"You look just like an ordinary bum to me."

"Well, I'll have you know, I'm more than an ordinary bum— I'm extraordinary."

"Who are you, then?"

"I'm Max, the egg king."

"What's your specialty?"

"I eat three dozen hen's eggs, two dozen duck's eggs, and one dozen goose eggs, all at a single sitting."

"Do you know our program?"

"What is it?"

"We give four shows every day."

"Yes, I understand that."

"Do you think you can do it?"

"I know I can."

"On Saturdays, we give six shows."

"All right."

"On holidays, we usually give a performance every hour."

"In that case, I'll have to have one thing understood before I sign a contract."

"What's that?"

"No matter how many performances in the day you've got to give me time off for my regular meals."

*

An impresario was interviewing the trainer of an act consisting of several performing mice of quite startling prowess. The mice could not only play a variety of tiny musical instruments, but they could sing in several languages.

The impresario was filled with enthusiasm.

"Why," he said, "this'll go over wonderfully here in Europe, but just imagine the impact on American television! And the clubs! New York! Las Vegas! Even Hollywood! We'll clear a million a year! When can you sail?"

"Sorry," said the trainer, "I'm afraid America's impossible for the act."

"Why you're crazy," pleaded the excited impresario. "Why ever not?"

"Well, there's just one difficulty. You see that one mouse second from the left who plays the guitar? He's a communist."

*

A man took his talented dog to a producer's office and put her through an hour-long routine of singing difficult operatic arias in perfect pitch.

But the producer said, "Opera singers are a dime a dozen. If she could only play the guitar and sing folk songs—"

*

Two showgirls were discussing a very successful theatrical producer. One girl rattled off a list of the hit shows he had produced.

"You know, Cynthia," she said suddenly, "I don't think he's ever produced a flop in his life."

"Oh, yes, he has," responded Cynthia. "I went out with his son the other night."

Shrewd

A customer at the delicatessen marveled at the owner's ability to handle figures. "What makes you so smart?" she asked.

"Herring heads," the proprietor answered. "Eat herring heads and you'll be positively brilliant."

"How much are they?"

"Thirty cents each."

The woman took half a dozen. In a few days, she was back. "Say, you charged me thirty cents for a head," she complained, "when I can buy the whole herring for twenty-five cents."

"You see," beamed the owner, "you're smarter already!"

*

Every day the Soviet factory was being robbed of vital materials. Finally, the commissars stationed guards to check every worker. A guard reported that one particular laborer departed each night with a wheelbarrow filled with sand.

For a month, the guards searched the sand for hidden valuables and found nothing. Finally, they challenged the worker.

"We will give you total immunity. You will not be punished if you'll just tell us the truth. What is it you're stealing?"

"You fools," the worker replied, "I'm stealing wheelbarrows!"

Smoking

Two men met on the street and one asked the other for a cigarette. His friend gave him the cigarette, commenting, "I thought you had quit smoking?"

"I'm just to the first stage," replied the other. "I've quit buying."

*

A man who was fighting the cigarette habit became so jittery that he left his job in mid-afternoon and started to walk home. On the way, he passed an automobile agency and saw a sports car on display. He went in, bought the car, and drove it off the floor.

As he was parking it in front of his house, his wife came out. "What's this?" she asked, pointing at the sports car.

"Well," he shrugged, "it was either that or a cigarette."

Sports

Watching a sandlot baseball game being played by very small boys, the stranger was quite amused to see the team in the field full of pep and ginger, although they apparently were taking a beating.

The stranger walked over to the first baseman, who was talking it up, and asked him the score. When he was told the team at bat was leading 18 to 0, the stranger wondered aloud why the team in the field wasn't downhearted.

"Downhearted," exploded the first baseman, "why should we be downhearted? We haven't come to bat yet."

*

A patient called his dentist for an appointment.

"So, sorry," said the dentist, "not today. I have eighteen cavities to fill."

Whereupon he hung up the phone, picked up his golf bag, and departed.

*

Son to his father who is watching a baseball game: "What are you watching, Dad?"

"Baseball."

"What's the score?"

"Six to three."

"Who's winning?"

"Six."

*

Few baseball characters have spawned more stories than Leo Durocher. One day, while managing the Brooklyn Dodgers, Leo was riding the plate umpire particularly hard on called balls and strikes. Along about the seventh inning, he raced from the dugout to the plate for perhaps the tenth time for another session over a called strike. Satisfied that he had made his point—and he had —Leo turned and walked back toward the dugout, muttering something just loud enough for the umpire to hear, but not for him to understand.

"What was that you said?" the umpire barked after him.

Leo turned like an actor on cue. "You've been guessing all day," he snarled triumphantly. "Guess again!"

*

The wife asked her husband, "Why don't you play golf with Frank any more?"

Her husband said, "Would you play with a fellow who puts down the wrong score and moves the ball when you're not looking?"

His wife said she wouldn't.

"Well," said the husband, "neither will Frank."

*

Some years ago when the New York Giants were playing an exhibition game with West Point at the Military Academy, one loud cadet sitting in the stands started to heckle Leo Durocher.

"Hey, Durocher," yelled the cadet, "how did a little squirt like you ever get into the major leagues?"

Leo's quick reply left the cadets' cheering section in stiff silence. "My congressman appointed me."

*

"Okay, men," said the football coach at the end of a discouraging practice session. "There's one more formation I want to teach you. It's pretty simple—everybody just form a circle around me."

The players gathered round. "Now start running toward the field house," he ordered.

"But, Coach," asked one player, "when will we need a formation like this?"

"If things go as I suspect," replied the coach, "it'll be needed after every game—to get me past the alumni."

*

It was the close of the season. The team had just lost again. The coach was despondently turning from the bench while a friend tried to comfort him. "After all, old man, your boys were always good losers."

"Good, hell," growled the coach, "they were perfect."

*

The golf match to end all golf matches was being played in heaven by Saint Peter and Saint Paul.

Saint Peter had the honor of the first tee and promptly made a hole in one. Saint Paul, undaunted, repeated the performance.

Saint Peter marked the scores down dutifully on his card, then remarked, "What do you say, Paul? Let's cut out the miracles and get down to business."

*

A minister was out golfing. He took a swing at the ball and watched it sail into a clump of trees. A moment later, a big bird flew up out of the trees, circled the ground, and dropped the golf ball in the cup. Looking upward, the preacher cried, "Father, please, I'd rather do it myself!"

*

A golfer was having a perfectly horrible day on the links. When he didn't hook, he sliced. When he didn't slice, he missed the ball completely. And each lie was worse than the one before.

Finally, on the eleventh hole, after missing three putts, he failed to sink an eight-incher. That did it!

He took all of his balls and tossed them into the brook. He broke three of his best clubs over his knee. There he sat by the hole on the eleventh green, crying—a perfect picture of total frustration.

"I've got to give it up! I've got to give it up! I've got to give it up!" he muttered over and over again.

"Golf?" inquired his caddy.

"No, the ministry."

Squelches

"Your wife tells me you didn't approve of the decorating job we did in your house," the painter declared to the seething homeowner.

"Well," was the controlled reply, "let's just say I can't make up my mind whether to pay you or have you arrested for vandalism."

*

The woman was berating her husband about the fact that their picture window had no drapes.

"Do you realize," she shouted, "that if I happened to be running around the house stark naked the neighbors could look in the window and see me? Do you?"

"Relax," said the husband calmly. "If the neighbors could see you stark naked, they'd buy the drapes."

*

The captain of the cruise ship was understandably irritated by the endless questions of one passenger.

"How far are we from land, Captain?" this human question mark finally asked.

"One mile," the captain said shortly.

"But that's impossible," the passenger protested. "I can't even see land."

"One mile," the captain repeated firmly, "straight down."

*

One night, at a gathering, Bernard Baruch was seated next to a bore who was monopolizing the conversation.

"Why don't you change your seat?" suggested another guest. "You know what a dreadful bore he is."

"I know," smiled Baruch, pointing to his hearing aid. "I haven't tuned him in in ten years!"

*

A girl's mother had opposed her daughter's marriage to a certain young man, but the girl went ahead anyway. The mother openly blamed her son-in-law for dragging her poor, innocent daughter to the altar, and missed no opportunity to make snide remarks about the marriage. Then the day came when the young couple informed her that they were expecting a baby.

"Oh, dear!" she wailed, looking at the young man with indignation. "First, you get married, and now this!"

"Well," smiled her son-in-law, "just be happy that it wasn't the other way around."

*

A missionary deep in the jungle came upon a witch doctor who was pounding his drum furiously.

"What gives?" asked the missionary, with some trepidation.

"We have no water," explained the witch doctor.

"So you're praying for rain?" ventured the missionary.

"No," snapped the witch doctor, "I'm sending for the plumber."

*

Insurance companies have discovered that people on the lower East Side of New York City live longer than they do elsewhere in the nation. So they sent a group of experts down to talk to the residents.

They found one man who was ninety-seven years old and asked him a lot of questions. Finally, they said to him, "Since you've lived here all these years, what would you say the death rate is in this community?"

"Well," the oldtimer declared, "I would say it's about one to a person."

*

A lawyer who prided himself on his vast knowledge of the law and a spongelike memory that soaked up and retained every bit of legislation was caught one afternoon carrying a number of law books under his arm.

"I thought you had no need for those things," a friend chided him.

"I don't," the lawyer said. "They're for the judges."

*

While a big-budget Western was showing at a movie theater in New York, two Indians were employed for advertising purposes outside the theater. Accosting one of the red men, an inquisitive woman asked, "You are a real Indian, aren't you?"

"Yes, madam," was the courteous response.

"How do you like our city?"

"Fine, madam. How do you like our country?"

*

The professor stepped up on the speaker's platform and, by way of breaking the ice, remarked, "I've just been asked to come up here and say something funny."

At this point, a student heckler in the back of the hall called out, "You *will* tell us when you say it, won't you?"

The professor replied, "I'll tell you. The others will know."

*

On a train during a tour of the United States, an Englishman fell into conversation with a Texan, who embarked on a long recitation of the wonders of the Lone Star State. "Maybe you didn't realize it while you were going through my state," the Texan wound up, "but all of Great Britain could fit into one corner of it."

"I dare say it could," said the Englishman dryly. "And wouldn't it do wonders for the place!"

*

George Bernard Shaw attended a dull party given by a society matron. After some minutes of tortured conversation, he retired to a corner. Spying him, the hostess rushed over.

"I do hope you are enjoying yourself, Mr. Shaw!" she gushed.

"Have no fear, madam," he replied wearily, "that's all I am enjoying."

*

Carol was a girl who couldn't help bragging about how men stumbled over themselves when they saw her.

"My dear," she confided to a companion, "I really do wish I could determine how many men will be made wretched when I marry."

Exclaimed the other girl in a shocked tone, "You're not thinking of becoming a bigamist, are you?"

*

There just wasn't any stopping him. Whether you wanted to listen or not he would pour streams of adjectives into your ear describing the unparalleled and exotic beauty of his girl.

"She's divine," he raved. "She just floated down from heaven and landed in front of me."

"Too bad," said someone who had been listening, "that she landed on her face."

*

A rich woman from New York was touring the West and finally arrived in Santa Fe. She noticed an old Indian with a necklace made from curious-looking teeth.

"What are those?" she asked.

"Those are grizzly bear teeth, madam," replied the Indian.

"Ah, yes," she nodded. "And I suppose they have the same value for you red men that pearls have for us."

"Not exactly, madam," replied the noble savage. "Anybody can open an oyster."

*

A father thought it was about time to lecture his young son, who was something of a scatterbrain.

"Jimmy," he said, "you're getting to be a young man now and I think you ought to take life more seriously. Just think, if I died suddenly, where would you be?"

"I'd be here," the kid replied. "The question is, where would you be?"

*

A cub reporter was sent to interview the town's Oldest Living Inhabitant, and of course the inevitable question came up. "To what," said the reporter, "do you attribute your long life?"

"Young feller," said the Oldest Living Inhabitant, "you can write it down that my secret of a long and healthy life is to eat some garlic every day."

"Ah," said the cub reporter, "but what makes you think it's a secret?"

*

"Can you give me a brief outline of the military campaign you've planned?" a reporter asked General Westmoreland once in Viet Nam.

The general peered at him intently. "Can you keep a secret?"

"Yes!" said the reporter.

"Well, so can I," replied the general.

*

"I notice you've got your arm in a sling," one man on the Florida Express said to another across the club car. "Accident?"

"No," said the second man, "I broke it trying to pat myself on the back."

"Well, well," said the first man. "What for?"

"For minding my own business."

*

He had been sitting next to her at the dinner table for the last hour and was admiring her beautiful arms and shoulders.

"Do you know," she said suddenly, "I've been in misery for a week. Sometimes I could almost scream with pain."

"Why, what's the matter?" he exclaimed.

"I was vaccinated last week and it has taken dreadfully."

His eyes fell and his gaze was curious, but he saw no scar. "Why, where were you vaccinated?" he asked.

She raised her eyebrows and smiled, "In New York."

*

The man who had been celebrating was returning home at dawn when he saw several policemen on the shores of the park lake.

"What're you looking for?" he asked.

"We're looking for a drowned man," was the answer.

The citizen thought this over solemnly and then inquired, "What d'you want one for?"

*

An elderly man complained to his doctor that he wasn't feeling well.

"I'm doing all I can to help you," said the doctor. "You know, I can't make you young again."

"I don't want to be young again," the man replied. "I just want to keep on getting older."

*

A bride and groom checked in at a hotel on their honeymoon and got a room on the twelfth floor. The groom turned on the water in the bathroom and forgot about it. The tub overflowed and flooded the room below. The man in the room below shouted and cursed at the top of his voice. The groom leaned out of his window and said, "Watch your language, sir, I have a woman up here."

The man below yelled, "Waadd'ya think I got down here—a duck?"

*

She was buying luggage for her husband. She kept coming back to a case made of alligator hide. Finally, she asked for the third time, "Are you sure this is alligator skin?"

"Positive," asserted the salesman. "In fact, I shot the alligator myself."

"That leather seems rather scuffed up on the side."

"That," the exasperated salesman blurted, "is where it struck the ground when it fell out of the tree."

*

"What flavors of ice cream do you have?" asked the diner.

The pretty waitress answered in a hoarse whisper, "Vanilla, strawberry, and chocolate."

Trying to be sympathetic, the diner said, "You got laryngitis?"

"No," replied the girl, with an effort, "just vanilla, strawberry, and chocolate."

*

A drunk fell out of a third-story window. Immediately, a crowd gathered.

"What's going on here?" shouted a cop as he pushed his way through the mob.

"I dunno, Offisher," hiccuped the drunk, "I just got here myself."

*

The only son announced his engagement.

"What? She's much too old for you," said Mother.

"She has red hair?" asked Auntie.

"I understand she is very fond of pleasure," said Grandma.

"She has no money," said Uncle.

"But she has one important quality," said the son.

"What is that?" asked the family chorus.

"She has no relatives."

*

A ferryboat captain shouted down to the crew's quarters, "Is there a macintosh down there big enough to keep two young ladies warm?"

"No," came the booming answer, "but there's a MacTavish here who's willin' to try!"

*

The nemesis of a large office of clerical employees was the office manager, an incorrigible braggart and pompous stuffed shirt who overlooked no occasion to dress down and humiliate an employee in the presence of the entire office for the pettiest of reasons.

One day, after a phone call from his wife, the office manager strutted into the office, chest puffed out in obvious self-satisfaction, and loudly exclaimed, "My wife's pregnant!"

After a moment of silence, a sweet young voice from the back of the room demurely asked, "Whom do you suspect?"

*

After an exciting whirl on the dance floor, the Don Juan of the small college town asked the pretty girl on his arm, "Do you tell your mother everything you do?"

"Of course not," she replied sweetly. "Mother doesn't worry. It's my husband who's inquisitive."

*

The club bore was boasting of his ability to distinguish between different beverages. Finally, one of the listeners took a flask from his pocket and asked the connoisseur to taste it and tell him what it was. The man tasted a mouthful and promptly spit it out.

"Great Scott!" he cried. "That's gasoline."

"I know," came the bland reply, "but what brand?"

*

A self-important stuffed shirt businessman came home from work one day more puffed up than ever. "I've just been made a vice-president of our firm," he boasted to his wife.

Thoroughly annoyed with him, considering all his previous boasts, she snapped: "So what? Vice-presidents are a dime a dozen. The grocery market where I shop, for example, has so many vice-presidents it even has one in charge of prunes."

The husband pretended to ignore his wife's remark, but it sorely bothered him. The next morning he decided to call the market to see if she was telling the truth.

He asked for the vice-president in charge of prunes.

"Packaged or bulk?" he was asked.

*

A very talkative woman buttonholed an angler who was reeling in his catch and said, "Aren't you ashamed of yourself? A big fellow like you might be better occupied than in catching poor little fish."

"Maybe you're right," said the fisherman, "but if this fish had only kept his mouth shut, he wouldn't have been caught."

*

A man had just bought a cigar in a department store and started to light it.

"Didn't you notice that sign?" asked the salesgirl.

"What!" exclaimed the customer. "You sell cigars in here but prohibit smoking?"

The salesgirl smiled sweetly, "We also sell motor boats."

*

A New Yorker was introduced to a man from California. Not hearing his name distinctly, he remarked, "I beg your pardon, sir, but I didn't catch your name."

"My name is a very hard one to catch," smiled the Westerner, "perhaps the hardest name you ever heard."

"Hardest name I ever heard? I'll bet you ten dollars my name is harder."

"All right," said the Californian. "My name is Stone—Alfred R. Stone. Stone is hard enough, isn't it, to take the ten dollars?"

"Pretty hard name," said the New Yorker, "but my name is harder." He paused.

"But what is your name? Let's have it."

"Harder—Thomas B. Harder."

*

Two fellows were discussing the fact that many girls' names were the same as the names of cities. Each came up with one, then another.

"Florence, Italy."

"Helena, Montana."

"Elizabeth, New Jersey."

"Indianapolis, Indiana."

"Just a minute. Indianapolis isn't a girl's name."

"Is that so? Do you know everybody?"

Strategy

A young couple who had received many valuable wedding presents established their home in a suburb. One morning, they received in the mail two tickets for a popular show in the city, with a single line: "Guess who sent them."

The pair were amused as they tried to identify the donor, but they failed to find out. They duly attended the theater and had a delightful time. On their return home late at night after the show, still trying to guess the identity of the unknown host, they found the house stripped of every article of value. And on the bare table in the dining-room was a piece of paper on which was written: "Now you know!"

*

A wealthy landowner in Ireland advertised for a chauffeur. From the letters of application, he selected the three most promising men. When they arrived for the interview, he took them to the top of a cliff near his home. He asked each how close he could drive to the precipice.

The first man boasted that he could drive to within a few inches.

The second man more modestly estimated he could drive to within a couple of feet.

The third man, nervous over the whole idea, gulped and said he wouldn't care to drive within a mile of the place. He got the job.

*

Timmy had only two pennies in his pocket. Undaunted, he approached the farmer and pointed to a luscious tomato hanging from a vine.

"Give you two cents for it," the boy offered.

"That kind brings a nickel," the farmer told him.

"This one?" Timmy asked, pointing to a smaller, less tempting specimen, which was not quite ripe. The farmer nodded agreement.

"Okay," said Timmy, and sealed the deal by placing his two pennies in the farmer's hand. "I'll pick it up in about a week."

*

He was the winner of many foot races and was boasting of his speed and achievements when the man sitting next to him interrupted.

"I'll race you any day," said the stranger. "And if you give me a couple of yards head start and let me choose the course, I guarantee you won't pass me."

The athlete looked at his challenger, a short and rather stout man, and laughed.

"I'll bet you twenty to one I'll win," he boasted. "Where's the course?"

"Up a ladder," replied his opponent.

*

An African tribe was having a terrible time with its crops. The natives went to the chief, who said: "What we'll do is send a telegram to the Russians telling them we are having agricultural problems and need their assistance. They will send us seeds and tractors and one hundred young technicians to help us. Then we'll send a telegram to the Americans telling them that the Russians are sending us seeds and tractors and technicians, and the Americans will send us seeds and tractors and one hundred technicians. When all the technicians arrive, we'll eat them."

Suburban Life

"I know it just snowed six inches," the defiant husband declared from his easy chair, "but a man's house is his castle."

"If you say so, dear," his wife gently replied. "But I think you should get out there and shovel the moat."

*

The suburban train was ploughing through the snow. After countless stops, it came to a dead halt, and all efforts to start it again were fruitless.

In the early hours of dawn, one of the passengers, numb with cold, crawled out of his compartment and floundered through the snow to the nearest telegraph office.

"Will not be at the office today," he wired to his boss. "Not home yesterday, yet."

Superstitions

A business executive was dining with his very private secretary in his hotel suite which was located on the thirteenth floor of a Chicago hotel.

Suddenly, there was a knock on the door. A woman's voice cried out, "Herman, I know you're in there with another woman. Open up, or I'll have the house detective break down the door."

The frightened executive cried, "That's my wife!"

"What shall I do?" asked the panic-stricken secretary.

The executive ran to the window, flung it open, and shouted, "Jump!"

"You must be crazy," his secretary protested. "We're on the thirteenth floor."

"Please!" pleaded her boss. "This is no time to be superstitious."

*

The professor was noted for his practical approach to life. He always insisted that there were logical and reasonable explanations for everything. Naturally, his friends were surprised to find a horseshoe hanging over the professor's door.

"Why did you put that horseshoe up there?" one of them asked. "Surely you don't believe that old superstition that a horseshoe will bring you good luck."

"Of course I don't believe it," growled the professor, "but I understand that it's supposed to work whether you believe it or not."

Tact

A swanky New York restaurant believes in tact, no matter what. One day, a customer walked in, sat down at a table, and tied his napkin around his neck. The maître d' was horrified. He took one of the waiters aside and said, "George, go over and make that fellow understand that that kind of thing isn't done here. But do it tactfully."

George thought for a minute, strode confidently over to the customer, cleared his throat, and quietly asked, "Shave or haircut, sir?"

*

A young man wise beyond his years paused before answering a widow who had asked him to guess her age.

"You must have some idea," she said.

"I have several ideas," said the young man, with a smile. "The only trouble is that I hesitate whether to make you ten years younger because of your looks or ten years older because of your intelligence."

Tall Tales

A farmer grew a crop of flax and then had a tablecloth made out of the linen. Sometime later, he bragged about it to a woman guest at dinner.

"I grew this tablecloth myself."

"Did you really?" she exclaimed. "How did you manage it?" It was plain that she had no idea as to how tablecloths came into being.

The farmer lowered his voice mysteriously. "If you promise not to tell anyone, I'll tell you."

The guest promised faithfully.

"Well," confided the farmer, "I planted a napkin."

*

A Houston millionaire owned six Rolls-Royces. A reporter who called on him for an interview inspected the estate and observed that there were only five in the garage.

"What happened to the sixth?" he asked.

"Oh, nothing," said the oil magnate. "Every thousand miles we send it to London for a grease job."

*

An important European lecturer, after delivering a speech, went to a bar nearby with a couple of newspapermen. In the course of the conversation, he began to boast about his expensive Swiss watch which, he said, never lost a minute and chimed each hour.

"That's nothing compared to American watches," one of the men said. "Why, I dropped my watch into the Mississippi River last year, and it's been running ever since."

"What!" said the lecturer. "The same watch?"

"No," said the newspaperman, "the Mississippi River."

Teachers

All the young ladies in the office were showering attention upon the handsome new employee. A long-married oldster looked on with sour disapproval.

One day, he cornered the young fellow and cautioned, "Don't pay them any mind—bide your time for some nice schoolteacher."

"Why a teacher?" asked the youth.

"She's the only kind of woman," replied the counsellor, "who can ask a question and then keep her mouth shut long enough to hear the answer."

*

It was evident that the pretty schoolteacher on the television

quiz show was a very nervous contestant. The master of ceremonies, seeking to relieve her tension, remarked kindly, "This
is just like school. After all, in school you know all the answers,
don't you?"

"Yes," replied the young woman, "but in school, I'm the one
who asks the questions."

Teen-agers

A tall, thin teen-ager had been sent to the principal's office for
fighting. Asked why she was always getting in fights, she said,
"As long as they call me 'Turnpike,' I'll fight."

"But why do they call you that?" exclaimed the principal.

"Not a curve in sight," said the girl sadly.

*

"All that criticism of the American school system in newspapers
and magazines is completely justified!" exclaimed a teen-age girl
just home from school.

"Do you really think so?" asked her mother.

"Yes, I do," replied the girl, "and if you want proof of how
bad it is, just look at the terrible marks on this report card."

*

The mother of a teen-age girl suffered through months of being
without the use of her telephone simply because her daughter
was always talking. Finally, in desperation, she gave her daughter
the ideal gift—her own phone. You can imagine her dismay when
she found her daughter engaged in lengthy conversation on the

family phone. "Susan!" she protested. "I gave you a phone to keep this line free. Why don't you use your own phone to call your friends?"

"Oh, I couldn't do that," replied Susan. "Then my line would be busy if somebody wanted to call me."

*

"Gee," said an enthusiastic young rock fan to her girlfriend, "do you know that some of those singers earn a hundred thousand dollars a year?"

"Do they?" exclaimed her friend. "Why, that's what the President of the United States gets."

"Yeah," snapped the first in disgust, "and the President can't sing a note."

*

The elderly bachelor moved into a house in a small town. He didn't realize it, but it was located on a dead-end street known as the local lovers' lane. One beautiful spring night, the bachelor went to bed early, but had a hard time getting to sleep because his dog kept barking. At last he went to the window, opened it wide, and called out, "Hey, Tiger, cut that out!"

The barking stopped, and through the stillness came a young man's voice, surprised but meek, "Yes, sir."

*

The young clerk asked his boss for a vacation, so he could get married.

"How long have you known the girl?" the boss asked the young man.

"I've known her for about ten days," was the clerk's reply.

"That's what I thought!" the boss exclaimed. "It's not nearly long enough to find out what a girl is like. I suggest that you wait a month or two—then, if you still want to get married, come and see me."

So in two months the young fellow was back in his boss's office to remind the old gentleman of his promise.

"Well, you still want to get married?" the boss asked. "I'm really surprised. These days, I didn't think kids stayed interested in the same girl for such a long time."

"I know, sir," answered the boy, "but this isn't the same girl— it's her sister."

*

Three men at the office were discussing what most people wanted in a new car.

"Dependability," said one fellow.

"Styling," declared another.

"Economy," said the third.

Just then a fourth man, who recently had bought a new car, entered the room. They decided to pose the question to him.

"What is the thing you'd like most to get out of your new car?" they asked.

"My teen-age son," he replied.

Tender Loving Care

A man walked along the street. He was moaning because of the pain caused by an agonizing toothache. He met his friend and asked what to do to relieve the pain. His friend said, "When I have a toothache or a pain, I go over to my wife, and she puts her arms around me and kisses and caresses me and comforts me till I forget all about the pain."

His friend brightened considerably. "Gee, that's wonderful— is she home now?"

Texans

A Texan had a small farm with just a few sheep. One day while his wife was dyeing some bedspreads blue, a little lamb fell into the bucket of dye. A passing motorist saw the lamb with the blue fleece and bought it for fifty dollars. So the Texan figured he had a good thing going and colored some more lambs, which brought big profits.

"Pretty soon," he recalled, "I was coloring them pink, blue, yellow, green, lavender, and you know—now I'm the biggest lamb dyer in Texas."

*

"Son," said a Texan to his offspring, "I just heard you asking that man what state he was from. Now, my boy, I want you always to remember this: if a man comes from Texas, he'll tell you; and if he doesn't, there's no need to embarrass him."

*

At the height of the tourist season, a huge Texan strode up to the desk of one of Miami Beach's most expensive hotels. He was followed by a caravan of bellhops, all of whom were carrying snowshoes, skis, ice skates, and other northern winter sports gear.

The confused clerk looked over the entourage and said to the new guest: "Sorry to have to tell you this, sir, but we never have snow here in Miami."

"That's okay, son," boomed the Texan. "It's comin' with the rest of my luggage."

*

A Texan was having dinner with friends in California when the conversation turned to talk about children.

"Someday when you're down our way," said the Texan, "I'd like to have you see my son's ranch. He's only sixteen, but he's already got himself a magnificent spread, and he earned it all—every bit of it."

Everyone wanted to know how a sixteen-year-old managed to earn a big ranch. The Texan replied, "By hustling. That boy," he drawled, "got two A's and a B on his report card."

*

An Easterner was being driven over a barren stretch of Texas by a rancher when a gaudy bird scurried in front of them. The Easterner asked what it was.

"That's a bird of paradise," the rancher informed him.

The stranger rode on in silence for a moment and then he said, "Long way from home, isn't he?"

Tipping

A man walked into a coffee shop during the lunch-hour rush, ordered a cup of coffee, gulped it down, left a dime on the counter and walked out. The waitress scooped up the coin and put it in her pocket—only to catch the cold eye of the owner glaring at her.

She hesitated a moment, then shook her head sadly. "What a screwball," she confided. "Leaves a ten-cent tip, then walks out without paying."

*

The meter registered just eighty cents for the trip from the railroad station to the nearest hotel. The cabbie received the exact amount from an obviously well-to-do passenger one day and frowned at the three quarters and a nickel.

"That's correct, isn't it?" asked the passenger.

"It's correct," replied the cabbie, "but it ain't right."

Tourists

An American tourist visiting London was being shown the sights by an English friend. They came to a park, and his friend pointed out an old cannon.

"We're very proud of this, old man. In the Battle of Bunker Hill, we captured this cannon from the Americans."

"That's swell," answered the American. "You've got the cannon—but we have the hill!"

*

An American in London had hired a guide to show him about the city.

"How long did it take to put that up?" he asked his guide as they passed a large hotel.

"Oh, about a year, I should say."

"A year!" exclaimed the Yank. "Why, it wouldn't take us more than six weeks to put up a building like that in New York."

They passed an office building which looked new.

"And how long did that one take?" asked the Yank.

"About six months," answered the guide.

"Six months!" said the Yank. "Now back home we'd build a place like that in less than a month."

Nothing more was said until they approached the houses of Parliament.

"Say, that's not a bad-looking place. How long did it take to build that?"

"Well, isn't that odd," replied the guide, "that building wasn't there when I crossed the bridge last night."

*

A Frenchman came to see America. When he returned to his homeland, he told his friends of the wonders of our nation and the hospitality of the people.

"Those Americans are the most generous people I have ever seen," he said. "You eat in the best restaurants—free! You ride around in high-powered cars and chauffeured limousines—free! You get beautiful jewelry—free! You get all the latest clothes—free! You live in a beautiful penthouse—free! I tell you, it's marvelous!"

"You mean all this happened to you?" asked his incredulous friend.

"Oh, no," he explained, "not to me—to my sister."

*

He had never been outside the United States and neither had she, but both were recounting their experiences abroad.

She bragged, "Asia, wonderful Asia. Never shall I forget Turkey, India, Japan—all of them. And most of all, China, the celestial kingdom. How I loved it."

He: "And the pagodas; did you see them?"

She: "Did I see them? My dear, I had dinner with them."

Travel

A woman from Washington who was making her first visit to Boston told her taxi driver that, despite the city's reputation for coldness, everyone she'd met had seemed friendly. "Yeah," said the driver, "they are—till ya get to know 'em."

*

Two Americans visiting Switzerland were discussing Europe. One of the Americans rather cynically said that there was nothing beautiful in Europe.

"Cathedrals are old and dusty; the castles are without bathrooms; the art is not beautiful and, for the most part, it is religious art, with none of the squares and circles that you find in our progressive American art; there is nothing beautiful in Europe," he said.

His compatriot, pointing to the Alps, said, "But don't you think Switzerland is beautiful?"

His answer was, "Take away the scenery and what have you got left?"

*

An Englishman was sent by his company to investigate the possibilities of drilling oil wells in the wilds of Venezuela. He had been there a few days and had become quite chummy with a man who spoke English well. He was uncertain, however, of the man's nationality. He might have been an American or he might have been a Venezuelan who had learned English.

One day, the Englishman asked the man, "Are you a foreigner here, too?"

The fellow gazed at him indignantly. "Foreigner?" he demanded wrathfully. "Hell, no! I'm an American."

*

A Russian traveler named Popov went to Poland and sent back a postcard: "Greetings from free Warsaw."

Next came a message from Czechoslovakia: "Greetings from free Prague."

Then he wrote a card from Hungary: "Greetings from free Budapest."

The final note from Vienna, Austria, said simply, "Greetings from free Popov."

*

The American traveler found an unpleasant insect in his railway compartment and wrote to the company with a strong protest.

He had not hoped that much could be done about the matter, but was somewhat mollified when he received a reply, couched in very courteous terms, expressing sincere regret.

His satisfaction was not enhanced, however, when he found a slip of paper, obviously left in error in the envelope by some railway clerk, on which was written: "Send this guy the bug letter."

Women

An explorer who had just returned from an African safari was describing some of his adventures before an audience of women.

"I suddenly came upon a tribe of wild women who had no tongues."

"What! No tongues?" exclaimed a few in the group. "How in the world could they talk?"

"They couldn't," he explained. "That's what made them wild."

*

A lady was telling her husband that she had put her first-aid lessons to good use that afternoon.

"I was crossing Main Street," she said excitedly, "when I heard a terrific crash. There was a man lying in the middle of the street. He had been thrown from his car. He had a compound fracture of the leg, a fractured skull, and was bleeding heavily. Quick as a flash, all my first-aid training came back to me. I sat down on the curb and put my head between my knees to keep from fainting."

*

A woman who had just finished a first-aid course saw a man lying face down in a flooded gutter. She rushed over to him, turned him on his back, and began to apply mouth-to-mouth resuscitation.

Suddenly the man sat up and pushed the woman away.

"I don't know what you have on your mind, lady," he said, "but I'm supposed to be clearing this drain."

*

The customer announced that she wanted to select three ensembles suitable for European travel. The alert saleswoman fitted her out with three complete wardrobes that included such accessories as hats, gloves, shoes, and purses.

The woman was delighted. After spending the entire morning at this pleasant task, she thanked the girl politely and said, "Well, those are just the sort of clothes I'll buy if my husband ever lets me go to Europe."

*

The housewife had put in a harrowing afternoon trying to balance her checkbook. When her husband came home, she handed him four neatly typed sheets, with items and costs in their respective columns. Listed were "Milkman, $11.25; Cleaners, $7.50," and so on.

Her husband was impressed as he glanced over the list, but he looked bewildered as he came to an item near the end: "ESP, $24.70." "What does that mean?" he asked.

"Oh," the wife said smiling, "that means Error Some Place."

*

A doctor met an ancient lady who claimed it was her one hundred eighth birthday. The surgeon was skeptical but the soul of cordiality.

"Well, congratulations," he said, "I hope I'll see you on your one hundredth ninth birthday."

"You will," the old girl cackled contentedly.

"I will?" he asked.

"Certainly," she said. "Very few people die between one hundred eight and one hundred nine."

*

A woman was trying to impress her friends at a party one afternoon.

"My family is very old," she said. "It dates back to the days of King John of England." Then turning to a woman sitting nearby, she asked condescendingly, "How old is your family, my dear?"

"I can't really say," replied the woman with a smile, "all of our family records were lost in the Flood."

*

"Julia, do you know what love is?" asked the young man intently.

"Yes," was the firm answer.

"But do you really know?" he asked again. "Have you ever been the object of an undying love as all-pervading as the air, as wonderful and sparkling as the stars? Have you ever loved and been loved like that, Julia?"

In an agony of suspense, he waited for her answer.

"Have I?" she murmured. "In my bedroom I have a trunk full of letters, a box full of photographs, and seven engagement rings!"

*

A successful but illiterate manufacturer who managed for years by signing his checks with two X's received a call from his bank.

"One of your checks came in today," a teller told him, "and it had three X's. Is it yours or is it a forgery?"

"It's mine," the manufacturer said. "My wife has social ambitions and thinks I ought to have a middle name."

*

A woman visited a divorce lawyer and told him that she wanted to leave her husband because he beat her and was cruel to their children.

The lawyer said, "He sounds like a real brute."

The wife said, "I came here to get advice about a divorce, not to hear my husband insulted."

*

A young miss presented a check to a bank teller for cashing.

The teller examined it, then said, "Can you identify yourself?"

The puzzled girl reached into her handbag and brought out a small mirror. For a moment she studied it, and then she smiled.

"Yes," she said, "it's me all right!"

*

A woman telephoned her friend and asked how she was feeling.

"Terrible," was the reply. "My head's splitting, my back and legs are killing me, the house is a mess, and the children are driving me crazy."

"Listen," said the caller, "go and lie down. I'll come over right away and cook lunch for you, clean the house, and take care of the children while you get some rest. By the way, how is Sam?"

"Sam?" the complaining housewife asked.

"Yes, your husband."

"My husband isn't named Sam."

"My heavens," gasped the first woman, "I must have dialed the wrong number."

There was a long pause. "Then you're not coming over?"

*

A wife was trying to persuade her husband to rent a beach cottage in Miami during his winter vacation instead of going on a trip to Canada.

"But you'll be stuck in the kitchen, cooking for the family," he protested.

"That's okay," she said. "All I want is a change of sinks."

*

During a bus strike, an attractive blonde was trying to get a ride to work. She wasn't having any luck, however, and was becoming desperate. A young man whose car was filled, seeing the trouble she was having, inquired, "Miss, why don't you try waving a white hankie?"

"Look, mister," she said, "I'm just trying to get a ride. I don't want to surrender."

*

A man spotted a young woman futilely edging in and out of a tiny parking space. Ten minutes later, thanks to his directions, the car was neatly parked in the space.

"Thank you very much," the woman said. "This is very nice, but I was trying to get out."

*

A movie star, loaded with jewels, was the last to leave the theater after a movie premiere. She noticed that one of the cleaning women was staring at her. Suddenly, there was a cry of "Mother!" and the two women rushed toward each other and embraced.

When the star, tears streaming down her cheeks, finally tore herself away and drove off in her limousine, the cleaning woman turned to her fellow workers.

"You gotta admit it," she said proudly. "My mother sure is a good-looking woman."

*

The young man waited patiently for the obviously expectant mother to finish with the drugstore telephone directory. After she had turned page after page, he finally said, "Madam, can I help you find the number you want?"

"Oh, I don't want a number," she replied. "I'm looking for a pretty name for my baby."

*

An elderly woman picked out two very handsome sweaters and mailed them to her son-in-law as a birthday present. Some weeks later, the mother-in-law paid a visit. Being a dutiful and peace-loving man, the son-in-law was wearing one of the sweaters when his mother-in-law arrived.

She looked him up and down and barked, "What's the matter, didn't you like the other one?"

*

A woman had given herself a fancy new permanent wave. Two of her neighbors were discussing the job after they had seen the results of her efforts.

"What do you think of it?" asked the first.

"Well, if you ask me," said the second, "it looks like her parole came through just as the warden pulled the switch."

*

The young couple had had their first quarrel, and for several hours neither would speak to the other. Finally, the husband decided to give in.

"Please speak to me, dear," he said. "I'll admit I was wrong and you were right."

"It won't do any good," sobbed the bride. "I've changed my mind."

*

The chic but blasé girl walked into the smartest department store in New York.

"I want a maroon flannel nightgown," she said.

The salesgirl was startled. "A maroon flannel nightgown—for someone as smartly dressed as you? I do not understand, mad-moiselle."

The chic chick shrugged. "You see, I'm getting married tomor-row and I've got to have something to surprise my husband."

*

Buying a magazine at a newsstand, a woman gave the man three dimes, and then took them back and paid for her purchase with a bill.

"I can't give you dimes," she explained, "because I have to save them for my flat tires."

"How do you change a flat tire with dimes?" asked the news vendor.

"Easy," the woman said, "I call the auto club."

*

"The nerve of that guy," protested the woman as she left the restaurant.

"Why, what did he do?" inquired her companion.

"He stared at me as if I hadn't paid my check," she replied.

"What did you do?" asked the other.

"I just stared back at him—as if I had," said the first woman.

*

A woman was fleeing a fire in her home. She carried a dog in her arms.

"Lady," a fireman called to her, "is your husband still in the house?"

"Yes," she said.

"Then why don't you get him out of the house instead of the dog?" demanded the fireman. "Do you want him to burn to death?"

"Don't worry, he won't burn," was the woman's nonchalant reply. "He's taking a shower."

*

A week after the robbery, a young wife called the police to report several valuable items missing. The investigating officer asked, "Why did you wait a week? When you found all of your bureau drawers pulled out and clothing scattered around, didn't you suspect a burglar had done it?"

"Why, no, Officer," she replied, "I just thought my husband had been looking for a clean shirt."

*

One of the guests turned to her hostess at dinner and said, "What a wonderful antique locket you're wearing. Does it contain some memento or family picture?"

Said the hostess, "It contains a lock of my husband's hair."

"But your husband is still alive."

"True," the hostess agreed, "but his hair is long gone."

*

During a bridge game, a shapely girl felt a foot run up and down the calf of her leg. She looked at the other three players, all men, and snarled, "If that's my husband, I bid three no trump. If it's one of you other guys, you're gonna get a punch in the nose."

*

At the amusement center, the woman in charge of the bowling concession noticed a young lady bowling first with her right hand and then with her left.

"Miss," she said, "you will improve your average if you just concentrate on one hand."

"Oh," replied the young lady, "I'm worried about my weight. I want to take some off this side and some off that side."

*

As they were entering a restaurant, two women discussed some acquaintances they had run into only a few minutes earlier.

"Did you see how pleased Mrs. Smith looked when I told her that she didn't look a day older than her daughter?"

"I really didn't notice," the other woman answered. "I was too busy watching the expression on her daughter's face."

*

The office beauty was regaling her bored companions with a tale of her adventures on the previous night.

"This fellow," she said, "took me up to his apartment and showed me a closet that contained at least fifteen absolutely perfect mink coats. And what do you know—he gave me one of them!"

"What did you have to do?" asked one of the girls skeptically.

"Just shorten the sleeves a little," was the reply.

*

An excited citizen waving a little black notebook rushed into the FBI office.

"I found this on the elevator," he shouted. "It's in code!"

The local FBI agent examined it and read: K1, P2, CO8," and so on. Putting the vast, intricate code-breaking system to work, he found that he couldn't break the code. He sent it to Washington for expert attention.

The young lady clerk quickly decoded it as follows: "Knit one, purl two, cast on eight."

*

A woman walked into a millinery shop and pointed out a hat in the window. "That red one with the feathers and berries," she said. "Would you take it out of the window for me?"

"Certainly, madam," the clerk replied, "we'd be glad to."

"Thank you very much," said the woman, moving toward the exit. "The horrible thing bothers me every time I pass."

*

"Hello! This is Mrs. Jones. Will you send over some nice cutlets right away?"

"I'm sorry, but we haven't any cutlets."

"Well, then a couple of nice lean chops."

"We haven't any chops either, Mrs. Jones."

"Oh, then a sirloin steak will have to do."

"We haven't any steak."

"For heaven's sake! Aren't you Smith the butcher?"

"No, I'm Smith the florist."

"Oh, well, send me a dozen white lilies. My husband must have starved to death by now."

*

An actress was making her first trip East, and her press agent made it a point to prepare each gathering she was scheduled to attend.

"Remember, boys," he warned a group of newspapermen, "she's an innocent little thing, easily startled. That's because she's so young and shy."

"She's shy, all right," admitted one of the reporters, "about ten years."

*

A lovely young motorist was speeding through the sleepy village when a policeman stepped out on the road and forced her to stop.

"What have I done?" she asked innocently.

"You were traveling forty miles an hour," replied the policeman, taking out his notebook.

"Forty miles an hour! Why, I haven't been out an hour!"

The policeman scratched his puzzled head with his pencil and then replied, "Go ahead, lady. That's a new one on me."

*

The bank was crowded with depositors waiting to draw out their money because a rumor had spread that the bank was in trouble. One woman waiting in line stepped out and approached the guard, saying, "Why is the line moving so slowly?"

The guard said, "Just be patient."

She refused to accept his advice and continued to annoy him. He said, "How much money do you have in the bank?"

The woman replied, "Who's got money? I'm waiting for a calendar."

PART
III
ONE-LINERS

One-Liners

ABILITY

Ability is what you need to get ahead if the boss doesn't have a daughter.

ACCIDENTS

Virtually all fatal accidents occur in traffic or at home, but most people won't stay out of cars or houses.

* * *

Most auto accidents occur when the fellow at the wheel refuses to let go of his clutch.

ACTING

Hollywood's best acting is done by stars congratulating Academy Award winners.

* * *

A Hollywood actress and her husband wanted to reconcile, but their lawyers couldn't see it.

* * *

There was an actress who was so dumb she should have been beautiful.

ADOLESCENTS

An adolescent is a discontented, confused teen-ager who will probably grow up to be a confused, discontented adult.

ADVERTISING MEN

Know what happens to kids who take two hours to eat a meal? They grow up to become advertising executives.

ADVICE

The trouble is—good advice, free advice, and bad advice are *all* expensive.

* * *

The trouble with good advice is that it usually interferes with our plans.

* * *

The hardest part of giving teen-agers advice is finding something they don't already know.

* * *

Advice is wonderful. Take it and you can make the same mistakes everybody else does.

* * *

It's when a man gets too old to set a bad example that he starts giving good advice.

AGE

If truth is beauty and beauty truth, how come all pretty girls lie about their age?

* * *

No one hates to hear a woman admit her age like her older sister.

* * *

Fewer women would conceal their age, if more men acted theirs.

AIRPLANES

Thanks to the tremendous speed of today's jets, you can have breakfast in New York and get to Los Angeles just in time to find out nobody's up yet.

* * *

On French airplanes, they don't show movies. They pass around French post cards.

ALASKA

The nights are so long in Alaska that some of the stores in Nome sell more pajamas than suits.

* * *

It's so cold in Alaska that when I was there, a snowman knocked at my door and asked for a hot-water bottle.

ALIBI
An alibi is what you use to explain that you weren't where you were.

ANNIVERSARIES
Anniversaries are like martinis; after you've had a few, you don't bother to count them.

APARTMENTS
Many of today's apartments have what are called "living-rooms." In the old days, they were walk-in closets.

*   *   *

In some modern apartments, the walls are so thin that you cannot only listen to your neighbor's TV shows, you can see them too.

*   *   *

The walls in my apartment are so thin that I recently asked a visitor a question and got three answers.

APPEARANCES
Appearances are deceiving—a dollar looks the same as it did ten years ago.

APPETIZERS
Appetizers are those little things you eat so many of you lose your appetite.

ARCHITECTS
It's remarkable what a good architect can do. He can make an old house look better just by talking about the cost of a new one.

ARGUMENTS
Isn't it strange how easily we can understand the two sides of any argument when it doesn't concern us?

*   *   *

After winning an argument with his wife, the wisest thing a man can do is apologize.

ASTRONAUTS

He would make a perfect astronaut. He's been fired from every place but Cape Kennedy.

* * *

I can't understand these astronauts. They go around the world a dozen times and don't come back with one hotel towel.

* * *

I wouldn't want to be an astronaut. As far as I'm concerned, there's no space like home.

* * *

Women would never make good astronauts. They'd all refuse to wear the same hat.

AUTOMATION

One of the great uncertainties of modern life is wondering what will replace automation.

* * *

Automation has a bright side. Look at all those new jobs which are created to keep track of the ones that are lost.

* * *

Automation is man's effort to make work so easy that women can do it all.

* * *

Automation hasn't cut out red tape. It just perforated it.

* * *

Automation has really progressed. Some computers are so human, they blame their mistakes on others.

* * *

I'll accept the fact that automation is here to say when I see a computer sitting on the boss's lap.

AVAILABILITY

Most girls find that the one quality they admire most in a man is availability.

AWKWARD AGE

Awkward age: That's when a kid is too old to cry and too young to swear.

* * *

Awkward age: When your daughter is old enough to have her own phone but too young to pay the bill.

BABIES

One of life's greatest mysteries is why a girl who has done a lot of baby-sitting ever gets married.

* * *

A man never wakes up his second baby to see it smile.

* * *

A baby-sitter is a teen-ager who gets a dollar fifty an hour to eat five dollars' worth of your food.

BACHELORS

A bachelor is a sportsman who plays the game of love and manages to retain his amateur standing.

* * *

A bachelor is a man who leans toward a woman—but not far enough to fall.

* * *

A bachelor is a man who has a cool head and cold feet.

* * *

A bachelor is a man who doesn't make the same mistake once.

* * *

Most bachelors have no idea of what marital bliss is. And neither do most married men.

* * *

Only good men stay single; they're too considerate to get married.

BARGAINS

The most difficult thing in the world is to convince a woman that a bargain costs money.

* * *

Bargain: A deal in which each party thinks he's cheating the other.

BATHING SUITS

Nowadays, when a woman is sewing tiny garments, it doesn't always means she's expecting a baby. She might just be repairing her bikini.

* * *

A bikini is like a barbed-wire fence. It protects the property without obstructing the view.

* * *

I spent a week-end at the beach and couldn't decide whether bikinis are getting smaller or girls are getting bigger.

* * *

With bathing suits being what they are today, the girls who complain they have nothing to wear are usually wearing it.

BEAUTY

Never marry a beautiful girl. She might leave you. If you marry an ugly girl, she might leave you too—but you won't care.

* * *

A beautician is a person who puts a price on a woman's head.

* * *

A beauty contest is an event where the judges crown the winners and the losers want to crown the judge.

BEHAVIOR

To really know a man, observe his behavior with a woman, a flat tire, and children.

BILLS

Try paying your bills with a smile. If that doesn't work, try money.

BIRTH CONTROL

I know a woman who took an aspirin instead of a birth-control pill. Nine months later, she had a baby who never got headaches.

* * *

Most of the people favoring birth control have already been born.

BIRTHDAYS
All some women want for their birthdays is not to be reminded of them.

* * *

A thoughtful man is one who gives his wife a birthday present without mentioning her birthday past.

BOARD OF DIRECTORS
A board of directors is a group of individuals who, as individuals, can do nothing, but who, as a board, can decide that nothing can be done.

BOOKS
A book is a success when people who haven't read it pretend they have.

BOSSES
A lot of guys who think their boss is dumb would be out of a job if he were any smarter.

BUDGETS
A balanced budget is when your earning capacity catches up with your yearning capacity.

* * *

A budget is merely a mathematical confirmation of your suspicions.

* * *

The trouble with the average budget is that it's hard to fill up one hole without digging another.

* * *

Some housewives carefully go over their budgets each month. Others just go over them.

BUSES
In buses today, old-fashioned chivalry is a standing joke.

* * *

Nothing makes a street corner colder than a crowded bus that doesn't stop.

BUSINESS

Business is what—when you don't have any—you go out of.

* * *

A businessman is a fellow who never discusses his business with his wife until she wants to buy something expensive.

* * *

Nowadays, to make a fortune, you have to come out with something that is low-priced, habit-forming, and tax deductible.

* * *

What with parking difficulties, household errands, and golf, it's almost impossible for a man to find any time for his business.

CALIFORNIA

California is a state that's washed by the Pacific on one side and cleaned by Las Vegas on the other.

CALORIES

Among the country's unmanageable surpluses are wheat, corn, cotton, and calories.

* * *

Destiny shapes our ends, but calories shape our middles.

CARDS

If you're lost in the woods, start playing solitaire. Someone's bound to show up and say, "Pardon me, but the red five goes on the black six."

CAREER GIRLS

A career girl is a woman who goes out and earns a man's salary instead of staying home and taking it away from him.

CARS

The only time some fathers get to use their cars is when they have to drive downtown to pay an installment on it.

* * *

If cars get any longer, parking lots will have to start charging by the inch instead of by the hour.

* * *

He's having trouble with his car. It won't start and the payments won't stop.

* * *

Compact cars are a threat to romance. It takes them too long to run out of gas

* * *

I figured out a way to avoid parking tickets. Remove the windshield wipers from your car.

* * *

It's estimated that the auto industry employs more than a million workers. Isn't it amazing that so many people can make a living from something nobody has paid for.

CHARGE ACCOUNTS

A charge account is what a woman uses to keep her husband from becoming too independent.

* * *

Remember the good old days when a woman occasionally retreated instead of continually charging.

CHEAPNESS

I wouldn't say he's cheap, but before he buys a round of drinks for the house, he makes sure he's the only one at the bar.

CHILDREN

Children are not only a comfort to a man when he reaches middle-age, they help bring it on.

* * *

What most children learn by asking is how to drive their parents crazy.

* * *

All a youngster wants out of school these days is himself.

* * *

Today's underprivileged child is the one who has to share the family car with his parents.

* * *

A problem child is one who puts two and two together and gets curious.

* * *

He comes from such a tough neighborhood that, when he was a kid, anybody who had all his teeth when he was six was considered a sissy.

* * *

All you can do about children these days is have them.

* * *

When he was a kid, they kept him in the refrigerator to keep him from getting spoiled.

* * *

Most kids only eat spinich so that they'll grow up to be big and strong enough to refuse it.

* * *

My child goes to progressive school. He's dating his teacher.

* * *

He grew up in a neighborhood so tough, the corner candy store had a bouncer.

* * *

When a child displays mature self-control—it's probably his mother's.

CHRISTMAS

Christmas is the time of year when both trees and husbands get trimmed. With a little luck, they both get lit, too.

* * *

Before Christmas, you receive cards from people you didn't send them to. After Christmas, you receive cards from people you did send to.

* * *

Driving a car on Christmas Eve is like Russian roulette—you never know which driver is loaded.

* * *

One good thing about Christmas shopping—it toughens you for January sales.

* * *

It's amazing how they put just enough after-shave lotion in a bottle to last from Christmas to Father's Day.

* * *

Funny thing about Santa Claus—he's got plenty of money, but he's always in the red.

* * *

Santa Claus comes down the chimney December 24, and he goes through the roof on the first of the month.

* * *

By the time a man has the shape for the job, his kids no longer believe in Santa Claus.

* * *

Some people's idea of celebrating the holidays is to have a Christmas they'll never forget and a New Year's they can't remember.

CIGARETTES
Once we talked out our problems over coffee and cigarettes. Now, they are our problems.

CLEAN
She never lines her shelves with newspapers. She doesn't want anyone to know when she cleaned them last.

CLERICAL WORK
Twice as many people are engaged in clerical work as in 1940. We may be more mixed up than ever, but at least we have a record of it.

CLOCKS
He who watches the clock remains one of the hands.

CLOTHES
Nothing puts a woman's clothes out of style quicker than her neighbor getting a new wardrobe.

* * *

Newest fad with the beachwatching set: imagining the girls with clothes on.

* * *

Remember when girls stayed home because they had nothing to wear?

* * *

If men dressed like girls, women would turn around and look, too.

* * *

If kids' clothes get any weirder, how will we know when the spacemen have landed?

* * *

The way the modern girl dresses, she is obviously a firm believer in "never leave off tomorrow what you can leave off today."

* * *

Some economists claim that women's hemlines go up when prices rise. This is a trend that bears watching.

* * *

Most husbands would like to have their wives wear their dresses longer—about two years longer.

* * *

Most women dress on the theory that a man can't think while he's looking.

* * *

Her dresses are stunning—when her husband finds out what they cost, he's stunned.

COLDS

Of the many remedies that won't cure a cold, whiskey is by far the most popular.

* * *

There's nothing like a bad cold to take your mind off your troubles.

COLLEGE

College applicants are being asked if they plan to concentrate on tests or protests.

* * *

Sending a youngster through college these days is very educational. It teaches his parents how to do without a lot of things.

COMMUNISM
A communist country is where the people name a street after you one day and chase you down it the next.

CONFIDENCE
Confidence is the feeling that you have before you really understand the problem.

CONFUSION
Nothing is more confusing to a man than driving behind a woman who does everything right.

CREDIT
Most department stores are willing to give a woman credit for what her husband earns.

*   *   *

Keeping up with easy credit takes plenty of hard cash.

*   *   *

What this country really needs is a credit card that will fit in a vending machine.

*   *   *

He figured out a way to cut down his wife's expenses. He hid all her credit cards.

CYNICS
A cynic is a person who thinks the only footprints in the sands of time are heels.

DANCING
If you really want to know just how ridiculous modern dances are —think of a monkey doing them.

*   *   *

Remember when African tribal dances used to look strange to Americans?

* * *

Some of the new dance steps are so wild that in some places they won't permit premarital dancing.

* * *

I went to a place that was so old-fashioned, the couples were dancing together.

* * *

Nowadays, when I'm in a night club and I see a man stumble, I can't tell whether it's a new dance or an old drunk.

* * *

It's funny that the people who like to live dangerously always seem to do it behind the wheel of a car.

DATES

Some girls break a date by going out with him.

DEBTS

Some people go into debt trying to keep up with others who already are.

* * *

There's only one way for families to stay out of debt, and most of them would like to know what it is.

* * *

He wants to consolidate all his debts so that he'll only have one bill collector to dodge.

DECEMBER

December is the month when employees everywhere are working their fingers to the bonus.

DEFICITS

A deficit is what you have when you haven't as much as when you had nothing.

DEMURE

She's the demure type—demure money he gives her, demure money she wants.

DIETING

Most of us don't know what poor losers we are until we try dieting.

* * *

She went on a banana and cocoanut diet. She didn't lose any weight, but she can climb a tree like crazy.

* * *

He went on a diet and lost so much weight that the battleship on his chest shrunk to a rowboat.

* * *

He has a sure fire reducing diet. He never eats when his wife is talking.

* * *

He went on a drinking man's diet. In only three weeks, he lost ten pounds and his job.

* * *

His idea of a balanced diet is a highball in each hand.

* * *

She went on a diet for a week and all she lost was seven days.

* * *

He went on a whiskey and vitamin diet. He didn't lose any weight, but he's the healthiest drunk in town.

* * *

The worst kind of reducing pill is the one who keeps on telling you how he did it.

DISAPPOINTMENT

The most disappointed people in the world are those who get what's coming to them.

DIVORCE

The only thing that can see through a man better than an X-ray is an ex-wife.

* * *

He gives her candy, furs, flowers, diamonds, everything but what she wants most—a divorce.

* * *

Last year there were a million and a half marriages and a quarter of a million divorces in the United States. The moral is: It pays to take a chance.

DOCTORS

Some doctors tell their patients the worst—others mail the bill.

* * *

Today, it isn't an apple that keeps the doctor away—it's his fees.

DOGS

If you think you have influence, try ordering someone else's dog around.

* * *

Did you ever notice how dogs win friends and influence people without reading books about it?

* * *

The reason a dog has so many friends is that he wags his tail instead of his tongue.

DRINKING

Isn't it funny that you never see a drunk spill a drink on another drunk?

* * *

The way the modern college students drink, tuition isn't the only thing that's high.

* * *

When it comes to drinking, he has wonderful self-control. He never drinks unless someone else is buying.

* * *

He's an antique fancier. He is particularly fond of anything that's aged in wood.

* * *

She drinks primarily as a beauty aid. She looks better slightly out of focus.

DRIVING

Drive as if you were early for an appointment with the Internal Revenue Service.

* * *

One-handed driving often leads to the church—either walking down the aisle or being carried up it by six men.

* * *

Watch out for Sunday drivers—especially those who started out on Saturday night.

* * *

He has his doubts about the driving school his wife is attending. The first thing they taught her was how to fill out accident forms.

ECONOMY

When a woman says she's going to economize, it means she's found a new place to spend money.

* * *

If all the economists in the world were placed end to end, they wouldn't reach a conclusion.

* * *

The role of the American male in our economy is to make almost as much money as his wife spends.

EDUCATION

Education is what's left over after you forget the facts.

* * *

If you don't think every American child is receiving a higher education, you're not a taxpayer.

* * *

Education is what you sometimes got when your father sent you to college, but what you always get when you send your son to college.

* * *

It won't be long before schools teach without books. Then, you'll really see some great football teams.

EFFICIENCY EXPERTS
Did you hear about the efficiency expert who really overdid it?
He put unbreakable glass in the fire-alarm boxes.

EGOTISTS
There are two kinds of egotists. Those who will admit it, and the
rest of us.

ELECTIONS
Elections are things that are held to see if the polls were right.

* * *

Things could be worse. Just suppose we had a presidential election every two years.

* * *

It's easy to pick out the conscientious worker on Election Day.
He's the one who goes to the polls during his coffee break.

ELEPHANTS
What do you get if you cross an elephant with peanut butter?
An elephant that sticks to the roof of your mouth.

EMOTIONS
He's so emotional, he cries when a traffic light's against him.

* * *

She's so emotional, she cries when a subscription expires.

ENERGY
He has so much energy, he gets around more than a virus.

ENVY
Every time you turn green with envy, you're ripe for trouble.

EXERCISE
If it weren't for the fact that the TV set and refrigerator are so
far apart, some of us wouldn't get any exercise at all.

EXPENSES

It's not difficult to meet expenses these days. I meet them every-where.

* * *

Few things are more expensive than a girl who is free for dinner.

EXPERIENCE

For every man who speaks from experience, there's a wife who isn't listening.

* * *

You can learn nothing more valuable from experience than not to rely on it.

* * *

There's no fool like an old fool. You just can't beat experience.

* * *

It's easy to pick out the guy who has no experience with women. He's the one who shows up early when he has a date.

EXTRAVAGANCE

An extravagance is anything you buy that is of no earthly use to your wife.

FAMILIES

The best way to keep the family together is to have only one car.

* * *

There are two ways to get old furniture—buy it or raise a family.

* * *

Definition of a family man: A guy who has replaced the currency in his wallet with snapshots.

FARMERS

A gentleman farmer is one who tips his hat to all the tomatoes.

* * *

In the United States, the farmer is the only one who can lose money every year, live well, educate his children, and then die rich.

* * *

A successful farmer is one who has the summer stock company held over in his barn an extra week.

FASHION

Why is it that women don't find mini-furs and mini-diamonds as fashionable as mini-skirts?

* * *

There are some women who show a lot of style, and some styles that show a lot of woman.

* * *

If her dress were any shorter, it would be a collar.

FENCES

Nothing makes a weathered picket fence look more quaint and attractive than being the guy who has to paint it.

FIGURES

Some girls have everything. The trouble is that it all settles in one place.

* * *

The only slim thing about her figure is her chances of getting it back.

FIRMNESS

Firmness is that admirable quality in ourselves that is stubbornness in others.

FISHING

One fellow is planning to manufacture glass-bottom boats so the fish can see how big the guy is they got away from.

FLATTERY

If you can't think of any other way to flatter a man, tell him he's the kind who can't be flattered.

* * *

Flattery is the art of telling another person exactly what he thinks of himself.

FLYING
In just a few more years, we'll be able to go around the world in three hours—one in the air and two getting to the airport.

FOG
It's so foggy in London that when English kids play hide 'n seek, they just stay where they are.

FOOD
He misses his wife's cooking—every chance he gets.

* * *

Accidents will happen. That's why there are so many different kinds of salad.

* * *

She served turkey for dinner and all the guests were tickled. She forgot to remove the feathers.

* * *

Doctors say you eat less if you eat slowly. This is especially true if you have a large family.

* * *

She's very sanitary. She doesn't even use a can of frozen orange juice unless she boils it first.

GAMBLING
Gambling is one sure way of getting nothing for something.

* * *

My luck is so bad that even when I'm cheating I can't win.

* * *

You never realize that a dog is man's best friend until you start betting on horses.

GARDENS
She took up gardening—and all she grew was tired.

* * *

When it comes to gardening, there's no better labor-saving device than a bad back.

* * *

Buying a load of topsoil is an educational experience. It teaches that while some things are dirt cheap, dirt isn't one of them.

GENERATIONS

Friction between the generations is inevitable. That's because the young and the old have all the answers, and those in between are stuck with the questions.

GIRLS

All it really takes to separate the men from the boys—is girls.

* * *

She uses her old flame to burn up her new boyfriend.

* * *

She's so short that she wears a mini-skirt as a full-length evening gown.

* * *

Scientists say that a duck is followed by ducklings because of the way she swings when she walks. Chicks have been followed for the same reason.

* * *

Have you ever noticed that a girl with bad legs never sees a mouse?

* * *

Considering the way some girls dress today, it's hard to believe that they really love clothes.

* * *

To get a man, girls should know how to play tennis, bridge, and dumb.

* * *

She showed him her new fall line—and he certainly fell for it.

* * *

Never try to change a girl's mind—let her have the satisfaction of doing it herself.

* * *

She's a home-loving girl—she wants a home in New York, Paris, and Rome.

GOLD-DIGGERS
A gold-digger is a girl who forgets all about the past and future and simply enjoys the presents.

* * *

A gold-digger is a woman who tries to take a man to the cleaners as soon as she spots him.

GOLF
Golf is like business—you drive hard to get to the green and then wind up in a hole.

* * *

Golf is no longer a rich man's sport. There are plenty of poor players.

GOSSIP
You know you're working for a large company when it takes a bit of gossip a week to get from one end of the office to the other.

* * *

Nothing is more annoying than to have someone refrain from telling you the piece of gossip you said you didn't want to hear.

* * *

Gossip is like a grapefruit. In order for it to be really good, it has to be juicy.

* * *

The trouble with inviting everyone you know to a cocktail party is that there's no one left to gossip about.

* * *

A gossip is a person who can leave bad enough alone.

GOVERNMENT
Any government that is big enough to give you everything you want is big enough to take everything you've got.

GRANDMOTHERS

Some grandmothers I know are so young they help Boy Scouts across the street.

* * *

Grandma may have worked harder as a housewife, but she never had to clean out the swimming pool, mix a martini, or get the power mower started.

GROWING-UP

You know she's growing up when she's dressing slower and spending faster.

GROUCHES

He's a real grouch. He'd complain about the noise if opportunity knocked.

HAIR

Years ago, some boys didn't get a hair cut until they were ten years old. Today, it seems that's their last one.

* * *

She's got long back hair running down her back. Too bad it isn't on her head.

* * *

Nowadays, a woman's first gray hair is usually her last one.

* * *

Today's boys let their hair grow so long that the only way you can tell the difference between the boys and the girls is to ask their mothers.

* * *

The reason so many modern girls wear hairdos that look like mops is because they don't know what a mop looks like.

* * *

With the new hair styles, from the back you can't tell if it's a man who needs a haircut or a woman who's had one.

HAPPINESS

Happiness is like perfume. Spray it on others and you are bound to get some on yourself.

* * *

Happiness is finding the owner of a lost bikini.

HEADACHES

Before television, no one ever knew what a headache looked like.

HEALTH

The best way to keep healthy is to eat what you don't want, drink what you don't like, and do what you'd rather not.

* * *

A man's health can be judged by which he takes two at a time—pills or stairs.

* * *

By the time a guy's successful enough to take several hours for lunch, the doctor limits him to a glass of milk and crackers.

HELPING HAND

The best place to find a helping hand is at the end of your own arm.

HEREDITY

Heredity is what makes the mother and father of teen-agers worry about each other.

HISTORY

One reason history repeats itself is that so many people weren't listening the first time.

HOLLYWOOD

It's hard to keep a Hollywood marriage secret. News of the divorce is bound to leak out.

* * *

Hollywood is where movie stars are marrying more these days, but enjoying it less.

* * *

I met an actress who does settlement work. Her lawyer sues and she gets the settlement.

* * *

I know a Hollywood couple who won't get a divorce until their son passes his bar exams. They want to be his first case.

HOMES

Here's a guaranteed way to make your home look better—go out and price some new ones.

* * *

I come from a broken home. My kids have broken everything in it.

* * *

Many a home has been "bugged" by miniature devices for several years. They repeat every word all over school, too.

* * *

One good thing about moving—you're not embarrassed when surprise guests drop in and the house is a mess.

* * *

A housewarming is simply the last call for wedding presents.

HONEYMOONS

The honeymoon is over when you're no longer drinking to her, but because of her.

* * *

The modern trend is toward shorter honeymoons—but more of them.

* * *

A honeymoon is the period between "I do" and "You'd better."

* * *

The honeymoon is over when the husband gets out of the car at a drive-in movie to wipe off the windshield.

HOUSEWIVES

Today's housewife has it easy. She only has to push a button to get her dishes washed. Her mother had to push her father.

* * *

The trouble with today's young housewife is that all she knows how to do is thaw foods. Why can't she be like her mother and open cans?

HUMAN NATURE

You can fool some of the people all of the time . . . and chances are if you're not careful you'll be one of them.

HUMILITY

It's not easy to be humble, but some of us have no choice.

HUMOR

One reason why there is so much humor in the world today is that so many people take themselves seriously.

* * *

A sense of humor is what makes you laugh at something that happened to somebody else which would have made you mad if it had happened to you.

HUSBANDS

Some women get even with their husbands by staying married to them.

* * *

When a woman butters up her husband, chances are she's preparing to put the bite on him.

* * *

The average man has probably thought twice about running away from home—once as a child and once as a husband.

* * *

The average husband prefers a clothes horse to a nag.

* * *

A truly henpecked husband is one who has more aprons than his wife does.

*   *   *

The average husband is thirty-six around the chest, forty around the waist, ninety-eight around the golf course, and a nuisance around the house.

IMPOSSIBILITY

Nothing is impossible to the man who doesn't have to do it himself.

*   *   *

There are only two things that are really impossible: putting toothpaste back in the tube, and getting off a mailing list.

IMPRESSIONS

If you really want to impress people, a Ph.D. isn't worth half as much as being greeted by name and getting a little salute from the cop on the corner.

*   *   *

She made a lasting impression on him. The doctors say the scar will never disappear.

*   *   *

You never get a second chance to make a good first impression.

INCOME

All most men want from their wives are affection, admiration, encouragement, and ability to live grandly on an inadequate income.

*   *   *

Every man's income runs into four figures—the real one, the one he reports to Internal Revenue, the one he tells his wife, and the figures she passes along to the girls.

*   *   *

Living on a small income wouldn't be so hard to do if it weren't for the effort involved in keeping it a secret.

*   *   *

He doesn't cheat on his income taxes. His accountant does it for him.

INFLATION
One of the benefits of inflation is that kids can no longer get sick on a nickel's worth of candy.

INSECURITY
His insecurities started when he was a Boy Scout. The little old lady he was helping across the street got run over.

INSULTS
The only gracious way to accept an insult is to ignore it; if you can't ignore it, top it; if you can't top it, laugh at it; if you can't laugh at it, it's probably deserved.

INSURANCE
With all of today's attractive accident policies, a man can't afford to die a natural death.

INTUITION
Intuition is what enables a woman to contradict her husband before he says anything.

JOBS
Some people try to hold a job by sitting on it.

* * *

He's a novelty worker. It's a novelty when he works.

* * *

He never puts off a hard job until tomorrow. He puts it off forever.

* * *

He got a job for a good cause—'cause he needed money.

* * *

The best way to keep a job is to get things so mixed up your first day on the job, the boss can't afford to fire you.

* * *

He's got a job where he works all the time. He's a picket.

JUNK
Junk is all that stuff that got in your way for ten years, which you threw away two weeks before you needed it.

JUVENILE DELINQUENCY
One day he went to school. He couldn't get a table in the pool room.

* * *

Juvenile delinquents in Texas are so rich they slash their own tires.

LANDLORDS
Guerilla warfare isn't new. It's as old as tenants and landlords.

LAWYERS
A lawyer is a guy who represents you just to make sure you get all that's coming to him.

* * *

If you can't get a lawyer who knows the law, get one who knows the judge.

LIBERTY
Liberty is the privilege of being free from things we don't like so that we can be slaves of things we do.

LIFE
Life is what passes you by while you're making other plans.

* * *

Life is like a crowded bus—it takes a sudden jolt for some people to know just where they stand.

* * *

Live your life so that you wouldn't be afraid to sell your parrot to the town gossip.

LIQUOR

Liquor is the stuff that can make your world go round.

* * *

When you think about all the booze that's guzzled, it staggers the imagination.

* * *

People who complain that Americans spend more money for liquor than education don't realize what you can learn at a cocktail party.

* * *

The young man who thought the world owed him a living is the old man who blames the world for his failure.

LOSERS

You can't help but like a good loser—unless you had a bet on him.

* * *

A born loser is the guy who sticks his hand out of his car window to signal a turn and smacks a cop in the mouth.

LOVE

Platonic love is like eating soup with a fork.

* * *

Love is like hash. You have to have confidence in it to enjoy it.

LUCK

He's always had bad luck. When he was a kid, he brought his teacher an apple and she found a worm in it.

* * *

He has terrible luck. His best friend ran away without his wife.

MANNERS

Good manners enable you to wait in silence while the loudmouth gets the service.

MARRIAGE

You can figure your marriage is on the rocks when your wife forgets to send your apron to the laundry.

* * *

Too many marriages end the way they began—with people throwing things.

* * *

You can always recognize a married man at the beach. His looks are quick and guilty.

* * *

If your wife doesn't treat you as you deserve—be thankful.

* * *

A well-informed man is one whose wife just told him what she thinks of him.

* * *

They were married on Friday the thirteenth. They had to blame it on something.

* * *

Once a man learns how to listen, he and his wife can remain on speaking terms indefinitely.

* * *

Before they're married, women want to know if there's a man in their future; afterward, they want to know if there's a future in their man.

* * *

Engaged couples should realize that a marriage will never be as good as she hopes or as bad as he expects.

* * *

Behind every woman in a mink coat is a husband who swore she'd never get one.

* * *

Marriage is a wonderful institution. If it weren't for marriage, husbands and wives would have to fight with perfect strangers.

* * *

If you want to know how your girl will treat you after you're married, just listen to the way she talks to her little brother.

* * *

A successful marriage is one in which one partner makes the living, and the other makes the living worthwhile.

* * *

Marriage is an institution that teaches a man regularity, frugality, temperance, forbearance, and many other splendid virtues he wouldn't need if he stayed single.

* * *

Marriage is the only lottery licensed by the state and supported by the clergy.

* * *

Marriage is a mutual admiration society in which one person is always right, and the other is always the husband.

* * *

Marriage is really a grind. You wash dishes, make beds, and then two weeks later, you have to do it all over again.

* * *

They say marriages are made in heaven. Maybe that's why married people are always harping at each other.

MECHANICS

The average mechanic is not choosey. He'd just as soon wipe his hands on the steering wheel of a Ford as on the wheel of a Cadillac.

MIDDLE-AGE

When a man reaches middle-age, he still has a lot of get up and go—his air, teeth, and virility *all* get up and go.

* * *

A man has reached middle-age when he is warned to slow down by the doctor, instead of the police.

* * *

Middle-age is when your feet hurt before you get out of bed.

* * *

You've reached middle-age when your weight-lifting consists of standing up.

* * *

Middle-age is the time when your clothes don't fit—and it's you who really needs the alterations.

* * *

A woman has reached middle-age when she worries more about the way her shoes fit than her sweaters do.

MINDS

Some minds are like concrete, all mixed up and permanently set.

MISTAKES

The quickest way to get somebody's undivided attention is to make a mistake.

* * *

The only thing that's worse than making a mistake is discovering that you're so unimportant, nobody noticed it.

MONEY

I'll never understand why they call money "dough"; dough sticks to your fingers.

* * *

Today's money-making gimmick is the tax loss. I plan to open a chain of bankrupt dance studios.

* * *

Among the things that money can't buy is what it used to.

* * *

By the time most men discover that money doesn't grow on trees, they're already way out on a limb.

* * *

Money is what you spend for luxuries and owe for necessities.

* * *

Once, a fool and his money were soon parted. Today, Uncle Sam doesn't make any distinction in intelligence.

* * *

Nowadays a miser is anyone who lives within his income.

* * *

Philosophy is something rich people use to convince the rest of us that it's no disgrace to be poor.

* * *

If prices keep going up, it won't be long before there'll be more marriages ending in bankruptcy than in divorce.

* * *

It won't be long until we have money to burn. It's almost cheaper than fuel right now.

* * *

The best way to double your money is to fold it up and put it back in your pocket.

* * *

Women call it pin money because they have to needle their husbands to get it.

* * *

If you don't think the modern kid knows the value of money, ask one how many record albums ten dollars will buy.

* * *

He's so broke, he just gave his bookie two weeks' notice.

MORNINGS

There ought to be a better way to start the day than getting up in the morning.

MOTHERS

Any mother can tell you that two heads are *not* better than one. That would mean four ears to wash.

* * *

Every mother will agree that the hardest meal for them to get is breakfast in bed.

* * *

Did you hear about the Eskimo mother who was so strict, she wouldn't let her daughter go out on a date without a noseguard?

* * *

A mother's patience is like a tube of toothpaste—it's never quite all gone.

MOVIES

Some of the films today are so sexy that Hollywood makes two versions—one for the local airlines and another for the European airlines.

* * *

Modern Westerns are okay, but when the Indians picket the fort instead of going on the warpath, that's ridiculous.

MUSIC

Every time I listen to the top fifty records, I shudder to think of what the bottom fifty must sound like.

* * *

One good thing about those rock songs. The kids can't whistle them.

* * *

Some of today's musicians carry a tune as if it were too heavy for them.

NAPS

Frequent naps will keep you from getting old—especially if you take them while you're driving.

NEIGHBORHOODS

Nothing ruins a neighborhood for the average husband like having an enthusiastic gardener move in.

NEW YEAR'S RESOLUTIONS

The weakness of most New Year's resolutions is that they go in one year and out the other.

NIGHT CLUBS

I've got a great idea for a night club show. All the chorus girls are fully clothed, but the audience sits there naked.

NONCONFORMITY

He's a real nonconformist. He has TV dinners for lunch.

OLD AGE

Don't resent growing old. A great many people are denied the privilege.

* * *

She's so old, she still carries a nickel for mad money.

* * *

I must be getting old. I can remember when I could get a penny postcard for two cents.

* * *

You know you're getting old when the doctor giving you a check-up is younger than you are.

* * *

You're getting old when you don't care where your wife goes, just so you don't have to go along.

OLD DAYS

I remember the old days when a quartet was four guys singing in a barber shop, instead of four guys who look like they never saw one.

* * *

In the old days, a boy would give his girl his class ring when they were going steady. Nowadays, he lets her use his hair rollers.

* * *

An old-timer is one who remembers when a man withheld his own tax from his take-home pay.

* * *

An old-timer is one who remembers when you could promise a kid the moon without having to buy him a space suit.

OPERATIONS

An operation may take only an hour to perform, but it takes the patient years to describe it.

OPPORTUNITY

This is the land of opportunity. That's why so many married men get into trouble.

* * *

Opportunity is hard for some people to recognize, because it goes around wearing work clothes.

PARENTS

One advantage of being a parent is that you don't have to take the same medicine you give the kids.

* * *

All a parent has to do to make a child thirsty is to fall sound asleep.

PARTIES

He livens up a party by leaving it.

* * *

The more at a party, the merrier; the fewer, the better fed.

PATIENCE

Patience is the ability to idle your motor when you feel more like stripping your gears.

PAWNSHOPS

Know what three balls in front of a pawnshop means? Two to one you don't get it back.

PEDESTRIANS

It's getting so a pedestrian isn't safe unless he's riding in a car.

* * *

There would be fewer pedestrian patients if there were more patient pedestrians.

* * *

I can't understand why motorists wear safety belts, when it's the pedestrians who aren't safe.

PEEPING TOMS

A Peeping Tom is a Doubting Thomas doing research.

PLASTIC SURGERY
Plastic surgeons can do anything with a nose, except keep it out of other people's business.

POLITICS
Politicians wouldn't promise the impossible, if people didn't expect it.

* * *

In an election year, the politicians just can't seem to leave welfare enough alone.

* * *

I can't understand why politicians invent lies about each other when the truth would be bad enough.

* * *

A politician is a man who approaches every subject with an open mouth.

* * *

Political platforms are for one party to stand on, and the other to jump on.

* * *

The trouble with political jokes is that they sometimes get elected.

* * *

The principal advantage of being a defeated politician is that you don't have to explain why you didn't keep your campaign promises.

* * *

What would happen if everybody believed what political candidates say about each other, and nobody won?

* * *

To err is human. To blame it on someone else is politics.

* * *

If a woman were elected President of the United States, would her husband be called "the first man"?

* * *

An honest politician is one who will fulfill his campaign promises, no matter how dishonest he has to be to do it.

POPULATION EXPLOSION

It is estimated that our population increases by one every ten and a half seconds. We can't control the population explosion, but at least we have it timed.

POVERTY

He's so poor, he can't afford to go window-shopping.

* * *

He's so poor, his wife has to sweep their dirt under a neighbor's rug.

* * *

He's so poor, he has to buy one shoelace at a time.

PRACTICE

Some folks practice what they preach; others just practice preaching.

* * *

Price ceilings are back—when you hear the price, you hit the ceiling.

PROGRESS

Progress is that continuing effort to make the things we eat, drink, and wear as good as they used to be.

PROSPERITY

Prosperity is that short period between the time you hide money at home and the time your wife finds it.

PSYCHIATRY

I know a psychiatrist who has great success with teen-age patients. He lets them phone in their problems.

* * *

Sometimes you go to a psychiatrist when you're slightly cracked, and keep going until you're completely broke.

* * *

I know a psychiatrist who is so expensive that for twenty-five dollars he sends you a get-well card.

* * *

A neurotic builds castles in the air. A psychotic lives in them. A psychoanalyst collects the rent.

PUNCTUAL

The worst thing about being on time is that everybody thinks you don't have anything to do.

PUNISHMENT

Children should be punished without a definite end in view.

RACING

What often keeps a man from making a fast buck is a slow horse.

* * *

He crossed a chicken with a racing form and got a chicken that laid odds.

* * *

I went to the racetrack yesterday, and I bet on a horse that was so bad it wouldn't even make good glue.

* * *

She was disappointed when she went to the race track. She thought they'd at least have curtains at the hundred-dollar window.

* * *

The Kentucky Derby is famous for three things: win, place, and show.

RAIN

Everybody enjoys walking in the rain except the people who have to.

REINCARNATION

I definitely believe in reincarnation. Did you ever notice how many dead people come to life every day at five in the afternoon?

REPUTATIONS

A good reputation may simply mean that you don't have inquisitive neighbors.

RESTAURANTS

I ate at a real health-food restaurant. Instead of waiters, they had interns.

* * *

I just ate at a restaurant that serves both Chinese and German food. One hour later, you're hungry for power.

* * *

I ate in a restaurant that was so swanky, the chef sliced tomatoes by throwing them through a harp.

RETIREMENT

Retirement is the time of life when you stop lying about your age and start lying around the house.

RUMORS

An "unimpeachable source" is the one who started the rumor.

SADISM

A sadist is a doctor who keeps his stethoscope in the refrigerator.

SAFETY

Highway toll booths are really safety devices. If it weren't for them, some motorists wouldn't slow down at all.

SALARIES

The way prices are today, I can't live on the salary I used to dream of.

* * *

Thanks to my wife, I never gamble away my salary. She spends it before I get a chance.

* * *

The guy who really understands cold cash is the one whose salary isn't so hot.

SALESMEN

A super-salesman is a guy who can sell American-made transistor radios in Japan.

* * *

Did you hear about the salesman who died and left an estate of five hundred hotel towels and two hundred hotel keys?

SAVINGS

It's easy to save pennies today. What else can you do with them?

* * *

If he keeps on saving for the next twenty years at the rate he's been saving for the past ten years, he'll be able to retire at sixty and owe one hundred thousand dollars.

SCIENCE

Know why there's no life on other planets? Because their scientists were a little more advanced than ours.

* * *

Science is strange. White mice do all the work and men take all the credit.

SEASONS

Summer is the only season when there are more redskins on the beaches than on TV.

* * *

Spring is the season that makes tired blood really tired.

* * *

The first sure sign of summer! My air conditioner broke down.

* * *

Autumn is that magic time of year when your pool is no longer filled with the neighbors' kids—now it's the neighbors' leaves.

SECRETARIES

If you want a job done, give it to a busy man. He'll have his secretary do it.

* * *

A good secretary is expected to look like a girl, think like a man, act like a lady, and work like a dog.

* * *

A good secretary is one who can keep up with her boss when he's dictating and keep ahead of him when he's not.

* * *

My secretary gets annoyed when she is late to work. It's not that she's conscientious; she's just mad because she missed a coffee break.

SECRETS

The trouble with secrets is that they're either not worth keeping, or they're too good to keep.

SHYNESS

She's a very shy movie star. It's taken her three whole years to fall in love with herself.

SMILES

Keep smiling! It makes people wonder what you've been up to.

SMOKING

What's the best way to stop smoking? Carry wet matches.

* * *

It would be a lot easier to quit smoking if they could prove that cigarettes have calories.

SNOBS

A snob is a person who only wants to know the people who don't want to know him.

* * *

He's becoming a snob. The other day, he asked the man at the liquor store to recommend the proper wine to go with a TV dinner.

SPEAKERS

A good speaker is one who knows how little time his two cents' worth should take.

* * *

The easiest way to stay awake during an after-dinner speech is to deliver it.

* * *

He's careful about his speech. The only time he has trouble with his English is when he mixes it with scotch.

SPEED

We are moving ahead at twice the speed of sound and half the speed of sense.

* * *

The driver who burns up the road often lands in the cooler.

SUCCESS

If success turns your head, you're facing in the wrong direction.

* * *

You are a success when your name is in everything but the telephone book.

* * *

One of the troubles with success these days is that you achieve it at just about the same time as you have a nervous breakdown.

* * *

A successful executive is one who can delegate all the responsibility, shift all the blame, and appropriate all the credit.

* * *

Success is the progression from frayed cuffs to frayed nerves.

* * *

Few people travel the road to success without a puncture or two. As soon as some people get up in the world, they start looking down on it.

SURVEYS

A survey shows that the nation's top executives spend eighty percent of their time talking. Oddly enough, it is the same percentage that junior executives spend listening.

SWIMMING

Nothing can replace the modern swimsuit—and it has.

* * *

Did you hear about the high-school senior who flunked out as a lifeguard, because he forgot to remove his bubble gum during a mouth-to-mouth resuscitation test?

TACT

Some people have tact. Other people tell the truth.

TAXES

Work may not be as hard as it used to be, but it certainly is a lot more taxing.

* * *

America is the land of opportunity. Anybody can grow up to become a taxpayer.

* * *

The only time the average child is as good as gold is April 15.

* * *

Making out an income-tax form is a lesson in addition, multiplication, and extraction.

TEEN-AGERS

My teen-age daughter is so popular that her phone rings even when it's off the hook.

* * *

The only thing the average teen-age girl is afraid of is a stack of dirty dishes.

* * *

A teen-age singer is trading in his new sports car. It's so small, he can't get his hair in.

* * *

Today's teen-agers have lots of leisure time. Look at how much time they save by not getting haircuts.

* * *

The average boy these days isn't interested in putting his shoulder to the wheel, all he wants to do is get his hands on it.

* * *

Homework is something a teen-age girl does between phone calls.

* * *

The children's hour is any time they're on the phone.

* * *

The telephone is a remarkable invention. It allows teen-agers to go steady even without being able to hold hands.

* * *

Today's teen-agers are on the phone so much, they won't even start talking until they hear a dial tone.

TEETH

Always be true to your teeth, or they'll be false to you.

* * *

His teeth are in very bad shape. He has so many cavities that when he talks, there's an echo.

TELEVISION

TV has made dull conversationalists of us all. It even has people to talk about the weather for us.

* * *

Television's most suspenseful moment is when the repairman presents the bill.

* * *

TV commercials should be applauded. They encourage family conversation.

* * *

TV is a wasteland sold by the minute instead of the acre.

* * *

TV is a risky business—one day you're in it, the next day you can't afford to have your set repaired.

* * *

Kids who watch TV for hours will go down in history—not to mention arithmetic, English, and geography.

* * *

TV has improved conversation. There's less of it.

* * *

Whoever is responsible for all the violence on TV should be beaten up, tarred, feathered, and burned alive.

* * *

Some of today's TV shows are so bad that many kids have gone back to doing their homework.

* * *

TV has done the impossible. It's changed a whole generation of kids from irresistible forces to immovable objects.

TEMPTATION
The man who is suddenly overpowered by temptation has probably been dreaming about it for a long time.

THOUGHT
Think twice before you speak—and you'll probably find that the subject has been changed.

* * *

He gets lost in thought because it's unfamiliar territory.

TIGHTWADS
He's a real tightwad. He takes his electric razor to the office to recharge it.

TIME
The best way to kill time is to work it to death.

TRAFFIC
Traffic is so bad that I'm not going to buy another car unless a stretch of highway comes with it.

* * *

The trouble with Sunday traffic is that you can't avoid it any day in the week.

* * *

Those who think the competitive spirit is dead ought to take another look at the American motorist in rush-hour traffic.

* * *

The motorist who weaves through traffic often winds up getting stitched.

* * *

A traffic light is a device for luring pedestrians out where the traffic is.

* * *

About the easiest thing to manage in downtown traffic today is a bent fender.

TRANQUILIZERS

I'm on a new tranquilizer diet. You don't lose any weight, but you don't care about being fat anymore.

TRAVEL

No matter where you go, you'll find somebody who'll tell you that by taking another route, you could have gotten there forty-five minutes sooner.

* * *

Foreign travel will broaden more than eight million American tourists this year. It will also flatten them.

* * *

A pleasure trip is when you leave the kids with grandma and go away without them.

TROUBLE

The trouble with trying to get away from it all these days is that most of it is portable.

* * *

If nobody knows the trouble you've seen, you're not living in a small town.

* * *

The trouble with trouble is that most of it started out being fun.

* * *

Troubles, like babies, grow larger if you nurse them.

* * *

It's better not to tell people your troubles. Half of them aren't interested, and the other half are glad you are getting what's coming to you.

UGLINESS

She was so homely that a tear rolled down her cheek, took a look at her face, and rolled back up again.

* * *

She was such an ugly baby that when she was born her father went to the zoo and threw rocks at the stork.

* * *

His name isn't in *Who's Who*, but his picture is in *What's This?*

UNHAPPINESS

Can you imagine anyone as unhappy as a woman with a live secret and a dead telephone.

* * *

Unhappiness is in not knowing what we want, and killing ourselves to get it.

THE U.S.A.

Washington bureaucrats have finally figured out how to balance the budget. They're going to tilt the country.

* * *

Everything is much simpler these days—instead of solving a problem, you just subsidize it.

* * *

One trouble with this country is the number of people who try to get something for nothing. Another is the high percentage of those who succeed.

* * *

What this country needs is a ways and mean-it committee.

* * *

Two-thirds of our citizens now live in or near big cities. The other third is on the expressway looking for an exit.

* * *

National problems are getting so complex that even cabdrivers don't know all the answers.

* * *

America is the only country where it takes more brains to make out your income-tax return than it does to make your income.

* * *

The future of America is in darned good shape. Just go to any beach for proof.

* * *

What the country needs is a good five-cent nickel.

VACATIONS

A European vacation is a great equalizer. People come back from them just as broke as their neighbors who couldn't afford to go.

* * *

Vacation time is the two weeks you devote to finding places you swear you'll stay away from next year.

* * *

A man works hard all year convincing the boss he's indispensable, so that he can get a two-week vacation to prove he isn't.

* * *

Whoever said you can't take it with you has never seen the family car packed for a vacation trip.

* * *

On a vacation, it's hard to tell which goes faster—time or money.

* * *

Isn't it wonderful to get home from your vacation and realize you don't have to worry about it again for a whole year?

* * *

One thing most people learn on their vacation is that no resort quite lives up to its postcards.

* * *

Don't tell a tired-looking person he needs a vacation. Chances are, he just had one.

VIRUSES
Statistics show that nine out of every ten people suffering from a virus infection never go to the doctor. They go to the theater.

WALKING
Walking is only a pleasure when you can afford to ride if you want to.

WEALTH
Only the rich can be eccentric. The poor have to be satisfied with just being nuts.

* * *

Money only brings misery. But with money you can afford it.

* * *

They didn't send him a tax refund. They just sent him a bridge they couldn't find a river for.

* * *

Wealth can be a curse, especially if your neighbors have it.

* * *

If there were a market for Get-Poor-Quick schemes, he'd be a rich man today.

WEATHER
The weatherman is right eighty percent of the time—it's the weather that's wrong.

* * *

Wouldn't it be wonderful if weathermen seeded the clouds with detergent? Then we would get our cars washed when it rains.

WEIGHT
She's finally done something about her weight. She's stopped getting on the scale.

* * *

She doesn't have trouble watching her weight. Wherever she looks, there it is.

WIVES

She has just what it takes to wear the latest styles—a rich husband.

* * *

Leisure time is when your wife can't find you.

* * *

He's leaving his wife because of another woman—her mother.

* * *

If American husbands aren't spoiling their wives, it's about time they found out who is.

* * *

It took her just three hours to get her new mink coat: one hour of shopping and two hours of tantrums.

* * *

My wife's very thrifty. She didn't want to buy an Easter bonnet, because she'd only wear it once, so she bought a mink coat suitable for all occasions.

WOMEN

The modern woman doesn't need an attic as long as she has a handbag.

* * *

I know a woman who's so vain, she even lies about her dog's age.

* * *

Wild horses couldn't drag a secret out of most women. Unfortunately, they seldom have lunch with wild horses.

* * *

No matter what you hear about how often women change their minds—have you ever heard of a groom being left at the church?

* * *

Women are not what they used to be. They used to be girls.

* * *

The average woman would never dream of marrying a man for

his money—if she could find any other way to get her hands on it.

* * *

Never underestimate a woman—unless you're talking about her age or her weight.

* * *

If you don't think women are explosive, try dropping one.

* * *

A woman will never be man's equal until she can have a large bald spot and still think she's good-looking.

* * *

No wonder women live longer than men. Look how long they spend being girls.

* * *

Stop praising a woman, and she thinks you don't love her any more. Keep it up, and she'll think she's too good for you.

* * *

There are two types of women. Those who can talk on any subject—and those who don't need a subject.

* * *

You know a woman is in love with her husband if she smiles at him the way she does at a traffic cop.

WORDS

Sharp words will upset your stomach, especially when you have to eat them.

WORK

People are still willing to do an honest day's work. Trouble is, they want a week's pay for it.

* * *

One advantage of planning your work carefully is that you may discover some way to get out of it.

* * *

Sixty percent of the working women in this country are married. This figure is subject to change as soon as the plans of the other forty percent work out.

* * *

Too many people quit looking for work when they find a job.

WORLD

The way the world situation is today, when you break a mirror it's good luck. It means you'll be around for another seven years.

* * *

This is a crazy world. We can invent a rocket that will shoot a man to the moon, but we still can't perfect a gum machine that works every time.

* * *

People say that the world is going to the dogs. And considering the condition it's in, that's a terrible thing to do to man's best friend.

WORTH

No man is completely worthless. He can always serve as a horrible example.

YAWNS

A yawn is nature's way of letting married men open their mouths.

YOUTH

If you want to recapture your youth, cut off his allowance.

* * *

More and more women are discovering the secret of youth—they lie about their age.

* * *

When you feel like criticizing the younger generation, just remember who raised it.

* * *

The secret of youth is keeping your age a secret.

* * *

Why can't life's problems hit us when we're eighteen and know everything?